DEMOCRACY IN A
DIVIDED AUSTRALIA

The Inners-Outers divide ripping us apart

MATTHEW LESH

Connor Court Publishing

Published in 2018 by Connor Court Publishing

Connor Court Publishing Pty Ltd
PO Box 7257
Redland Bay QLD 4165
sales@connorcourt.com

www.connorcourtpublishing.com.au

Phone 0497 900 685

ISBN: 978-1-925826-10-4

Cover design: Joshua Stranger & Matthew Lesh

Printed in Australia

Contents

"Shall we, therefore, tamely submit to the
mad freaks of this unconstituted few —
shall we bow our neck to the yoke, and
see vanish into thin air the hopes which
have buoyed us up against all adversities?
…But rather let us say,
We dare and will be free.
We will not submit to misrule
or oppression in any form."

The Great Confederated Anti-Dray and Land Tax League
South Australia, 18 May 1850

FOREWORD

In December last year I sat down with a senior cabinet minister from the Howard Government to discuss the state of politics. Looking back now it feels like barely a prime minister ago. Suffice to say, we both agreed that not all is right. There is a lack of ambition and vision. Australians have lost faith in our leaders and institutions. And our assumptions about Australia's liberal democracy, namely that we all share a common commitment to personal liberty and responsibility, to free expression and the idea that the law should apply to all individuals equally, no longer holds.

The next day I invited Matthew Lesh to my office, recounted the conversation and asked: what is going on in Australian politics? Matthew's answer was that Australia is divided.

Outers are the instinctively traditionalist, stability seeking, culturally conservative grouping whose identity is primarily based on their sense of belonging to family, community and nation. Outers are frustrated but barely heard in public life. That's because of Inners' domination across politics, bureaucracies, trade unions, civil society, corporates, universities and much of the media. Inners are cosmopolitan progressives, they seek and benefit from rapid change. They have created a separate value system – primarily based on academic and professional achievement – and are dismissive of those who do not fit the mould.

The Inners and Outers tribes overlap and complicate the economic left-right divides of the past. The factions within the

the major parties, which grab media attention day to day, are merely microcosms of a much larger story. We are being ripped apart by an increasing divergent cultures, lifestyles and identities, and a corresponding fundamental misunderstanding of each other. *Democracy in a Divided Australia* does not just assert these claims, it backs them up with a plethora of evidence from a multitude of sources.

The Inners-Outers divide is not only driving political mayhem; it is undermining Australia's egalitarian ethos. Egalitarianism is the principle that no matter who you are or where you come from, you should have an equal voice in our democracy. I am better than no man and no man is better than me.

Australia is built on egalitarian roots. The need to grow, to develop, to survive left no room for the class based society of Mother England. Millions have arrived on our shores, in generation after generation and from every part of the globe, seeking a better future for themselves. Australia was attractive not because life would be easy. People came to Australia seeking a society that no matter who you are or where you come from you would receive equal respect, dignity, and opportunity. While we have often failed to live up to this ideal in practice, there can be no truer sense of what it means to be Australian than our larrikin dismissal of illegitimate authority, of the idea that someone else has the moral authority to tell me how to live my life.

Democracy in a Divided Australia shows how this egalitarian ideal is being undermined by the rise of a new tribe who think they are better than the rest – and want to rule over others in a technocratic and paternalistic manner. This group have been at their worst in recent history as events have led them to question democracy altogether. Following Brexit and the election of Donald Trump many elites expressed their absolute disgust at the unthinking, ignorant mob duped by 'fake news'. These are the type of people who call themselves 'experts', demand to be listened to, and expect to be in positions of power over other people's lives.

We are living in a uniquely uncertain political era. More than any time since the end of the Cold War, the future is undefined. The core plea from *Democracy in a Divided Australia* is a pluralist response. Matthew argues that both Inners and Outers should have a say in how our society is governed. This is the fundamental democratic egalitarian ethos that must guide us into the future.

Democracy in a Divided Australia is Australia's answer to Charles Murray's *Coming Apart: The State of White America, 1960-2010*, and David Goodhart's *The Road to Somewhere: The Populist Revolt and the Future of Politics*. The local dynamics and contours of Australia's divide may be unique, but Matthew successfully explores how the divide between the new elite and the rest has arrived in Australia – and begins to outline how we should respond.

I have no doubt that Australia is capable of overcoming the challenges the lie ahead. The Australian people are resilient, hard working, and ambitious. We live in a land of great opportunity and potential. *Democracy in a Divided Australia* is not an argument for despair – it is the case for a better future built on a renewed understanding of our equal moral worth.

John Roskam
Executive Director, Institute of Public Affairs

PREFACE

Learning to live together

I am a quintessential Inner. I am a young, inner-city living, unmarried, highly educated professional. I finished editing this book at an Australian café in London, eating smashed avocado on toast while drinking mimosas and cold brew coffee. (If the editor asks, they were non-alcoholic mimosas.)

Nevertheless, over the last few years I have spent much time critiquing the Inner-centric monoculture at Australia's universities. This contradiction was pointed out by a commentator named William on an article in *The Australian* about my report on campus free speech issues. He called me 'the sort of person who most commenting here disparage.' William is right. He had looked up my biography and concluded that my education and lifestyle are no different from the Inners that I criticise.

My grandparents came to Australia fleeing European antisemitism and the darkest hour in human history. They sought to establish new lives for themselves and their family as far away from their perilous homelands as they could reach. They expected and got little from government and worked hard to rebuild their lives in a new land. They were members of an often-marginalised minority. They were welcomed with open arms and achieved impressive success in Australia. They flourished in odd jobs, as labourers and in small businesses. They built comfortable lives, were deeply engaged in their communities and sought the best education for their children. I am the beneficiary of their success.

I had the privilege of being educated at a private school and have graduated from the University of Melbourne and the London School of Economics. I work in a knowledge economy job. I am excited by innovation, technology and progress. I travel widely and love to meet new people. My state member of parliament is from the Greens – and he defeated a Liberal at the last election. When I write about cocktail sipping and café brunching Inners I am referring to some of my favourite pastimes.

I tell the story of Australia's Inners and Outers as a reminder. Your lifestyle, opportunities, temperament, interests and journey are unique. We live but one life. While this may sound limiting, an awareness of our narrow perspective is empowering. It helps us remember that others have different experiences, opportunities and values.

This book is not just an intellectual exercise. A good book will change the way you see the world. I have written what follows in the hope of maybe, just maybe, reshaping the way we understand ourselves and others. This is a plea for Inners, like myself, to increase our self-awareness. With great power comes great responsibility. Inners must use our cultural, social and political influence to do good, not evil. Individuals should be free to make choices, local communities should set their destiny and we should not disparage Inners' or Outers' differing lives and values. Pluralism is essential. Inners *and* Outers are both legitimate voices in Australia's national debate.

If I am right, there will be more division in the years ahead. This challenge should be viewed as an opportunity, not a curse. In the end, we will be stronger if we can learn to live together.

§

If it takes a village to raise a baby, it took an entire nation to write this book. What follows is not merely my work – it is the amalgamation of ideas from many people who are much wiser and harder working than myself. As Isaac Newton wrote, 'If I have seen further it is by standing on the shoulders of Giants.' These thinkers are listed across the text, notes and bibliography.

There are many who have helped directly. First and foremost, my colleagues at the Institute of Public Affairs. The IPA not only provided me with the time to research and write this book but also ample feedback and direction on the journey. This project grew in size like a bad rash. It began as a short opinion piece, then became a potential report and eventually the book length exploration that follows. I thank my colleagues John Roskam, Simon Breheny, Dr Chris Berg, Scott Hargreaves and Andrew Bushnell for providing helpful ideas, feedback and comments. I thank Dr David Kemp and Dr Jill Sheppard who expertly reviewed the draft. I also wish to thank many friends who provided helpful ideas including Andrew Norton, David Kitchen and Matthew Kilcoyne. There are many more who made the mistake of asking me what I am writing about – and subsequently received an unsolicited lecture, showed interest and provided useful ideas. All errors and omissions are my own.

Matthew Lesh
Melbourne, Australia
September 2018

INTRODUCTION

A divided Australia

Australian politics is a mess. There is widespread and growing dislike of politicians, the political process and lacklustre policy outcomes.[1] Australians think that the system is being stacked against them, their communities, families and potential for human flourishing. In many respects, they are right.

As the tentacles of the state have expanded, and traditional class divisions declined, policymaking has become dominated by a new tribe. This new tribe has a different lifestyle, cultural attitude and identity to most Australians.

Policymaking is an iceberg. On the surface, politicians, bureaucrats, corporate leadership, trade unionists, journalists and academics – who went to similar universities, live in near identical suburbs and have comparable values – argue about a narrow set of policy options.

There is consensus below the surface. Almost all legislation has bipartisan support.[2] Many issues are never discussed and only a small subset of policy options is considered. The daily slanging match in Canberra is confected. Decisions that impact millions of lives are made by bureaucrats and regulators away from the public eye. Most Australians feel they have little say.[3]

Public debate is shallow. The media fill up column inches and airtime with relentless leadership speculation, titbits about parliamentarians' personal lives and meaningless minuscule changes in opinion polls. Politics is presented as a sport with daily winners and losers. This is a sport that most Australians do not like and do not play.

Australians are frustrated, disengaged and pessimistic.

'Public satisfaction with our democratic processes and public trust in the politicians we elect are at some of the lowest levels ever recorded,' Professor Ian McAllister of the Australian National University, who has been studying public attitudes for decades, surmised after the 2016 election.[4] Only a quarter of Australians think that government can be trusted, the lowest since when the question was first asked in 1969.[5] Just a third of Australians are satisfied with the way that democracy is working.[6]

Australians feel like their voice is not being heard. Three-quarters think that 'our government does not prioritise the concerns of people like me' – among the highest proportion in the developed world.[7] Australians have lost faith in political institutions.[8] Just 6 per cent have a lot of trust in federal parliament and only 2 per cent place a lot of trust in political parties.[9] Meanwhile, most Australians are gloomy about the future. Less than a third think that Australia is heading in the right direction.[10]

The consensus below the iceberg's surface is driving policy paralysis. As commentator Paul Kelly has argued, the era of reform is over.[11] Policymakers are ignoring long-term challenges:

- Australia has a record gross national debt of over $535 billion, projected to reach $684 billion by 2028. If the trend continues, that will reach $2.8 trillion by 2055.[12] Both sides of politics have broken promises to return the budget to surplus at the expense of household incomes in the short and long term.[13]

- Australia's population is ageing. In 1975 there were 7.3 people in the workforce for every person in retirement, that has now declined to 4.5. By 2055 it is projected to reach 2.7.[14] Australia's household debt has reached $2.47 trillion, an astonishing $99,000 per person.[15]

- We are not saving for the future. There will be fewer workers and more demands on government in the decades to come. This will mean lower quality services and higher taxes on 'those who are to be born.'[16]

- Politicians and bureaucrats in tandem with big business and big unions have created mountains of red tape – which is costing Australia's economy $176 billion a year.[17] This bureaucratic mess is limiting job creation, holding down incomes, pushing up prices and undermining democracy.

- Australia's economy is showing signs of weakness. There are 723,700 people unemployed and many more who are underemployed or left the workforce altogether.[18] Business investment has dropped to just 12 per cent of GDP, lower than the Whitlam era.[19] Entrepreneurship has declined.[20] Real wage growth has stagnated over the past two years.[21] Australia is falling in international measures of economic competitiveness.[22]

The divides in Australian society is driving our shambolic political predicament. We are not merely divided in our politics; we are divided in our identity, lifestyle and culture.

Inners base their identity on educational and professional achievements. They are confident and assertive. They value change, autonomy and diversity. They are younger, highly educated and live close to city centres. Inners have cosmopolitan liberal political attitudes. They have educational advantages and academic intelligence. Inners dominate both sides of politics, bureaucracies, trade unions, civil society, corporates, universities and much of the media.

Outers base their identity on family, community and national identity. Outers are instinctively traditionalist. They value stability, safety and unity. They live in suburbia, have low to middle incomes and less education. They are under relentless pressure in our ever changing world. Despite their higher numbers Outers are marginalised

We should welcome the influence of Inners in many fields. Inners-led campaigns on issues ranging from racial equality and women's liberation to gay rights have made Australia a more tolerant, interesting and forward looking society. Inners influence on economic matters, particularly the promotion of free trade, has helped Australia to become prosperous. The danger Australia faces is not that Inners are a part of the debate, it is that Inners dominate and Outers are poorly represented.

Australian politics is too Inners centric. Inners have taken over Australia's political, economic and cultural institutions. Inners lead, staff and influence both major parties. Since the 'consensus' driven reform era of the 1980s, policymaking has become a debate between Inners of the political left and political right.[23]

Inners pursue technocratic and paternalistic governance by the supposedly best and brightest, that is, decision making by themselves.[24] The growth and complexity of the regulatory state empowers Inners to make policy in their interests, often excluding Outers voices.[25] Outers are frustrated and losing faith in a political system dominated by people unlike themselves.

Australia is not alone in these trends. The 'Inners' and 'Outers' are inspired by British author David Goodhart's *The Road to Somewhere*.[26] Goodhart argues Britain is split into two tribes: the Anywheres, the educated, mobile middle class which values autonomy, openness and fluidity; and the Somewheres, the less educated, more rooted, working class which values security and group identity.

While Australia has not had a circuit breaker moment such as Brexit in the United Kingdom or the election of Donald Trump in the United States, there are similar underlying values divides and growing frustrations. We might not end up with our own Trump in the Lodge, but it is not impossible to imagine.

Historically, Australia's stable politics was predicated on strong support for the two major parties.[27] The working class voted Labor and middle to upper class voted Liberal. The Inners-Outers divide overlaps and often overrides the traditional left-right class distinctions of yesteryear. Working class Outers who feel disillusioned by Labor's strong Inners focus are increasingly voting for the Liberals; meanwhile, middle class Inners who are disappointed by the conservative political right are opting for Labor and the Greens.[28]

The social basis of both major parties is now mixed. The Liberal and Labor machines depend on the votes of *both* Inners and Outers. This dependence complicates matters. The major political parties must appease two distinct value sets. The Labor Party tries to win votes from young, highly educated professionals in the inner-cities of Melbourne, Sydney and Brisbane (Inners); while simultaneously trying to appeal to the suburban fringe (Outers). The Liberal Party tries to appeal to both blue-ribbon inner-city cosmopolitan values in wealthy electorates like

Higgins and Wentworth (Inners), while also trying to broaden their appeal in conservative suburbia such as western Sydney (Outers).

The major parties are struggling to be all things to all people. The outcome is insincerity and opportunism, which drives futher frustrations, instability and fracturing across the political spectrum.[29] Voters are unshackling from traditional party loyalties, swinging between the major parties and voting for minor ones. In 1967, 72 per cent of Australians voted for the same party at each election and in 1990, 60 per cent stuck with one party.[30] Today, just 37 per cent of Australians identify with a particular political party.[31]

There is also growing minor party support. In 1993, almost 9-in-10 Australians voted for one of the two major parties. A recent poll found nearly half of Australians had either decided or were actively considering not voting for a major party at the next election.[32] The most successful of the non-major parties is the Greens, who attract disillusioned Inners. More recently, One Nation has enticed some disillusioned Outers.

Australians increasingly feel that the government does not affect the economy.[33] Therefore, we can expect non-economic issues associated with the Inners-Outers divide to become more prominent in public debate in the years ahead. This includes topics such as Australia and Anzac Day, educational content, immigration and asylum seekers, the environment, constitutional change, law and order and identity politics.

The divides have also contributed to leadership instability, both by creating intractable splits among members of parties, and weakening traditional party loyalties causing rapid movements in opinion polls, which trigger leadership changes and shorter governments. Between 1945 and the end of the Howard era, prime ministers served for seven and a half years on average, since 2007 prime ministers have averaged just over two years.[34] As each new leader fails to manage the underlying division, negative sentiment about politicians increases.

§

Australia is facing an era of intense political tribalism in which groups with different sets of values compete for a finite resource: the power to dominate the other.

Sometimes Outers win a battle, but it is the Inners that are winning the war. Each skirmish leaves a substantial minority (and occasionally a majority) feeling alienated and frustrated. The winner-takes-all approach to politics leaves both sides scarred and full of mistrust. Meanwhile, the fight goes on and on, turned up another notch. This is a recipe for relentless conflict.

Australia faces immense challenges in the coming years. Can a severely divided Australia learn to live together? Can the viewpoints and priorities of the underrepresented feature in public debate?

This book combines an empirically grounded understanding of Australia's political tribes with an explanation for how they have grown and the impact the divisions are having on Australian policymaking as well as beginning to chart a course forward in a divided Australia.

The response to a divided Australia is not to allow one tribe to govern over anyone else, as is often the case today. We should ensure that everyone is represented. We should treat everyone with equal respect. We should have more freedom to decide within our communities, families and individual lives.

I call this *Liberal Populism*, in which frustrations with the elite-driven system are harnessed to protect our democracy, we rediscover Australia's egalitarian creed, we strengthen localism to empower communities, we maximise freedom to allow individuals to flourish, we treat everyone with equal dignity and we find unity.

PART I:

The Inners-Outers Divide

ONE

Australia's political tribes

On Tuesday, 15th September 2015, Malcolm Turnbull successfully challenged Tony Abbott for the leadership of the Liberal Party and became Australia's 29th Prime Minister. 'This has been a very important day in the life of the nation,' Turnbull posted on *Facebook*.[35] Following the perfunctory nod to his predecessor and declaring how humble he was to become the leader, Turnbull went on to declare that:

> 'We cannot be defensive, we cannot future proof ourselves. We have to recognise that the disruption that we see driven by technology, the change is our friend if we are agile and smart enough to take advantage of it. There has never been a more exciting time to be alive than today and there has never been a more exciting time to be an Australian.'

A few months later the 'never been a more exciting time' slogan became the centrepiece in the Turnbull Government's $28 million 'Ideas Boom' advertising campaign.[36] There is much truth to Turnbull's assertions. Humans are living longer, safer and more prosperous lives than at any time in our history.[37] Australia is among the freest and most successful nations on Earth.[38]

Turnbull's comments, however, failed to resonate with many Australians. A poll during the 2016 election campaign found that the majority of voters do not agree with the statement 'there's never been a more exciting time to be an Australian.'[39] The slogan fell flat electorally and received harsh criticism following Turnbull's mediocre 2016 election result.[40] 'Canning isn't going to be the next Silicon Valley,' Liberal MP Andrew Hastie told his local newspaper. 'A lot of what we were campaigning on nationally just wasn't resonating with everyday Australians.'

The 'never been a more exciting time' slogan is quintessential Turnbull. It reflects his identity and life experience: academically and financially successful, optimistic and excited about change and unashamedly ambitious. Turnbull's defenders told *Fairfax Media* that it 'played to his strengths and he was clearly in his element on that topic.'[41]

	Economic left	Economic right
Inners 30%	The New Elite: Highly educated Greens, Inner-city progressive Labor	The Old Establishment: Inner-city middle class 'Turnbull' Liberals
Outers 50%	The Left Behind: Working class traditional Labor	The Aspirational: 'Howard Battlers' Liberals
	One Nation, Australian Conservatives	

Figure 1. 'Inners' and 'Outers,' who sit on both sides of the economic left–right divide, is the new divide in Australian politics

The Inners

Turnbull does appeal to some Australians. They are the highly educated professional knowledge economy workers, the instinctive cultural progressives who reside in the inner-city.[42] They are academically talented and adapt to new technologies with ease. They are well suited to our era of rapid technological and economic change.[43] They are the 31 per cent of Australians who agreed with Turnbull's 'never been a more exciting time' slogan.[44] These habitual optimists are what I call the Inners.

Inners have cosmopolitan liberal political instincts.[45] They are post-materialist, profoundly secular and progressive on social issues. Inners are for abstract 'equality.' They voted overwhelmingly for same-sex marriage, express concern about the treatment of asylum seekers and support action on environmental issues. They value tolerance and diversity.[46] Life and work for Inners is about autonomy, self-actualisation and flexibility.[47] Inners like to meet new people, visit different places and try new foods.[48] They can afford domestic help, eat out often and travel to Europe regularly.

Inners swung *towards* the Liberal Party at the last election, delighted to see the end of Tony Abbott's leadership. They live in wealthy inner-suburban electorates such as Melbourne, Brisbane and Perth that recorded first preference swings towards the Liberal Party under Malcolm Turnbull, as well as swings to the Greens, at the 2016 election.[49] They were, nevertheless, disappointed by Turnbull whom they hoped would be 'more' progressive.[50]

Inners' 'achieved' status is the basis of their identity.[51] Inners did well in school tests, go to top universities and occupy the 'best' knowledge economy jobs. They are the innovators and entrepreneurs. Creativity, skills, abilities and effort defines their self-worth.[52] Because their achievements provide self-confidence, they do not need to derive their identity from where they happen to live or the traditions of the past.[53]

On a Friday evening Inners are sipping cocktails and on a Sunday morning they are eating smashed avocado on toast with goats cheese sprinkled with superfood seeds.[54] They have tried out yoga, downloaded a mindfulness app, regularly visit art galleries and go to the theatre and enjoy documentaries and drama on the *ABC*.[55] Inners think they are better than those with menial jobs and 'lower' cultural tastes like watching reality television or holidays in Bali.

When it comes to politics, Inners are highly engaged, information rich and influential.[56] They eschew traditional party loyalties and aggressive partisanship.[57] Inners of the 'left' and 'right,' have their differences on economic policy; however, Liberal, Labor and Greens voting Inners have very similar cultural attitudes, career paths, education and incomes.

Not every individual Inner pulls a lever of power. But almost every lever of power is pulled by an Inner.[59] Inner values are mostly unchallenged at the top of Australian society. Although they are a minority in number, Inners dominate politics, corporates, universities, civil society, bureaucracies and the media.[58] Inner values are well-represented in public debate by opinion formers and decision makers.

Inners often do not understand their cultural domination and nor do they realise that their attitudes are frequently in the minority.[60] I estimate Inners to be about 30 per cent of Australia's population, as I outline in more detail later in this chapter.

Inners, like their opposite group, the Outers, sit across the traditional left-right economic spectrum. Those on the economic right, **The Old Establishment**, are the archetype middle class Liberal Party voter. They went to the best independent schools, the top universities and live in blue ribbon seats such as North Sydney and Wentworth in Sydney, Higgins and Kooyong in Melbourne, Ryan in Brisbane and Curtin in Perth.[61] While many of their parents were lower middle class Liberal voters, Menzies'

Forgotten People, these persons now veer towards the upper end of the income scale.

The Old Establishment have succeeded in professional and managerial jobs. They vote Liberal but are not socially conservative. They reside in some of the most socially progressive seats in the country. Many traditional Liberal heartlands in wealthy inner-suburbia voted overwhelmingly in favour of same-sex marriage. Higgins in Melbourne voted 84 per cent 'Yes', Wentworth in Sydney was 81 per cent favourable, Ryan in Brisbane was 73 per cent; meanwhile, Curtin in Perth was 72 per cent in favour.[62] However, for *The Old Establishment*, social issues are not paramount when it comes to election time – like most Australians, economic concerns primarily motivate their vote.[63]

The New Elite are the younger, university educated, professional managerial class that form the post-materialist new left.[64] They come from a mix of backgrounds, made it into university and now have well paid knowledge economy jobs in the inner-city. They earn less than *The Old Establishment* but are wealthier than most Australians. They work in high income professional jobs – they are academics, architects, town planners, doctors, lawyers and bureaucrats. They live similar lives to *The Old Establishment*, but they care less for economic issues, instead focusing their political attention on cultural and social progressivism. They are internationalists and identity as global citizens, highly value autonomy and are dismissive of tradition.

The New Elite live in an information bubble. They read *The Guardian* and the *Buzzfeed News* and follow a limited clique on social media which reinforces their perspective.[65] Though some vote Labor, they are epitomised by the Greens.

Greens voters were most supportive of the leadership change

from symbolic Outer Abbott to symbolic Inner Turnbull (69 per cent).[66] They live in the same electorates as *The Old Establishment*, as well as Labor's traditional inner-city heartlands which are under threat by the Greens such as Melbourne, Melbourne Ports, Batman and Wills in Victoria, Sydney and Grayndler in New South Wales and Fremantle in Western Australia.[67]

Inners are highly vocal, extremely visible, and have come to dominate Australian political, social and corporate life. They are not going anywhere. But neither are the Outers.

The Outers

On the other side of this divide are the **Outers**, the many Australians who were not attracted to Turnbull's Ideas Boom. They see the world from a different place. They grew up and live in outer suburbia, small towns and rural Australia.[68] They are unlikely to have gone to university, have low to middle incomes, are a bit older and more likely to be married and have kids. They have trade qualifications and technical certificates, or no post-school education. They grew up in an era when relatively few went to university, fewer jobs required a university education and respectable decently paid jobs were aplenty.[69] I estimate Outers to be about 50 per cent of Australia's population.

Outers are more likely to be in jobs that require physical activity.[70] An Outer might be a plumber, mechanic or builder. While they do find their jobs interesting and rewarding, work for them is less about self-actualisation or helping society.[71] Outers work hard because they are financially and socially distant from the top. They are more materialistic than Inners, thirsty for the opportunity to succeed on their own terms.[72]

On a Friday evening they are at home with their families

and on a Sunday they are more likely to be in Church – though their religious observance has declined.[73] They enjoy commercial television and are passionate about their football teams. Outers enjoy a pub meal much more than Asian fusion and read the *Herald Sun* or the *Daily Telegraph*.[74]

Outers have an 'ascribed' identity. Their identity is grounded in the local community where they grew up, the sports teams their families have barracked for across generations and the nation which they are proud to belong.[75] Patriotism is an important part of their identity. It is this devotion to nation that underpins a rejection of proposals based on a negative vision of Australia, such as changing the date of Australia Day or disparaging Anzac Day.[76] Outers are viciously opposed to those who threaten Australia's safety and security and more broadly the Australian way of life.[77] This concern drives high levels of apprehension about rising crime and terrorism.

Outers are concerned about reduced status of non-graduate employment and the lower prestige of technical education and apprenticeships compared to university.[78] Outers have less in savings, lower incomes and larger families to support and are therefore thirsty for job security.[79]

Outers are struck by the rapid pace of social, economic, technological and demographic change in recent decades. They often look at modern Australia as a foreign country.[80] Outers are not technophobes, but they do want some stability in their lives, which is often lacking in an era of social media, AI and blockchain. Rapid change is unsettling and threatening to their natural thirst for stability and familiarity.[81]

For Outers change is not inevitable nor merely to be accepted. They support necessary change. However, change for change's sake is rejected. Outers are the reason 38 of Australia's 44 referendums to modify the constitution failed to receive public support.[82]

Immigration raises complex issues for Outers. They welcome immigrants who successfully integrate and contribute. However, concern about cultural change, jobs, congestion and local amenities and exploiting the welfare system drives less support for immigration from Outers compared to Inners.[83]

Outers are culturally conservative, they want to preserve Australia's political and social institutions and have traditional moral and social mores.

Outers are not bigots, despite the way some Inners portray them.[84] While they may be conservative in their own lives, most Outers have tolerant liberal views towards women, homosexuality and race. This follows the wider liberalisation in attitudes over the past thirty years.[85] On specific social policy issues, however, they have mixed opinions. Same-sex marriage split Outers – some voted 'Yes' for personal empathy, while others voted 'No' to the Inners driven agenda.[86]

Outers are substantially less politically engaged.[87] They are not watching Question Time on weekdays, *Q&A* on Monday evening, or *Insiders* on Sunday morning.[88] This disengagement is because they live busy lives raising families and working hard, and because no matter whom they vote for life does not change much.[89]

Outers are sick of the chaos in Canberra, the relentless attempts to control their lives by edict and the inaction on issues which impact on them such as energy prices. Outers' politics is more local and pragmatic, focused on issues such as school quality, the cost of their bills and the dog fouling on their street.[90] They want tangible results to real life problems, not abstract utopianism.[91]

The Aspirational are the conservative voting working to lower-middle class. They are 'Howard's Battlers' or 'Tony's Tradies', families who have risen into moderately comfortable lives in the suburbs. While some did go to university, most have a trade qualification, certificate, or no post-school qualification. They are self-made small to medium business owners who want a brighter future for their children. They want their kids to get a good education, their parents to get a decent standard of healthcare and when it comes to election time consider the economy to be the most crucial issue. They take community life seriously and are more likely to attend church, sports and voluntary organisations which give them a sense of purpose.

The Aspirational often come from Labor families. However, they do not feel at home in the modern Labor Party dominated by union officials and tertiary educated technocrats. It is not that they left the Labor Party, it is that the Labor Party left them. Labor's posturing on environmentalism and identity politics (of limited relevance to their lives) pushed working class voters increasingly into the hands of the Liberals. *The Aspirational* are self-sufficient and do not see the government as the solution to the world's problems. They want a hand up, not a handout. They want the freedom to flourish and are sick of outside forces, particularly government, getting in their way.

The Left Behind is the old guard left wing working class. They are the remnants of Labor's blue collar voting base, which has substantially declined because of the transformation away from manufacturing and towards services. They feel out of place in modern Australia, left behind by the rapid pace of change. They grew up in an era of stability, economic growth and job security and strong family ties. Today, however, their place in society has been diminished. Australia's graduate focused economy and society has downgraded their skills, education and attitudes.

The dominance of Inners on the political left, both within the Labor Party and in the upper echelons of the unions, has diminished the working class voice. Historically trade unions were controlled by the working class and their emergence in the 19th century provided a platform for representation and participation as equals with the middle and upper classes. Today though, unions and Labor are dominated by university graduates, not the working class. *The Left Behind* lack a political home and are willing to look for new options. Some voted for the Liberal Party under John Howard and Tony Abbott but were also attracted to One Nation in 2016, Palmer's United Party in 2013, and the Shooters, Fishers and Farmers and Jacqui Lambie. While the Greens were most likely to support the rise of Turnbull, One Nation supporters were the least likely. Just 11 per cent of One Nation voters at the last election supported the handling of the leadership change from Abbott to Turnbull.[92]

The divide

The 'Inners' and 'Outers' are an analytical model to better understand the divides that have emerged in Australian society. Inners and Outers are loose alignments of sentiment and worldview, not precise or stable. They are identifiable values clusters, not groups with hard borders and explicit memberships. The Inners-Outers dichotomy explains something, but it does not explain everything.

No party and no person fits perfectly into either tribe. Parties are vote seeking entities that move between contradictory positions. Consequently, there is substantial crossover in party support and appeal between the groups (See Figure 2).

Australia's Political Divides

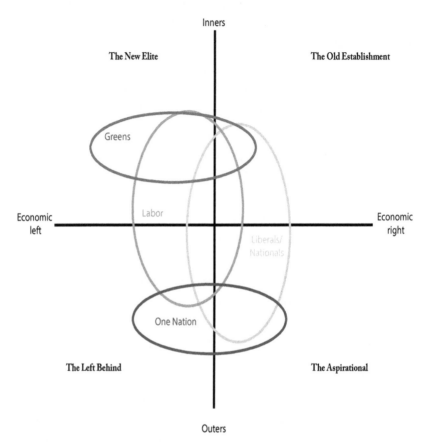

Figure 2. Australia's political divides and party crossover

Individuals are multifaceted and will inevitably break the mould in some of their views and attitudes. No analysis can precisely explain the diversity in the social world. Each individual has a wide array of viewpoints and different identities.

There is also a large group of **Betweeners**, about 20 per cent of Australians, who express both Inner or the Outer tendencies. For example, some individuals from *The Old Establishment*, the Liberal voting middle class, have conservative social and cultural attitudes. The subset is closer to Inners in education and career; however, nearer to Outers in values. Despite the complexities, surveys and data analysis reveals the existence of the Inners and Outers value divide. Furthermore, it is possible to identify differences in attitudes by education, geography and occupation.

The response to survey questions that tap into ideational, lifestyle and cultural issues reveals the 30 per cent Inners and about 50 per cent Outers dichotomy. The Outers are the 53 per cent of Australians who identify primarily as national citizens, and the Inners are the 31 per cent of Australians who identify as citizens of the world.[93] Outers are the 54 per cent who express a 'great' deal of pride in and feel 'very close' to Australia, the 55 per cent who are worried about Australia losing its culture and identity and the 52 per cent who say that Australia sometimes feels like a foreign country.[94]

Outers are the 49 per cent who think that Australia should deal with its own problems and let other countries deal with their issues, while the Inners are the 32 per cent of Australians who do not believe that national borders make the world better.[95] The Outers are the 50 per cent who think that sharing national customs and traditions is very important to be truly Australian.[96]

The Inners, by contrast, are the 35 per cent of Australians who think that patriotic feelings lead to intolerance and negative feelings towards immigrants and the 26 per cent of Australians who want an increase in immigration.[97] Outers are the 53 per cent of Australians who do not want change of historical statues; the Inners are the 32 per cent who do want change.[98]

The divide also emerges on questions of issue priority. When asked what the most important issue is, 70 per cent prioritise the economy and crime – indicating strong support for economic and safety concerns by both Outers and Betweeners.[99] Meanwhile, 30 per cent of Australians, the Inners, think that 'support for a less impersonal and more humane society' and a society 'in which ideas count more than money' is more important than economics or security.

The divide emerges prominently on policy issues that link to safety concerns. Outers are the 56 per cent who believe the government could do more to prevent terrorist attacks; Inners are the 25 per cent who are concerned that counter-terrorism laws have gone too far.[100] Similarly, Outers are the 53 per cent who support turning back boats carrying asylum seekers; the Inners are the 29 per cent that disagrees.[101] The Outers are the 55 per cent of Australians who prioritise keeping energy costs down and maintaining reliability, unlike the Inners who want to prioritise reducing carbon (15 per cent) or somehow want all three (22 per cent).[102]

The Inners-Outers divide is *not* the same as the social conservatism versus social liberalism axis that has previously overlaid the left-right economic axis in many political compasses.[103] While social conservatism has not wholly disappeared in Australia, it has substantially diminished. There has been a rapid and widespread liberalisation of attitudes on homosexuality, abortion, divorce and sex before marriage (See Table 1). The successful campaigning by Inners has persuaded most Outers. The new divide in Australian politics is not about social issues; it is about culture, lifestyle and identity.

I am not the first to explore values divides in Australian society. In 1999, academic Katharine Betts wrote *The Great Divide: Immigration Politics in Australia*. Betts describes the 'new class' of Australians who feel superior because of their education – which

'Never justifiable'	1984	2014
Homosexuality	39%	13%
Abortion	29%	16%
Divorce	15%	4%
Euthanasia	22%	15%
Sex before marriage	-	6%

Table 1. Attitudes to social issues (Source: World Values Survey 1984 & 2014)

gave them critical thinking skills making them confident with open-ended systems of meaning.[104] Betts contrasts the group with those who learn from life experience and submission to authority. She has called the two groups the 'cosmopolitans,' who are supportive of immigration, and the 'patriots,' who are sceptical about immigration.[105] The cosmopolitans, Betts writes, 'have built their claims to honour and prestige by painting a negative picture of parochial Australians and distancing themselves from that picture.'[106]

In 2002, former Labor leader Mark Latham described the 'insiders' and 'outsiders,' and argued that each has a distinctive political culture. 'The powerful centre of our society, concentrated in the international heart of the major cities, talk a different language to suburban communities. In lifestyle and political values, they are poles apart,' Latham said in a London speech.[107]

In 2013, journalist Nick Cater wrote in *The Lucky Culture and the Rise of an Australian Ruling Class* about the 'cultural divide,' that drives Australians apart.[108] Cater describes 'the new ruling class' as the 'people who did not simply feel *better off* but *better than* their fellow Australians':

'they were cosmopolitan and sophisticated well read (or so they would have us believe) and politically aware. Their presumption of virtue set them apart from the common herd: they were neither racist nor sexist, claimed to be indifferent to material wealth, ate healthily, drank in moderation, and if they were not gay themselves, made a show of solidarity with lots of friends who were. Their compassion knew no bounds: the vulnerable of the world could rely on their support, in principle at least. They were plastic bag refuseniks and tickers of carbon offset boxes, for they knew what the science was saying, and it could not be denied. People like them should be running the country, they thought, or more accurately, ruling it.'

Other analysts have used different labels to describe multi-dimensional divides within Australian society. In 2016, *Crikey* reporter Guy Rundle identified four new political groupings: the old bourgeoisie (*The Old Establishment*), the progressive-knowledge class (*The New Elite*), the working-middle class (*The Aspirational*) and the excluded (*The Left Behind*).[109] Rundle noted, following the election of Donald Trump, how this was making politics more difficult for the political left.

A survey by academics Jill Sheppard and Nicholas Biddle of the Australian National University, which analysed economic, social and cultural capital identified six 'latent' classes: the 'precariat' and 'ageing workers' (*The Left Behind*), 'new workers' and 'established middle' (*The Aspirational*), 'emerging affluent' (*The New Elite*) and 'established affluent' (*The Old Establishment*).[110] The clusters group together people by income and assets, social networks and cultural tastes – such as watching sport or going to the opera.

Fairfax Media, in collaboration with ANU's Social Research Centre, found similar trends in their Political Personas Project. The study group used a public survey to deduce geographic patterns.[111] On the one end, in the inner-city of Sydney and Melbourne there is a clustering of progressive cosmopolitans and activist egalitarians (*The New Elite*) and ambitious savers and lavish mod-cons (*The Old Establishment*). Meanwhile, in the outer suburbs reside prudent traditionalists (*The Aspirational*) and anti-establishment types (*The Left Behind*).

The geographic characteristics of the divide between Inners and Outers emerges in voting patterns. The support for the Greens is strongest in the inner-city. One Nation voters are most likely to be found in the outer suburbs and regional areas. The Grattan Institute found that the further you travel from the centre of Australia's capital cities the higher the support for One Nation and other minor parties.[112]

§

The worldviews of Inners and Outers are legitimate and should form *part* of Australia's political debate. However, Australia's party system, which is designed around a disintegrating class structure, is struggling to handle the divide. There is a disproportionate representation of Inners at the top of Australian life. Inners dominate the major political parties, bureaucracy, media, universities, trade unions, not-for-profits and corporates. Consequently, Outer viewpoints receive less attention. The divide also helps explain internal divisions within parties and the growing polarisation, political conflict and instability that makes reform difficult.

The major parties will, more likely than not, endure into the future. Incumbency provides advantages. The major parties are organised, have relatively large memberships and links to corporates. Labor has historic links to the union movement. They also receive media attention and benefit from single member electorates in the House of Representatives. The parties have also created laws that benefit themselves: public funding, membership requirements for new parties, exemption from privacy law and donation law which favours existing parties. Additionally, party allegiance has weakened, but it has not entirely disappeared. About a third of Australians still vote for the same major party, Liberal and Nationals, or Labor, at every election and an additional large segment only swing between the major parties.[113]

Nevertheless, the divide within the parties complicates matters. Labor and Liberal parliamentarians, party members and voters are a mixture of Inners and Outers. Politicians often try to hide the divides on cultural and identity issues by concentrating on policy issues that unite their potential voters.[114] The Liberal Party can attract both *The Old Establishment* and *The Aspirational* by focusing on the economy. For Labor, highlighting welfare, healthcare and education appeals to both *The New Elite* and much of *The Left Behind.*

The major parties are struggling to stick to their traditional strengths and hide from the divisive issues. Challenged by the rise of the Greens in their historic inner-city heartland, Labor is struggling to appeal to the post-materialist policy interests of *The New Elite* while also attracting *The Left Behind* and *The Aspirational* who reside in marginal suburban seats. The Liberal Party similarly struggles to appeal to *The Old Establishment* in blue-ribbon electorates such as North Sydney and Wentworth while also trying to reach out to *The Aspirational* in suburban Australia, such as Western Sydney. Political parties do worse in the polls and at elections when they narrowly appeal to only Inners or Outers.

Meanwhile, many Labor MPs with an Inners disposition

represent Outer Labor electorates and, in other cases, Outer Liberal MPs represent Inner Liberal seats, and vice-versa. This situation raises questions about the nature of representation. Should Labor's Member for Chifley, Ed Husic, have followed the party line in favour of same-sex marriage or his electorate's vote against in the plebiscite? Similarly, should Liberal MP Tony Abbott have followed his constituency, Warringah, who supported same-sex marriage or stick to his personal conviction?

In political practice, as a matter of arithmetic, Outers *should* be more prominent. Most marginal seats are suburban contests between different types of Outers, *The Left Behind* and *The Aspirational*, which become Liberal and Labor races, where the Greens receive limited support.[115] There are few marginal seats made up of Inners. That is, contests between *The New Elite* and *The Left Behind*, between Labor and the Greens, are rare. Electoral battles between *The Old Establishment* and *The New Elite*, between Labor, Liberals and Greens, are even rarer.

Nevertheless, the priorities of Inners are prominent beyond their raw numbers. The situation arises because Inners, the new managerial-professional elite, dominate Australia's political, economic and cultural institutions.

The following chapter explores how the rise of the Inners has reshaped the divides in Australian politics.

TWO

Australia's political realignment and the rise of Inners

I did not expect much support at La Trobe University – located in Melbourne's working class northern suburbs – when I visited to debate in favour of capitalism against the Socialist Alternative. The caricature of La Trobe is a left wing heartland. It is often flippantly labelled 'La Trot,' after socialist Trotskyists. The reality is different.

After the debate, in question after question, the audience critiqued the socialist's arguments. 'How do you justify your ideology in the face of the absolute failure of Marxist implementation?' one young woman asked. 'Not only the rich are getting richer, but the poor as well,' a gentleman of South Asian background commented. A few dozen supportive audience members followed me and my fellow debater, John Hajek, out of the room afterwards. John, who has debated the socialists three times before at other universities, said he has never seen such a positive audience response.

The Socialist Alternative is the latest far left campus activists who claim to represent 'workers.' However, the organisation is dominated by students from a middle class background.[116] One of their mistakes during the debate was to repeatedly describe menial, strenuous jobs, the type done by lower income Australians, as 'monotonous.' The label did not go down well with the working class audience.

Solmaz, an 18-year-old politics and psychology student, expressed her anger at how the speakers repeatedly dispaged the dignity of work.[117] 'My question is for the socialists,' she said:

> 'What do you suggest people who are doing hard physical work now do? Because my Dad is a panel beater and he loves his job and although it's really hard what else is he meant to do? He didn't finish high school. He grew up in a third world country, which, to borrow a phrase from President Trump, is a "shit hole country". He can't come here and work as a doctor. He's a panel beater. That's what he does.'

That's what he does. Solmaz explained her question to me after the debate. 'I've grown up in a family where [strenuous work] is viewed as a good thing… and the reason my parents work so hard is because they want me and my brother to end up in a better position than they have,' she said. Solmaz comes from a working class background; however, she felt alienated by the contemporary left – the people who are supposed to represent her class interest.

Australia's Inners of the political left, *The New Elite*, are not particularly interested in economics and, ironically considering their claims to represent the working class, are often condescending to workers. Even the *Socialist Alternative* have limited interest in economics and class – they do talk about income inequality; however, they are just as likely to be campaigning for same-sex marriage, multiculturalism, the environment and refugees, as they are for the working class.[118]

Solmaz's frustration with the left is common. The traditional association between the parties of the left and the working class, and parties of the right and the middle class, has disappeared across developed countries. A new middle class cohort has emerged, made up of highly educated, well-paid white collar professionals and public servants, who are wealthy enough to be interested in non-economic issues and now vote for parties of the political left. Partly in response, an aspirational working class has emerged, who feel alienated by the contemporary left's focus on cultural, identity and lifestyle issues and are increasingly voting for parties of the right.

The end of class?

It was not always so. Australian politics used to be easy to explain: the working class, in manual jobs, voted for Labor Party and the middle class, in non-manual jobs, voted for the Liberal Party.[119] Elections were fought on a left-right political pendulum and both parties campaigned to a relatively small number of swing voters who sat on the fence between working and middle classes.[120]

In 1963, political scientist Robert R. Alford wrote that 'Australia's politics have been dominated by class cleavages before and since its foundation as a nation in 1901.'[121] Similarly, in 1970, political scientist Solomon Encel concluded 'the correspondence between class identity and voting is so close... that the two may be regarded as largely alternative measures of the same general outlook.'[122]

Australia was not unique in this regard. American political scientist Seymour Martin Lipset wrote in 1960 that 'For most of the twentieth century, working class voters in developed countries generally supported Left-oriented parties, while middle and upper class voters supported Right-oriented parties.'[123] In Australia, the class groupings also had religious and gender undertones. The standard narrative was that working class male Catholics voted Labor and middle class female protestants voted Liberal.[124]

The traditional class, religion and gender divides in Australian politics have substantially declined if not entirely disappeared. Political scientist, and former federal minister, David Kemp was the first to comprehensively analyse the breakdown of traditional groupings in the Australian context.[125] Kemp argued in 1978 that the decline of blue collar jobs, and the rise of white collar jobs and the public sector, was undermining class and other divides in Australian politics.

Kemp argued that '[changes in occupations were] inexorably pushing the party structures and their electoral bases of support out of alignment.' Kemp found, from an extensive analysis of available electoral and survey data, a substantial decline in class, religion, region and urban-rural divides in Australian politics. Essentially, blue collar voters were becoming more conservative and white collar voters more progressive. The trend has accelerated since Kemp wrote his thesis (See Figure 3).[126] In 1987, almost two-thirds of self-identifying working class voters opted for the Labor Party. At the last election, a working class voter was more likely to vote for the Liberals and Nationals (42 per cent) than they were for Labor (37 per cent).

Meanwhile, parties of the left and the right attract middle class voters (See Figure 4). At the last election a small majority of middle class voters opted for the Liberal and Nationals (52 per cent). The rest are split between Labor (26 per cent) and minor parties such as the Greens (22 per cent). There has not

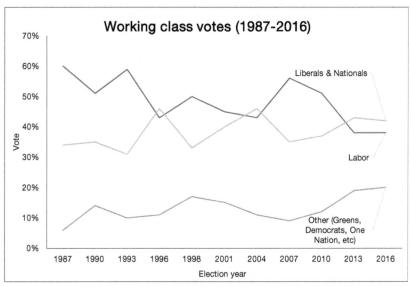

Figure 3. Self-identifying 'working class' vote in the House of Representatives (Source: Australian Election Study 1987-2016)

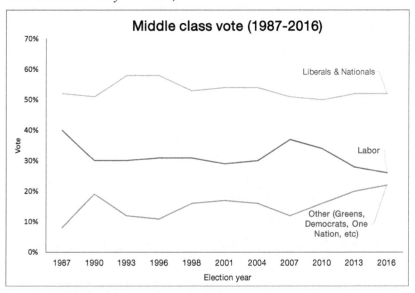

Figure 4. Self-identifying 'middle class' vote in the House of Representatives (Source: Australian Election Study 1987-2016)

been a substantial change in the proportion of Australians who identify as working class (44 per cent), middle class (54 per cent), or upper class (two per cent).

Historically, the key voting divide was between manual workers, who voted for parties of the left, and non-manual workers who voted for parties of the right. Today, however, both Labor and Liberal attract a similar proportion of professionals and trade workers (See Figure 5). Overall, Liberal voters are more likely to be managers and Labor voters are more likely to be community and personal service workers. The Greens vote is dominated by professional workers, while One Nation's vote is made up of a high proportion of community and personal service workers.

On education, Labor and Liberal voters are university graduates in similar numbers; Liberal voters are slightly more likely to have a trade qualification (See Figure 6). Greens and One Nation supporters, on the other hand, sit at the opposite ends of the spectrum. The Greens disproportionately represent graduates and few tradespeople. The largest proportion One Nation voters are trade qualified and very few are graduates.

There are some remaining distinctions in voting. The Liberals and Nationals continue to receive more support from self-employed than Labor, as well as more support from higher income earners.[127] The income split relates dually to many high-income voters opting for the Greens, hence bringing down the average income of Labor voters. It also reflects the continuing Liberal Party support from financially successful Australians who are mostly interested in economic issues.

Labor still receives stronger support from union members.[128] However, trade unions have declined in size and are no longer

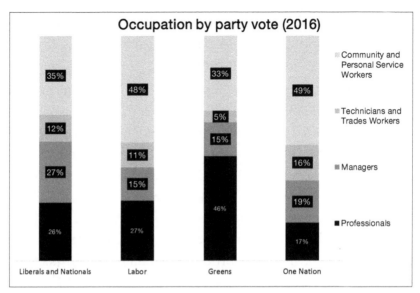

Figure 5. Occupational categories by voting in the Senate, 2016 election (Source: Australian Election Study 2016)

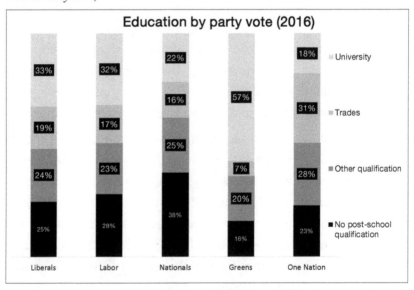

Figure 6. Education level by voting in Senate 2016 election (Source: Australian Election Study 2016)

predominately made up of blue collar workers. Just 9 per cent of private sector workers are members of a union and there are more union members in professional and managerial jobs than blue collar labourers.[129] Graduates are more likely to be a member of a union compared to those without post-school education.[130] The situation reflects the growth in public sector unions – 38 per cent of public sector workers are members of a union – representing graduate bureaucrats, teachers and health professionals. Labor receives much stronger support from public sector workers, who make up a large proportion of unionised voters.

Australia is not unique in these trends.[131] Across western democracies there has been a decline in class voting as incomes and education rise, economies shift from manufacturing to services and a growth in small firms and technology.[132] In Britain, the working class are increasingly voting for the Conservatives and the middle class are voting for Labour.[133] Similarly, in the United States professional white collar workers are more likely to support the Democrats and working class blue collar workers have increasingly opted for the Republicans.[134]

The rise of the cognitive elite

In his early work on the decline of class voting in Australia, Kemp identified attitudinal differences between university graduates and the rest of society on issues such as the royal family, military service and faith in institutions. Kemp predicted that Labor would have to change over time to accommodate their new middle class and the declining number of working class voters. Kemp also predicts a new political divide 'between certain sections of the upper middle class and the rest of society' and 'new tensions… within political parties.'[135]

The rise of a cognitive elite, defined by their experience of higher education, is central to Australia's political realignment. Australia has become increasingly defined by the values divides between the new graduate tribe and the rest. Historically, a small number of Australians received a university education. In 1960, there were just 53,633 students at all of Australia's universities and in 1982 fewer than 7 per cent of Australians had a university degree.[136] Graduates were numerically few and of limited direct consequence during elections.

The creation of more universities and student places has substantially expanded university education since World War II. John Dawkins, who served as education minister from 1987 to 1991 in the Hawke Government, was particularly fervent. Dawkins converted 46 technical colleges into university campuses, increasing the total number of universities to 32 by 1991 and introduced the HECS higher education loan scheme to expand student numbers.[137]

Today, there are over 1 million domestic students at Australian universities, overall about 30 per cent of adults and 40 per cent of Australians aged 25 to 34 have a degree.[138] The growth has established a new, sizeable and influential faction within the Australian electorate.

Graduates are Australia's new middle class; they have different politics, culture and motivations to the middle class of the past. The old middle class were associated with the Liberal Party and defined by their conservative attitudes: virtue, self-discipline and the Protestant work ethic.[139] The new middle class are associated with the upper echelons of the Labor Party and the Greens and premise their identity and social status cognitive abilities, university education, mastery of knowledge and prestigious careers.

Australians with higher education do the jobs with the highest level of prestige – the highest paying, most socially respected occupations (See Figure 7).[140] Graduates are dominant in high-status careers such as surgeons (98 per cent), solicitors (98 per cent), architects (91 per cent) and civil engineers (86 per cent), and high influence careers such as secondary school teachers (95 per cent), economists (95 per cent), university lecturers and tutors (94 per cent) and journalists (71 per cent). Lower prestige occupations such as forklift drivers (four per cent), labourers (five per cent) and textile machine operators (six per cent) contain few graduates.

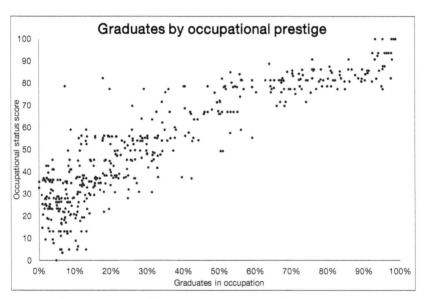

Figure 7. Graduates and occupational prestige, each dot represents an occupational category (Source: ABS census 2016, ANU Australian Socioeconomic Index 2006)

Although not every graduate is powerful, it is graduates who staff political parties, the bureaucracy, corporates, unions, media, universities, civil society and other major institutions.[141] Consequently, the graduate viewpoint have disproportionate weight at the top echelons of Australian society. Graduation from university provides access to the best jobs, higher incomes, social status, confidence, access and influence.

Across a wide array of measures, the differences between the lives of graduates and non-graduates are stark. Graduates are, according to the Australian Bureau of Statistics (ABS) General Social Survey, more likely to be in the workforce and employed, have better health and even feel safer when walking home.[142] Sixty-four per cent of graduates are in the top 40 per cent of income earners and graduates earn on average a $1 million extra across their lifetime.[143]

The Grattan Institute's higher education program director, Andrew Norton, argues that while higher education has increased social mobility, by providing an opportunity for many Australians to *improve* their socioeconomic standing, it is 'facilitating a more unequal labour market.'[144] Graduates have both the skills and cognitive ability to take advantage of high paying professional jobs at the centre of Australia's post-industrial economy.

The Australian economy has transformed from heavily reliant on manufacturing and agriculture to an economy almost entirely dominated by services over the last 50 years. In the 1960s, around a quarter of Australians were employed in manufacturing, 10 per cent per cent in agriculture, 1 per cent in mining and the remaining 64 per cent in services.[145] Today, 7 per cent of Australians are employed in manufacturing, 3 per cent work in agriculture and 2 per cent in mining and the remaining 88 per cent have a service sector job, ranging from finance, public administration, healthcare and education to retail and aged care.

Service sector jobs are diverse. There is evidence across developed economies of growing divides in the labour market between the professional economy workers at the top and the rest at the bottom. American economist Tyler Cowen argues that modern economies are splitting into two groups – a highly educated, self-motivated and cognitively capable group that masters technology and the majority that earn relatively little working within automated production systems, such as retail and hospitality.[146]

Following Cowen's model, Australia's job market is increasingly polarised between graduates in highly paid 'abstract' jobs and the rest paid less in lower skill jobs.[147]

In the context of assessing the impact of technological change on Australia's labour market, economists Jeff Borland and Michael Coelli of the University of Melbourne found a substantial increase in demand for 'abstract' jobs that require a high level of cognitive skill and a corresponding decline in demand for routine and manual jobs.[148] Borland and Coelli conclude that while overall there are not fewer jobs available, 'Technological change also creates winners and losers.' The losers tend to be 'concentrated among workers with lower levels of educational attainment.'

The bifurcation of the labour market is having a particularly strong impact on working class men. Gideon Rozner from IPA found a decline in participation of working age males from 95 per cent in the mid-1960s to 79 per cent today, leaving 650,000 men outside of the workforce.[149] These labour market trends will likely accelerate. The OECD predicts the less educated will struggle in the future as technology and automation drives further changes in the job market.[150] These changes are likely to benefit the highly educated while leaving everyone else behind.

There is a cross-generational element to these societal divides. Graduates partake in a process known as 'assortative matching,' graduates marry graduates and non-graduates marry non-graduates.[151] Today's graduates will likely carry their abilities, identity, lifestyle and culture across the next generation by having and raising similar children in the future.[152] The situation creates intergenerational advantages for the graduate class and leaves non-graduate families with fewer opportunities in the longer term.

Graduates at the centre

In early 2016, shortly before the vote by Britain to leave the European Union, academics Will Jennings and Gerry Stoker argued that growing work and political divides were creating 'two Englands':

> 'A dynamic of global economic development means that many countries are experiencing uneven development and their citizens are increasingly split between those who can access high-skill jobs and those who cannot. As a result some citizens are living in cosmopolitan areas of growth and others in backwater areas of decline.'[153]

The situation, they found, is having substantial political implications:

> 'In cosmopolitan areas we find an England that is global in outlook, liberal and more plural in its sense of identity. In provincial backwaters we find an England that is inward-looking, relatively illiberal, negative about the EU and immigration, nostalgic and more English in its identity.'

Australia is facing a parallel divide. We are becoming segregated between the prosperous inner-cities and the stressed periphery and regions.[154] Graduates cluster near the centre of cities, the location of well-paid professional jobs in finance, information technology and engineering which are key to Australia's economic growth. They are also close to the amenities such as public transport and live in areas that have experienced dramatic growth in housing values.[155]

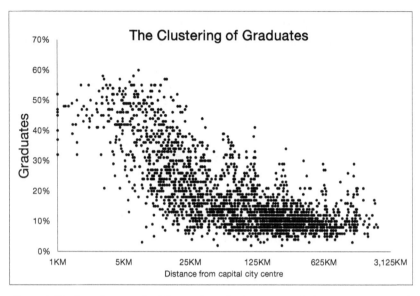

Figure 8. Graduates by postcode of distance from the city centre, each dot represents a postcode (Log scale: 5; Source: ABS census 2016)

Individuals who live near to Australia's city centres are twice as likely to have a bachelor degree than the national average, three-quarters more likely to be in a professional job and two-thirds more likely to have a high household gross income over $3,000 a week.[156] The limited remaining manufacturing and manual jobs have been pushed to outer suburbia and the regions – where people have less education, earn lower incomes, commute longer to work and more likely to experience social and economic disadvantage.[157]

Birds of a feather flock together, people with similar jobs and incomes, are more likely to live close to each other. Graduates are substantially more likely to live close to Australia's city centres (See Figure 8). Half of Australia's graduates live within 30 kilometres of our capital cities and two-thirds within 100 kilometres.[158] Inner-city suburbs have the highest concentration of graduates. This includes Yarralumla and Deakin in Canberra (60 per cent graduates), Nedlands in Perth (57 per cent graduates), Princes Hill and Fitzroy North in Melbourne (57 per cent graduates), North Sydney and St Leonards in Sydney (57 per cent graduates) and Bardon (54 per cent graduates) in Queensland.[159]

The postcodes, with a higher number of graduates, also contain higher numbers of professional job holders (See Figure 9) and higher income earners (See Figure 10). There are notable exceptions – for instance, mining towns such as Nullagine in Western Australia which have high incomes and a low number of graduates.

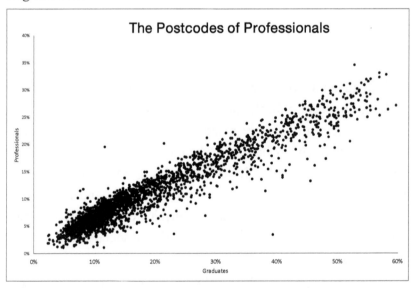

Figure 9. Graduates and professionals by postcode, each dot represents a postcode (Source: ABS census 2016)

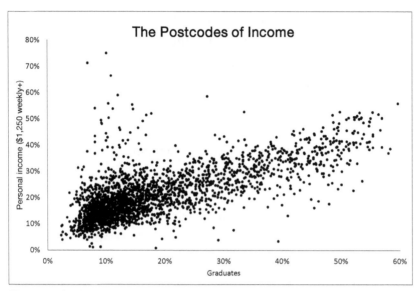

Figure 10. Graduates and personal income by postcode, each dot represents a postcode (Source: ABS census 2016)

Sociologist Charles Murray has idenified the educated elite living separately in the American context.[160] Murray identified 882 'Super Zips' where, other than low level service workers, the highly educated well-paid only interact with people like themselves. The new upper class, Murray argues, have a completely different set of attitudes and culture; meanwhile, the lower class is facing a weakening of family and community bonds.

Against the popular notion that the world is shrinking and we are becoming more mobile, evidence suggests that people in developed nations are moving *less* compared to 50 years ago. In Australia, Professor Martin Bell and collaborators found there has been a 'consistent and accelerating decline in migration intensities' across all distances. Despite a growing population, the number of people who have moved between region types, for example from outer suburbia or the regions to the inner-city, has declined from 334,000 between 1976–1981 to just 135,000 between 2006–2011. They argue the drop relates to housing availability, life choices and an aging population. The young and the highly educated are markedly more mobile; however, most people only move short distances and are likely to live near to where they grew up.

The declining internal migration, particularly over distance, is contributing to social and economic segregation. Demographer Bernard Salt has found a growing divide within Australia's cities between rich and poor suburbs, 'each world tends to beget and envelop its own.'[161] Consequently 'the richest and the poorest can live out their lives without bumping into each other.' Salt predicts that as the cities grow the poor will be pushed further out and consequently 'social mobility will drop as each of the city's bubbles tightens around its kin.'

The clustering of graduates in cities should be expected and, for many reasons, welcomed in an advanced economy.[162] Network effects and economies of scale mean that cities are more efficient with resources and more economically productive. Every time a city doubles in population there are 15 per cent fewer petrol stations, roads and electrical cables per capita; meanwhile, incomes and the number of patents are 15 per cent higher per capita.[163]

The clustering of highly capable individuals and innovative industry in cities has substantial economic benefit. However, there are political, social and cultural consequences for those who live outside cities and far from the city centre. There is an influential group at the physical heart of Australia's cities and the centre of power in Australia's political, economic and cultural institutions. This is creating a divided society, in which a small cohort, judged based on their professional and academic resume, dominate.

The achievement society

In 1958, British sociologist Michael Young devised the word 'meritocracy' to *criticise* a society that places academic and professional achievements above all else. Following the extensive positive use of the term 'meritocracy,' Young argued in 2001 that while people should be appointed based on their capabilities, merit itself has become a social class. 'With an amazing battery of certificates and degrees at its disposal, education has put its seal of approval on a minority, and its seal of disapproval on the many who fail to shine from the time they are relegated to the bottom streams at the age of seven or before,' Young wrote.[164] A society which emphasises a limited idea of merit creates a demoralised underclass.

The rise of higher education, the polarisation of the labour market and growing tribal clusters are having serious social, cultural and political impacts. We have established social status in academic and knowledge pursuits over others. As Andrew Norton has written, 'higher education creates its own status system that converts intelligence and academic effort into prestige':

> 'Higher education also increases occupational prestige; as with qualifications this is reflected in the way jobs are classified. It makes professions harder to get into and more exclusive. Over the twentieth century, many jobs that were once open to people without a university education came to require a bachelor degree. Now some professions want a masters degree.'[165]

David Goodhart has written that 'Cognitive ability, of the exam-passing kind, has in recent decades come to overshadow other criteria, such as character, competence or experience as the currency of career success from school days onwards.'[166] We have increasingly placed faith in quantifiable metrics of a person's value, such as standardised testing in school education.[167]

Testing is, of course, necessary to assess student progress and improve outcomes. However, if there are rewards for teachers or schools that do well on standardised testing pressure mounts to teach for the tests. A survey of teachers following the introduction of Australia's NAPLAN schools testing regime found that teachers are 'choosing or being instructed to teach to the test.'[168] The shift leads to less focus on other curriculum areas and character-building pursuits and reinforces social status in test taking

Those who are incapable of doing well on tests are at a disadvantage. In the past school leavers had a wider array of potential career paths, including university, technical, apprenticeship and relatively plentiful jobs. Today it is almost impossible to walk into a well-paying, prestigious job without a degree. Many young people are now left behind altogether; 15 per cent of Australian school leavers are neither in work or education.[169]

The cultural prestige of universities, combined with their government funding, is discouraging young Australians from considering vocational education. In many cases, technical education is more appropriate *and* can lead to better paying jobs than university degrees. The overemphasis on graduate education is increasingly being recognised, even within the university sector. Vicki Thomson, the CEO of the Group of Eight which represents Australia's top universities, has said that 'There is too much pressure on students that they must attend a university.'[170]

A 2017 study of over 6,000 primary and secondary school students in New South Wales found that the social pressure to attend universities begins at a young age.[171] 'There's a big push to go to uni,' Polly, a year nine student at a provincial school, told researchers in a focus group interview.[172] Participating students also told researches that technical education is 'lower' than university and for 'lazy' people. Calais, a year ten student, said that apprenticeships are 'just for if you can't get anything else I reckon.'[173] The bias towards higher education translates into post-school intentions. Two-thirds of young Australians, aged 15-19, say that they want to go to university, compared to 13 per cent who are considering TAFE and 9 per cent who are planning to undertake an apprenticeship.[174]

Student preferences are reinforced by public policy which has expanded higher education while providing declining support to vocational and apprenticeships. The introduction of the demand-driven university places system, which committed the government to fund as many students as universities could enrol, has led to 242,000 more places and a 40 per cent increase in commencing students in just eight years.[175] Over the same period, the number of Australians doing apprenticeships declined by two-thirds.[176]

The focus on university education has been detrimental for many young Australians. The upturn in university places has increased university drop-outs. Further, there are now more graduates than are required for high-skill occupations, leaving many graduates underemployed on lower salaries despite their costly degrees.[177]

Those who do physical or technical work receive less respect and social status compared to graduates. In the context of automation, Greens leader Richard Di Natale said that in the future 'having a full time job may not be possible or indeed desirable' for many.[178] Di Natale said that Australia should introduce a universal basic income, a liveable, unconditional payment to all citizens. The UBI could end up creating a permanent underclass by encouraging those with low education to leave the workforce altogether.[179]

The premise of Di Natale's remarks is that only some jobs are desirable and other work is not worthwhile. This condescending attitude overlooks that work provides meaning and purpose even for those without high status careers. Four-in-five Australians are satisfied with their job and three-quarters say they would work even if they did not need the money – and there are no substantial differences between graduates and non-graduates in job satisfaction despite doing different types of work.[180]

Work is a key driver of dignity.[181] People can have fulfilling lives whether they work on construction sites as a plumber or they manage an art gallery. No matter the nature of the work, people receive intrinsic gratification from their work, from giving to society and providing for themselves and their family. Even menial and repetitive occupations provide a reward for effort and an income that can be used to support themselves and others without a handout.

People also receive dignity through other methods such as raising a family, being an active member of their community and volunteering. There are many paths to human flourishing other than a university education, a professional well-paying job and a fast-paced inner-city lifestyle. While this path has delivered positive outcomes for the cognitively capable and career focused, it leaves much to be desired for the majority in society who might not want to, or cannot, reach the top. The achievement society priorities a single type of lifestyle and approach to the world over others and creates an underclass among those who do not meet the criteria.

Working class to the right, middle class to the left

Across the western world, the working class has increasingly become frustrated by parties of the political left, which have become dominated by the cosmopolitan progressive values and priorities of graduates. The decline of blue collar jobs, and the rise of the professional and technical sector, is associated with 'the new political culture': an increasing focus on non-economic issues such as the environment, animal rights, and identity politics.[182]

These new political issues have, most prominently, been adopted by parties of the political left – moving them away from their working class roots and attracting votes from graduates. In Australia, educated middle class voters are now increasingly voting for Labor and the Greens.[183] Working class voters, whose concerns revolve around family, community and nation, and are politically more interested in economic management and service delivery, have been driven into the hands of the political right, the Liberals and Nationals.

Yale academic Amy Chua discusses how the progressive left have alienated the working class. Chua points to the Occupy Wall Street protests, led by the privileged activists with a limited association to working class Americans. Chua quotes a rural South Caroline student talking about the protest:

> 'I think protest is almost status symbol for elites. That's why they always post pictures on Facebook, so all their friends know they're protesting. When elites protest on behalf of us poor people, it's not just that we see them as unhelpful; it seems they are turning us, many of whom have a great deal of pride, into the next "meme." We don't like being used as a prop for some else's self-validation.'

Chua argues that 'America's elites today, especially progressive ones, often don't realize how judgmental they are.' The progressive elite has disdain for the cultural symbols, lifestyle and patriotism of the working class. This condescension has driven working class voters away from the political left. 'There is nothing more tribal than elite disdain for the provincial, the plebian, the patriotic,' Chua writes. The same sentiment is held by Australia's new elite, the tertiary educated, alienating many working class voters from the left of politics.

Political scientists Murray Goot and Ian Watson noted a shift during John Howard's premiership of older, less educated and Catholic voters towards the Liberals and Nationals, while Labor was receiving more professional voters. 'Although Labor's pursuit of professional workers may not have delivered it many votes, its loss of support among blue collar workers and, to a lesser extent, among white-collar workers has made it more dependent than ever on the professional–managerial class,' Goot and Watson write.[184]

The political left often responds to the loss of blue collar workers with a 'false consciousness' model: the working class has been *duped* by 'racist' messaging into voting against their economic interest.[185] This simplistic argument ignores that working class voters have a different set of values to the graduate class which attracts them to conservative parties.

Social psychologist Jonathan Haidt's *The Righteous Mind* identified the gap in moral foundations between educated cosmopolitan progressives and conservatives.[186] Haidt finds that progressives respond strongly to the harm of others and injustice. These moral foundations drive policies such as increasing government spending on the downtrodden and concern about the environment, refugees and identity politics.

Conservatives, on the other hand, have a wider moral pallet. Conservatives are sensitive to care and fairness, *as well* as loyalty to the in-group, responsibility to superiors and disgust in response to potential dangers. Accordingly, conservatives are more focused on their families, want to protect their community and are less welcoming of potentially risky change.

Australian politics, particularly when it comes to cultural, identity and lifestyle issues, activate the moral foundations which Haidt describes. Terrorist incidents, crime and boat arrivals trigger the conservative instinct to protect the community from danger. Meanwhile, policies that aim to combat terrorism, are tough on crime and limit refugees activate the progressive concern about human suffering. The conservative and progressive disposition to policy is driven by opposing moral foundations.

A prominent dividing line between conservatives and progressives is nationalism.[187] Progressives think nationalism is a form of bigotry, an exclusionary mindset designed to lock out those who come from the non-majority race. Conservatives think that their national culture and society is unique and important to preserve. Instinctively, humans want to help those with whom they are close. Conservatives want their government to place the welfare of its citizens above that of foreigners – just like we care more about our partners, family and friends than we do about strangers.

Nationalism is not necessarily bigotry and hatred of outsiders. You can feel proud of your country while also feeling ambivalent or positive feelings about other countries. Haidt uses the example of your spouse: you love them because they are your own, not because you think your spouse is necessarily superior to others.[188] Furthermore, a shared identity, norms and history is necessary for social trust and cohesion and the basis for moral obligations between the government and citizens.

Haidt contends that progressives have lost support from the working class because they have only appealed to a limited set of moral instincts – and ignored their thirst for community, loyalty and respect. 'Are voters really voting against their self-interest when they vote for candidates who share their values?' Haidt asks,

'Loyalty, respect for authority and some degree of sanctification create a more binding social order that places some limits on individualism and egoism. As marriage rates plummet, and globalisation and rising diversity erodes the sense of common heritage within each nation, a lot of voters in many western nations find themselves hungering for conservative moral cuisine.'[189]

Australian politics has closely followed this model. As political scientist Judith Brett writes:

'In Australia the intellectuals' traditional scorn for suburbia has slipped easily into a scorn for Australian nationalists. Nationalists for their part still virtue territorial sovereignty, and place their obligations to their fellow nationals much higher than to those outside the boundaries of the nation.'[190]

The feeling that the progressive cosmopolitans do not prioritise the interests of Australians has driven many working class voters abandoning the Labor in favour of the Liberals and Nationals.

§

A mixture of social, cultural and economic changes has created serious divisions at the heart of Australian society. The traditional political parties are struggling to handle these divides. Australia's political parties were established under the old paradigm of left-right economic battles. Today, voters are split. On the one hand, there are those who prioritise their economic interest – wealthy Inners who vote Liberal for free market economic reasons and working class unionist Outers voting for Labor. On the other hand, there are those who have changed their vote for cultural, identity, and lifestyle reasons – wealthy Inners who vote Labor or Greens because of their liberal values and working to middle class Outers sick of Labor's cosmopolitan focus and now voting Liberals or a minor party such as One Nation.

The following chapter explores how the values divide within the major parties makes Australia increasingly difficult to govern.

THREE

The politics of Inners and Outers

'So let's be very clear: Labor is increasingly sceptical and today's revelation [about a scientific report], if true, is incredibly disturbing, and if Adani's relying on false information, that mine does not deserve to go ahead,' Labor leader Bill Shorten declared, indicating a turn against the proposed Carmichael coal mine by the Adani Group in northern Queensland.[191]

Adani is a divisive issue for Labor. On one side, Labor is attempting to appeal to Inners, who are captivated by climate change ('the biggest moral challenge of our time,' Kevin Rudd declared) and are fervently against coal. On the other, Labor is trying to appeal to Outers, who are attracted to the jobs and opportunities that the new mine will bring and want lower energy prices.

Shorten's remarks were at the campaign launch of Ged Kearney, Labor's candidate for the by-election in Batman, an inner-city Melbourne electorate. Batman is supposed to be a Labor stronghold. In 2001, the first time Greens candidate Alex Bhathal contested the seat, Labor received a *primary* vote of 59 per cent. The Greens achieved just 12 per cent, behind the Liberals. By 2016, Bhathal reached 36 per cent in 2016 and 39 per cent at the 2018 by-election. Labor relied on preferences to win the seat in both cases.

Batman represents of a divided Labor. The electorate has rapidly gentrified, earning the nickname 'Land of Tofu.'[192] It attracts a high number of Greens voting, highly educated, well-paid middle class professionals, particularly in the southern parts of the electorate. Meanwhile, the working class, located north of Bell Street reliably vote Labor.[193]

'It's hipsterville. When I moved in there were nine pawn shops on the main drag,' Malcolm, a resident of Northcote who moved to the area twenty years ago, told the *Herald Sun*, 'Now there's 26 restaurants and a loaf of bread at that bakery over there is $9.'[194]

Shorten was criticised from within his party for speaking against Adani and reversed his rhetoric.[195] Within just a few weeks, Shorten declared that there is a 'role for coal' and that Adani is just 'another project.'[196] These comments were made in the humid climate of Townsville, over 2,000km away from leafy inner-city Melbourne. Townsville, a marginal Liberal-Labor seat, is set to benefit economically from the mine.

While Labor struggles the most, the centre-left is not alone in needing to appeal to both Inner and Outer sensibilities. The divided electoral base is a challenge for the major parties established along 20th century class divides. Although Outers are more numerous, the major parties depend on votes from both Inners and Outers at elections. The split dependence is making Australian politics increasingly divided and bitter.

The limited rise of post-materialism

In 1970, political scientist Ronald Inglehart theorised that the peace and prosperity in the post-war period were fundamentally reshaping the value structure of western societies.[197] Inglehart argued that as younger generations, who were growing up in more safe and prosperous times, would move from 'survival values' to 'emancipative values': less concern about material and personal safety and a growing yearning for belonging, self esteem, aesthetic beauty and intellectual progress. Following Maslow's Hierarchy of Needs, humans could pursue 'belonging', 'esteem' and 'self-actualisation' following the realisation of 'psysiological' (breathing, food and water) and 'safety' (physical) needs.[198]

Inglehart called these 'post-materialist' values. Post-materialists are less conformist, open to new ideas, more tolerant, secular and socially progressive. Post-materialists 'prioritize freedom over security, autonomy over authority, diversity over uniformity and creativity over discipline.'[199] When it comes to politics, post-materialists are relatively apathetic about economic policy and most interested in environmentalism, animal rights, and gender, sexuality and racial equality.

Inglehart has identified an increase in post-materialists; however, they remain a minority within western societies and particularly in Australia.[200] There has been what Inglehart calls a move from 'traditional values' to 'secular values': liberalisation of attitudes towards gender, homosexuality, euthanasia, and abortion. These attitudinal changes follow the success of activist movements.[201]

However, there has not been a widespread turn towards 'emancipative' post-material values in issue priority.[202] In other words, Australians express increasingly liberal views on social issues; however, they still *prioritise* materialist concerns; Australians care more about economic and security issues than self-expression or the environment.

Inglehart assesses the rise of post-materialism using questions about issue priority in the World Values Survey. Materialists are said to prioritise 'managing the economy' and 'fighting crime.' Post-materialists prioritise having 'more say at their jobs' and want to 'make the countryside more beautiful.' The data for Australia indicates that there are relatively few post-materialists, despite what Inglehart would have predicted in a safe and prosperous country such as Australia.[203]

The World Values Survey's 12-item index finds three-quarters of Australians lean materialist and just a quarter are on the post-materialist end of the spectrum. Australia's post-materialists are most likely to vote for the Greens, and to a lesser extent, Labor. Only a small proportion select the Liberals and Nationals. Meanwhile, materialists are most likely to be found voting for the Liberals and Nationals, to a lesser extent Labor and relatively few choose the Greens (See Table 2).

	Post-materialists (24% of Australians)	Materialists (76% of Australians)
Liberals/Nationals	26%	56%
Labor	29%	32%
Greens	38%	8%
Other	4%	4%

Table 2: Post-materialists and voting in Australia. (Source: World Values Survey 2014)

Post-materialists are what critics of experimental psychology have called the WIRED: Western, Educated, Industrialized, Rich and Democratic.[204] Most behavioural psychology studies use WIRED subjects, students at universities and residents of nearby towns and cities. The sampling has proven problematic because the WIRED demographic are outliers in their motivations and behaviour compared to the rest of society.

Inglehart argues that birth era – growing up during a

prosperous and peaceful time – is the chief explainer for post-materialist values. He argues that people living safer and materially prosperous childhood, in contrast to those who lived through the world wars, were being socialised people into post-materialist values. Subsequent research, however, has found stronger links between education and post-materialism.[205] Graduates are more likely to be exposed to the post-materialist ideas during their university studies.[206] Graduates also have access to higher paying jobs, which provides for the material prosperity that is necessary to focus on issues such as the environment and identity politics.[207]

In Australia, post-materialist values are most likely to be found among young graduates, primarily from arts, humanities and social science backgrounds, on the political left. These individuals are university educated professionals and live in the inner-city. From the perspective of their high earnings and middle class status, they would have historically been expected to support the Liberal Party. Today, however, the majority of young graduates vote the quintessential post-materialist party the Greens, or Labor, and relatively few opt for the Liberal and Nationals (See Table 3).

Senate voting	Graduates under 35
Liberal and Nationals	30%
Labor	20%
Greens	35%
One Nation	0%
Other (i.e. Science, Arts, etc.)	15%

Table 3. Senate voting by graduates under 35. (Source: Australian Election Study 2016)

When it comes to their politics, the post-materialist minority has closely interlinked progressive political views. Of the 28 per cent of Australians who oppose asylum seeker boat turn backs, 91 per cent believe that Aboriginal land rights have not gone too far, 85 per cent support same-sex marriage and 73 per cent are against the death penalty.[208] There is nothing inherently similar about these issues – asylum seekers, Aboriginal land rights, gay rights and the death penalty. Nevertheless, they interrelate to non-material rights issues that appeal to the post-materialist mindset. The left of Australian politics, initially the Labor Party and more recently the Greens, have effectively appealed to this group by taking highly progressive stands on issues. A sizeable segment of the educated middle class is now voting for the political left, an important historical change.[209]

In the short term, the shift has been of limited damage to the political right, who have increased their appeal to the more numerous materialists and placed limited importance on the post-materialists. The Victorian Liberal Party have discussed not nominating candidates for inner-city Melbourne state seats with a high Greens vote, such as Melbourne, Brunswick, Richmond, Northcote.[210] Completely abandoning this group, however, could prove problematic. Despite their small size, it is important to not understate the cultural, social and political influence of post-materialists. They dominate the Labor Party, the Greens, arts, media, universities, unions and much of corporate Australia.[211] Accordingly, the political right cannot afford to completely surrender post-materialists for risk of being locked out of cultural influence in Australian society.

It's still the economy, stupid

Scientist Charles Darwin, during his 1836 visit to Sydney on the *HMS Beagle*, observed that 'The whole population, poor and rich, are bent on acquiring wealth; amongst the higher orders, wool and sheep grazing from the constant subject of conversation.'[212]

Similar remarks about politics and the role of the state reverberate throughout Australian history. In 1964, Donald Horne wrote in *The Lucky Country* that 'Australia is not a country of great political dialogue or intense searching after problems (or recognition of problems that exist). There is little grandiose ideology and politics is usually considered to be someone else's business and a dirty business at that.'[213]

Political scientist Hugh Collins seminally described Australia as having a 'Benthamite' utilitarian political culture: Australians weigh perceived costs and benefits of policies based on their capacity to improve our standard of living, not an ideological framework.[214] Politicians are expected to find 'practical' solutions and shun explicit ideology.

David Kemp argues that Australians want the state support them in the achievement of individualist ends, stepping in when required, however, generally allowing individuals to pursue their chosen ends.[215] In practice, for most Australians, the primary role of the state is to ensure that the economy is functioning and that services, such as healthcare and education, are adequately provided.

Surveys consistently reflected these priorities. Most Australians are primarily interested in the economy and services; few decide their vote on post-materialist concerns. At the 2016 election, 4 in 5 voters selected economic issues or service delivery to be the 'most important' during the campaign, 16 per cent selected 'post-materialist' issue, such as the environment, climate change, refugees or the treatment of Indigenous Australians and 4 per cent selected security and foreign policy issues (See Figure 11).

The precise issues of concern vary from election to election. In 1998, the GST was the central issue and 80 per cent of

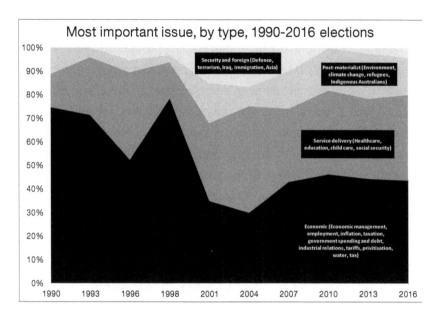

Figure 11. The most important issue, by type, 1990-2016; different topics are asked at each election (Source: Australian Election Study 1990-2016).

voters selected an economic issue. In 2001 and 2004, at the beginning of the 'war on terror' and Australia's commitment to Iraq, there was more concern about security and foreign issues. Nevertheless, at most, just one-fifth of Australians selected a post-materialist issue in 2013 and the number *declined* in 2016. Moreover, even this analysis exaggerates the resonance of post-materialism because voters often have a security concern about refugees as was the case in 2001 and 2013.

There is, however, a notable divergence in concerns by education levels and voter groups. University graduates are twice as likely to consider the environment to be the most important issue compared to those with no post-school qualifications.[216] Labor voters are more concerned with health and education and Liberal and National voters with economic concerns.

The most substantial divergence in issue priority is between Greens voters, the most post-materialist party, and the rest (See Table 4). Just over half of Greens voters select a post-materialist concern, including the environment, global warming and refugees and asylum seekers, to be the most important. Greens voters are almost six times more likely to select a post-materialist issue than Liberal, Labor or the Nationals voters. Meanwhile, just 15 per cent of Greens voters picked an economic issue, compared to two-thirds of Liberal and Nationals voters and a third of Labor voters.

Most important issue	Economic	Service delivery	Post-materialist	Security and foreign
Liberals/Nationals	66%	21%	7%	6%
Labor	28%	58%	12%	2%
Greens	15%	32%	52%	1%

Table 4. Number one issue by type, by party, 2016 election (Source: Australian Election Study 2016)

A nation divided

Outside of a relatively small group of highly educated Greens and Labor voters, there has not been widespread adoption of post-materialist priorities. Nevertheless, the growth of education has established underlying divisions within supporter basis of both major parties. The internal divides help explain the fracturing of Australia's political system, the growing support for minor parties that more closely reflect voter preferences and declining party identification. The increasing salience of non-economic issues exacerbates the divides. Two-thirds of Australians, up from half in 1990, think that the government does not affect the economy for better or worse.[217]

Australia's major political parties are divided. Labor faces divisions between their traditional working class voters and new middle class graduates leading the party. Meanwhile, middle class Liberal voters, attracted by the free market economic message, have not wholly been displaced by working class Liberals with conservative cultural attitudes.

Australia is not alone in these trends.

There are strong divisions within political parties of the left and right across the developed world. The dividing line in the Republican Party in the United States has emerged between people who are more of a supporter of President Donald Trump and those who are more supporter of the party. A *Wall Street Journal/NBC* poll found that economic issues, such as Trump's tax cuts, unite both sides.[218] However, the older and less educated Trump supporters are less supportive of immigration, trade, action on climate change and diversity. Meanwhile, Democrats are divided between the liberal progressive 'professional class' and more conservative 'blue collar' workers and 'old guard' elderly Democrats.[219]

Australia faces similar dividing lines. On economic issues, graduates and non-graduates who support the Labor and Liberals and Nationals have similar views. However, on a range of questions that tap into identity, cultural and lifestyle issues, large divisions emerge between graduates and those with less education (See Table 5). Liberal and Nationals voters are on the more conservative side of these issues. Nevertheless, the difference in views by education level is often larger than the gaps between the parties. The most substantial divide emerges between the extremes, One Nation and the Greens.

Issue	Education		Party			
	Graduate	No post-school	Liberal/Nationals	Labor	Greens	One Nation
Policy						
Death penalty reintroduction for murder*	24%	51%	44%	41%	14%	76%
Strongly agree with stiffer sentences for those who break the law*	16%	32%	29%	28%	10%	42%
The number of migrants allowed into Australia has gone 'too far'*	25%	53%	47%	34%	12%	90%
Less spending on defence*	19%	41%	16%	29%	58%	14%
More spending on police and law enforcement*	25%	58%	58%	48%	23%	65%
Politics						
Approve of the way the Liberal Party handled the leadership change from Abbott to Turnbull*	62%	47%	53%	54%	69%	11%
Strongly favour compulsory voting*	58%	46%	51%	55%	57%	32%
Australia should become a republic*	62%	43%	42%	65%	70%	43%
ANZUS treaty is very important for protecting Australia's security*	38%	52%	56%	40%	22%	51%
High income tax makes people less willing to work hard*	38%	50%	53%	42%	24%	68%
Equal opportunities for migrants have not gone far enough*	28%	14%	22%	10%	50%	1%
Identity and the future						
Anzac heritage is very important to my sense of what it means to be Australian#	34%	67%	62%	50%	25%	-
The true Australian way of life is disappearing so fast that we may have to use force to save it#	20%	56%	47%	33%	15%	-
I am afraid there isn't going to be as much freedom in Australia as time goes on#	51%	66%	61%	59%	47%	-
My standard of living will improve in the next ten years*	56%	38%	48%	41%	39%	31%

Table 5. Australia divided by education and party (Source: *Australian Election Study 2016; #Australian Social Science Survey 2014)

This dynamic is the Inners-Outers divide in Australian politics. At one extreme sits the Greens, who represent the graduate post-materialist graduate tribe; while at the other extreme sits One Nation, who represent more conservative values. In between, the two major parties attempt to balance voters with a diversity of viewpoints.

The dynamic emerges on a range of issues. Graduates support policies that are softer on crime and more supportive of migration. They are more likely to approve of the Abbott-Turnbull leadership change, favour compulsory voting and the republic, less likely to think that high taxes discourage work. Graduates view Anzac heritage as less important, are less concerned about society changing and loss of freedom and are more confident of higher living standards in the future.

Further divides emerge when drilling down into opinions *within* the voter base of the major parties. That is, the Inners-Outers divide exists *within* the party supporter basis. Labor and Liberal/National graduates and Greens voters hold similar opinions on many of these non-economic issues. Labor and Liberal/National with less education and One Nation supporters also have much in common.

The divide is prominent on law and order issues. On the one side, Outers are driven by the instinct to secure one's self, family and community.[220] Inners feel safer in their surroundings, have less concern for crime and have a softer perspective on criminal justice. This tendency emerges on the question of whether people who break the law should be given stiffer sentences (See Figure 12).

Greens voters are four times less likely to strongly support stiffer sentences for lawbreakers than One Nation voters. A similar proportion of Liberal and Nationals and Labor voters favour tougher sentences. However, differences of opinion exist *between* the Inners and Outers within parties. Labor and Liberal and Nationals voters with no post-school qualification are almost twice as likely to support harsher penalties compared to those with a degree. The split within Labor by education is even bigger. A similar proportion of Labor graduates and Greens voters support stricter judgements. Labor graduates, however, are four times less likely to support stiffer sentences than Labor voters with a trade qualification – whose views sit closest to One Nation voters. There are similar divides on reintroducing the death penalty for murder, another law and order issue (See Figure 13).

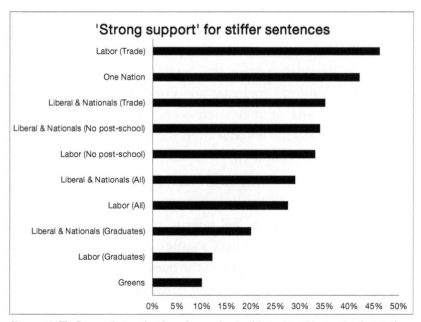

Figure 12. The Inners-Outers divide on law and order (Australian Election Study 2016)

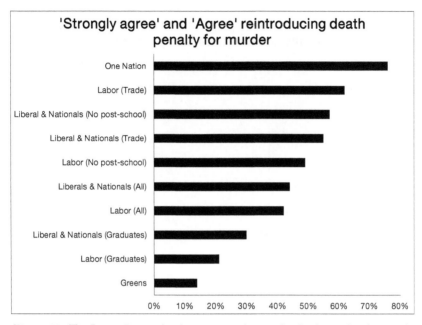

Figure 13. The Inners-Outers divide on reintroducing the death penalty for murder (Australian Election Study 2016)

These divides also emerge on the question of immigration (See Figure 14). The decision to allow additional people to join the nation is a core issue that divides Outers – who want to protect their community from outside danger – and Inners – that are defined by their confidence, openness and cosmopolitan attitude.[221] While almost all One Nation voters think that migration to Australia has gone too far, this view is very rare among Greens voters. The issue divides major party supports as well. Labor, Liberal and Nationals graduates have relatively similar attitudes to Greens voters on immigration; while Labor and Liberal & Nationals trades qualified voters and those with no post-school education are closer to One Nation voters.

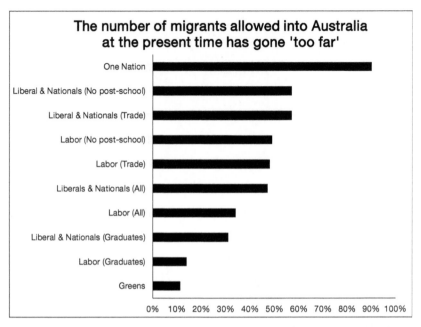

Figure 14. The Inners–Outers divide on immigration (Australian Election Study 2016)

The split also emerges on identity issues. Inners, with their achieved identity, are substantially less nationalistic than Outers whose ascribed identity is covered in the Australian flag – occasionally literally much to the scorn of Inners. The rift has led Anzac Day to become a location of 'cultural war' debates. Graduates from both parties think that Anzac Day is much less important to their identity compared to non-graduates (See Figure 15). The division on cultural issues has often sparked furious debate. In 2017, commentator Yassmin Abdel-Magied was forced to apologise for tweeting 'Lest We Forget (Manus).' In 2018, comedian Catherine Deveny was criticised for dismissively called Anzac Day 'Bogan Halloween' and claimed it leads to 'fetishisation of war and violence.'[222]

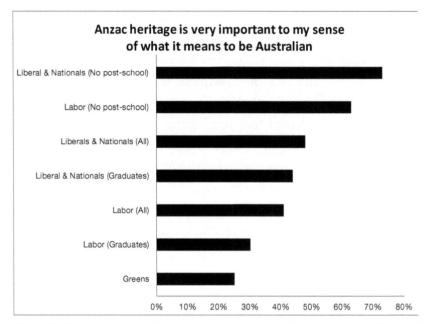

Figure 15. The Inners-Outers divide on identity, Anzac Day (Source: Australian Survey of Social Attitudes 2014)

The rise of higher education, and economic and social changes, has restructured Australia's party system and created underlying divisions within the parties. Labor's new highly educated and old working class supporters divide the party. Similarly, the Liberals are divided between less educated conservatives and graduate economic liberals.

Are Labor candidates more Green than the Greens voters?

In the last week of 2017 an unruly party at a rented Airbnb property in Melbourne's west escalated to police being pelted with rocks by dozens of youth.[223] This event, combined with other violent incidents by young offenders in Victoria, led to the emergence of a furious law and order debate.

Since Labor came to power in Victoria in 2014, there has been an increase in violent crime.[224] The Liberals have blamed the rise of crime on the weakening of bail law for young offenders, loosening anti-gang laws and lack of investment in the police.[225] However, ministers in the Victorian Labor Government as well the Victorian police leadership denied that youth gang delinquency is in itself a problem.[226] The focus on violence committed by young people of African descent led some progressive commentators to label the concern about violence 'clearly racist.'[227]

Despite Labor's attempts to downplay the issue, polls identified voter concern and internal divisions emerged within Labor Party on how to address law and order. 'We've got African gangs running wild and he's [Victorian Premier Daniel Andrews] going on about equality and social policy,' one Labor parliamentarian told the *Herald Sun*.[228]

Concern about crime is a litmus test that separates Inners from Outers. Graduates are less concerned about traditional material and personal safety issues and are less supportive of harsher sentences, the death penalty and more spending on law and order.[229] In contrast, Outers have a strong reaction to anything that threatens the safety of their community and society. Surveys have found Australians are becoming more concerned about violence.[230] A poll found 68 per cent of Victorians believe the state government is failing to do enough to tackle youth violence.[231]

The concerns were found to be particularly strong in outer-suburban seats held by Labor. Eighty-three per cent of voters in Cranbourne in Melbourne's south east and 85 per cent of voters in Tarneit in Melbourne's west said that crime and anti-social behaviour is 'very important.'[232] Both electorates contain a below average proportion of university educated professionals.[233]

While Inners and Outers can be found voting both Labor and Liberal, parliamentarians tend to be Inners. Almost all members of parliament have academic qualifications and almost all were managers or professionals before entering parliament (See Table 6). The different educational backgrounds and career choices contribute to substantial lifestyle, culture and values divide between the elected and the governed.

MPs	Academic qualifications	Managers and administrators	Professionals	Non-manager or professional
Liberals/ Nationals	86%	68%	25%	7%
Labor	87%	66%	33%	1%
Greens	90%	50%	50%	0%
One Nation	75%	100%	0%	0%

Table 6. Background of Members of Parliament (Source: Parliamentary Handbook 2017, Parliamentary Library)

Historically, Labor parliamentarians came from the working class ranks of the union movement. Today, the Labor Party is dominated by the professional, middle class following the collapse in union membership and weakening of class political divides.[234] Labor politicians are a mixture of political staffers, union lawyers, and union organisers (who are recruited from Labor's university politicians, not from the working class). Liberal parliamentarians are similarly from a narrow set of background including former staffers, professionals such as lawyers, accountants, and management consultants. Labor politicians are no longer from the working class and Liberal politicians are unlikely to come from a small business background.

It is not inherently problematic that most parliamentarians are highly educated; however, the disconnect, from geography to life experience, is concerning. Discussing the fate of the modern Labor Party, Hawke government minister Barry Jones argues there has been an exaggeration of ideological differences between Labor factions. 'Parties have become closed corporations, oligarchies. Political operatives have become traders,' Jones said, 'The bitterest fights in parliament are not on major issues, but on personalities, relative trivialities and "gotcha" moments.'[235] The consensus within the parties is divorced from the views of the public.

The divides between the elected and voters are most prominent on the Labor side of politics. There are substantial values differences between Labor's political class, who hold the views of their highly educated voters, and their overall voting base that is more conservative. The Australian Candidate Survey, which is undertaken by the same researchers as the Australian Election Study at each election, shows that Labor candidates are much closer to post-materialist Greens voters in their views than they are their supporters (See Figure 16).

The divides emerge on the identity and cultural issues which separate Inners and Outers. This includes the relative importance of global warming, the number of migrants coming into Australia, government help for Aborigines, spending on defence, stiffer sentences for lawbreakers, turning around asylum seeker boats and whether Australia should be a republic. Labor candidates are six times less likely to support stiffer sentences and five times more likely to select 'global warming' as the most important issue, than Labor voters.

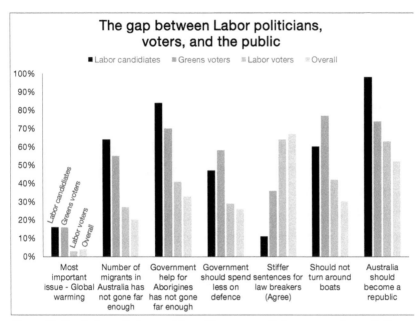

The gap between Labor politicians, voters, and the public

■ Labor candidates   ■ Greens voters   ▨ Labor voters   ▨ Overall

Figure 16. On the issues, Labor candidates, Greens voters, Labor voters and overall (Source: Australian Candidate Survey 2016, Australian Election Study 2016)

The contemporary Labor Party is fixated by identity and cultural issues. *The Australian*'s economics editor Adam Creighton found, from analysis of Labor's national platform, a strong focus on identity politics issues – gender, sexuality and race – and a lack of discussion on economics.[236] Labor's platform has more mentions of gender (126) and 'intersex,' (63 times), than 'wealth' (61) 'inequality' (47), 'poverty' (23), 'ownership' (12), 'production' (18), 'distribution' (10), or 'cost of living' (2). Creighton concludes Labor's focus on identity reflects the capturing of the party 'by well-paid, highly educated interests.'

The disconnect between the voters and the governed raises serious questions about the nature of representation. This issue has fascinated political thinkers for hundreds of years. Edmund Burke's *Speech to the Electors of Bristol* in 1774 argued for the national interest over the local. 'Parliament is not a congress of ambassadors from different and hostile interests,' Burke said, 'but parliament is a deliberative assembly of one nation, with one interest, that of the whole.' As noble as Burke's sentiment, there is an inevitable danger of politicians pursuing their interests, or the interests of one group, under the smokescreen of appeals to the supposed 'national interest.' Burke, who told the electors of Bristol that they were welcome to remove him from office, was voted out shortly afterwards.

The American founding fathers were acutely aware of the danger of a minority interest governing for themselves. In the Federalist Papers, the United States' fourth president, James Madison, warned about the danger of factions which are 'united and actuated by some common impulse of passion, or of interest, adversed to the rights of other citizens, or to the permanent and aggregate interests of the community.'[237] Madison noted that the issue could only be completely solved by either taking away liberty altogether, which is 'worse than the disease' it is trying to fix, or giving each citizen the same interests, which is 'impracticable' because human opinions are too diverse. 'The latent causes of faction are thus sown in the nature of man,' Madison states.

Madison is also dismissive of the possibility of an 'enlightened statesman' to manage the conflict. There is too much chance that they will pursue their interest. Economist F. A. Hayek, in the context of economic planning, also highlighted this problem. 'It is inevitable that they [the central planner] should impose their scale of preferences on the community for which they plan,' Hayek wrote in *The Road to Serfdom*.[238] The danger with the disconnect between politicians and the people they are supposed to represent is politicians governing in their interest. This is a recipe for popular frustration with the political system and the major parties, particularly for the Labor Party where the gap is the largest.

The disconnect between Labor's Inner politicians and Outer voters raises severe dangers for the Labor Party's future. Across Europe parties of the centre left have achieved miserable election results in recent history because of their loss of the working class. In countries such as Germany, Italy and Hungary, the historically dominate centre-left parties are now receiving just 20 per cent of the vote. The parties abandoned their traditional working class base, who are now voting for parties of the political right or further left. Editor-at-large of *National Review* John O'Sullivan writes that 'In pursuing progressive cultural politics, including European integration, to win middle class support, they have alienated their much larger traditional working class constituency, which showed it had somewhere else to go. It proved to be a poor exchange numerically.'[239]

Labor in Australia is facing both declining working class support and losing progressive cosmopolitans to the Greens. Labor's last two election results, 33.4 per cent primary vote in 2013 and 34.9 per cent in 2016, were the worst since 1949.[240] Labor leader Bill Shorten is not unaware of the danger of losing Outers. In the context of cracking down on 457 visas, Shorten delcared that 'We will buy Australian, build Australian, make in Australia and employ Australians.' He went on to say that ' My party will heed the lessons of Detroit, Michigan, of Ohio and Pennsylvania. We're not going to lose our blue-collar voters like the Democrats did.'

In the short term, preferential voting and single member electorates in the House of Representative has delivered Labor a disproportionate number of seats; however, the danger of losing popular support is substantial for the party's future.

§

Australian society is facing a new type of division. The rise of the 'new class,' inner-city living cosmopolitan liberals, is reshaping the political system and undermining the traditional left-right class divides of the past. While most Australians are primarily concerned with the economy, services and security issues, major party voters are a mix of Inners and Outers. The rift is creating difficulties for both sides of politics, who are struggling to appeal simultaneously to two segments of the electorate who hold conflicting views.

The following chapter explores how voters have responded by increasingly opting for the extremes, One Nation and the Greens, who fuel each other.

FOUR

Greens and One Nation: An equal and opposite reaction

There was a table selling cleanings rags, located between the Refugee Action Collective and the Greens stall, at the Brunswick Music Festival in the inner-north of Melbourne. These cloths were not the usual colourful apolitical affair. One cloth included an image of federal minister Christopher Pyne's face with the text 'Can He Fix It? No He Can't'. The next rag across was about Australia Day. On the top right, it had an Australian flag with '26 January' and on the right a series of words: White, Drunken, Wife bashing, Racist, Bigot, Redneck, Flag-waving, Bogan Day.

Australia Day is one of the latest battles in the 'cultural wars.' It divides Inners, particularly of *The New Elite*, and Outers. The 'Change the Date' of Australia Day campaign has gained momentum in recent years. The Greens have declared that the arrival of the First Fleet had 'catastrophic and tragic' consequences for Indigenous Australians and argue that 26 January is not an appropriate day to celebrate Australia.[241] Several Melbourne councils no longer celebrate Australia Day.[242] ABC's Triple J has changed the date of Hottest 100 music countdown previously held on Australia Day.[243]

For Inners, whose identity is defined by their achievements, not the nation which they happen to belong, Australia Day is a symbol of an intolerant and closed society. At the 'Invasion Day' rally held on Australia Day in Melbourne in 2018, one speaker hyperbolically called for Australia to be abolished. 'We have not organised this to change the date. We have organised this to abolish Australia Day because f..k Australia. F..k Australia, I hope it f..king burns to the ground,' Miriki Onus, the leader of the Warriors of the Aboriginal Resistance movement, reportedly said.[244]

Many commentators have claimed that Australia has a particularly shameful past. Blogger Yassmin Abdel-Magied declared Australia has a 'deeply racist history.'[245] Curtin University academic Dr Hannah McGlade wrote on *ABC News* that Australia is full of 'racist violence,' following allegations of abuse at the Don Dale Detention Centre in Northern Territory.[246] In 2017, the SBS hosted a week of programming that called for Austraia to 'Face up to Racism'.[247]

There has been a substantial backlash against changing the date. Former Prime Minister Malcolm Turnbull opposed the date change, appealing to the 70 per cent of Australians who support celebrating Australia Day on 26 January.[248] One Nation leader Pauline Hanson has declared that Australia Day is 'under attack' and backed celebration of the annual holiday.[249]

Australia Day is a divisive issue. The largest gap in attitudes is between supports of the Greens and One Nation. Just 32 per cent of Greens say that the date should not be changed, compared to 92 per cent of One Nation supporters.[250] The Greens and One Nation supporters sit at the opposite poles on a range of cultural, identity and lifestyle issues (See Table 7).

Identity issues	Party / All		
	Greens	One Nation	All
Leave Australia Day as it is*	32%	92%	65%
Support changing historical statues*	63%	14%	32%
'A great extent' of pride in the Australian way of life#	32%	79%	54%
'Strongly agree' that maintaining the Australian way of life and culture is important#	24%	92%	54%
Australia is in danger of losing its culture and identity~	34%	91%	55%
Australia has changed beyond recognition and sometimes feels like a foreign country	32%	85%	52%
Speaking English is important to being Australian*	33%	-	69%
Must share national customs to be Australian*	51%	-	69%
Tradition is important^	51%	-	69%
Willing to fight for Australia in case of war^	45%	-	64%

*Table 7. The Greens-One Nation divide (*Newspoll 2017 #Scanlon Survey 2017 ^World Values Survey 2014 * What It Takes to Truly Be 'One of Us', Pew 2017 ~Australian Population Research Institute Research Report 2017)*

One Nation and Greens voters epitomise the extreme ends of the Inners-Outers divide, while Liberal and Labor voters sit somewhere in the middle (near to Anthony Downs' median voter).[251] The party which attracts the highest concentration changes over time.[252] In the case of Inners, from the Australia Party and the Australian Democrats to the Greens. In the case of Outers from parties including the Shooters, Fishers and Farmers and the Palmer United Party to One Nation. While the precise party may change over time, the existence of minor parties that seek support from disaffected Inners and Outers is the new normal in Australian politics.

Isaac Newton's third law of motion, 'For every action, there is an equal and opposite reaction,' aptly describes the dynamic between the Greens and One Nation. The two parties feed off each other. The Greens and One Nation represent everything the other despises. The more one grows, the more there is a cultural backlash against the other. One Nation feeds off the perceived threat posed by The Greens and vice versa.

The disaffected anti-elite: One Nation

A regional Liberal state parliamentarian says that the quickest way to identify a One Nation voter in their electorate is a comment like "Did you fly here by helicopter?"[253] One Nation supporters think all politicians are useless, out of touch and greedy. They feel out of place in modern Australia. Their high-paying, high-status jobs are gone. The culture has changed. They are angry and nobody is listening. One Nation has effectively channelled frustrations that many share – including those who would never vote for One Nation's often vulgar politics.

The rise of populism, including the success of populist parties from Hungary and Poland through to Austria, Italy and France, the election of Donald Trump in the United States and Brexit in Britain, has shocked the political class. Voting for populist parties, accordingly to a calculation by Dani Rodrik of Harvard, has increased from less than five per cent in 1961-1980 to 20 per cent in 2011-15.[254] Some have linked the rise of populism to the end of liberalism and democracy.[255]

Progressives often assert that populism can be explained and resolved by addressing economic inequality, globalisation, unemployment and economic exclusion.[256] Greens leader Richard Di Natale has blamed the rise of populism on economic factors. 'Our communities are becoming more and more sharply divided as corporate profits skyrocket and wages flat line... And these conditions generate grievance. Racism thrives and hard right populist movements get a foothold,' Di Natale said.[257]

This argument fits pre-existing problem dimensions of the political left, who view the world in crass Marxist class terms.[258] The reality is more complicated. The political discontent that drives populism is not the absolute economic situation, it is 'relative access to the good things in life, about feeling of loss and sometimes humiliation, about disappointed expectations and about the conflicting worldviews of elites and masses,' David Goodhart explains.[259] Populist party voters are not the financially better off, however, nor are they the worst off.

Political scientists Ronald Inglehart and Pippa Norris conclude, from 13 years of European voting patterns, support for populists is not associated with income level.[260] They argue that the rise of populism is a cultural backlash against social change and rule by elites. Inglehart and Norris found that populist voting is most common 'among the petty bourgeoisie, not unskilled manual workers' who are 'most likely to feel that they have become strangers from the predominant values in their own country, left behind by progressive tides of cultural change which they do not share.' Norris finds no correlation between voting for authoritarian populist parties and the levels of economic inequality.[261]

In the United States, voting for Donald Trump was more strongly associated with the fear of losing status than economic hardship.[262] Just 35 per cent of Trump voters had a household income below US$50,000 per year.[263] Support for Brexit is correlated with cultural attitudes and not financial circumstances.[264] In Australia, the *Grattan Institute* concluded that support for minor parties, such as One Nation, 'rose most when wages grew strongly and inequality was stable.'[265] A visceral hatred of the establishment and the associated elites who hold a different set of values – not economic dislocation as is often asserted – drives populism.

A range of Australian political parties and politicians have attracted populist discontent. This includes Bob Katter, Jacqui Lambie, Clive Palmer's Palmer United Party, which received 5.06 per cent of the Senate vote in 2013, and the Shooters, Fishers and Farmers.[266] Pauline Hanson's One Nation epitomises Australian populism. Pauline Hanson established One Nation in 1997, following her dis-endorsement by the Liberal Party in the 1996 election for the seat of Oxley in Queensland.

One Nation achieved initial success by winning 11 seats in the 1998 Queensland election, however attained just a single Senate seat in 1998. The party had no further federal parliamentary representation until 2016, when, in an unexpected result, the party won four Senate seats and 4.29 per cent of the Senate vote. One Nation is now polling 6 to 10 per cent in national opinion polls.[267] They will win more seats in the future if the trend is maintained.

Amy Chua, in the context of Donald Trump's supporter base, explains that a 'powerful antiestablishment identity' has formed among the working class who are disillusioned by cosmopolitan progressive politics.[268] One Nation voters exhibit similar features of populist voters in other western democracies. Cultural anxiety and the perception that politics has become dominated by an elite clique in a conspiracy against the majority drives support for One Nation. An astonishing 83 per cent of One Nation voters express no confidence or not very much in Australia's political system.[269]

A driving element for populism is the perception that the political system is unfair or rigged. Political scientists Dalibor Rohac, Sahana Kumar and Andreas Johansson Heinö found that support for 'authoritarian populists are associated closely to corruption,' while other explanations, such as unemployment, inequality or immigration, could not explain the rise.[270] They theorise that corruption weakens political trust, which is exploited by populists. One Nation voters lack confidence in key institutions, including parliament, universities and Australia's political system.[271] Eighty per cent of One Nation voters think that Australia's system of government 'should be replaced' or 'needs major change.'[272]

Journalist David Marr describes One Nation voters as 'nostalgic, gloomy, and anti-government.'[273] Marr found that they feel economically worse off, express negative sentiments about immigration and strongly agree with boat turn backs, dislike the current government and are tough on crime. One Nation voters are most likely to self-identify as working class (60 per cent), however, do not necessarily have the lowest incomes, nor are they more supportive of redistributive policies.[274] They are three times more likely to be 'very pessimistic' about Australia's future than average.[275]

The disaffected elite: The Greens

Inners vote in the highest concentration for minor parties such as The Sex Party (renamed the Reason Party), the Animal Justice Party, Pirate Party and most prominently, the Greens. These parties attract disaffected Inners who feel their values are not represented by the 'old parties,' the Greens term for the major parties.[276] This disaffected subset of Inners feels threatened by Outers values, which they see as backwards and driven by bigotry that must be stomped out.

Australia's first graduate dominated political party was The Australia Party, a breakaway from the Liberal Party established in 1969. The Australia Party opposed the Vietnam War, the alliance with the United States and supported legalisation of abortion and homosexuality. The Australia Party received just one per cent of the vote in 1969 and two per cent in 1972; however, by directing preferences to Labor, helped Gough Whitlam's 1972 election victory.[277]

Approximately 50 per cent of Australia Party voters had a degree, despite just 7 per cent of Australians being graduates at the time.[278] Their supporters had middle incomes, were markedly less religious and were most likely to be found in the Australian Capital Territory. 'Far from being a non-sectional party [as they claimed], the Australia Party was probably the most highly selective of all the political parties in its appeal, attracting a very narrow section of the electorate,' David Kemp notes about the Australia Party.[279] Similar remarks could be made about the Greens today.

The Australia Party was the forerunner to the Australian Democrats, founded in 1977 as a breakaway from the Liberal Party led by Don Chipp, a former Liberal minister.[280] The Democrats received 11 per cent of the vote in the 1977 election and reached an electoral peak in 1998 with eight parliamentarians and the balance of power in the Senate. The Democrats platform highlighted tolerance, democracy and environmental sustainability. They received the bulk of their support from the young, middle class, highly educated inner-city cohort.[281] Today, the Greens fill the void for educated post-materialists disillusioned with the major parties.

Greens voters are the disproportionately highly educated, highly paid, professionals. They are almost twice as likely to have a degree as Liberal or Labor voters and are most likely to identify as middle class, live in inner-city, have a supervisory role at work, no religion and are unlikely to have a trade qualification or diploma.[282]

Greens voters are substantially more likely than major party voters to identify as middle class (68 per cent), post-materialist (58 per cent) and have a professional job (45 per cent).[283] Four-in-five Greens voters have a partner who is a graduate.[284] These trends are even stronger among active Greens members, 81 per cent of whom are university educated.[285]

Greens voters come from a mixed political pedigree. The voting background, while leaning left, also includes a path from Liberal voting to Greens voting through the post-materialist perspective. Of those who know how their parents voted, half had Labor supporting parents, a third come from Liberal parents and the remainder other minor parties.[286] The Greens have been dismissively described as the 'interaction between rising ecological consciousness and the development of a highly educated stratum of the contemporary labour aristocracy.'[287]

There are many rhetorical similarities between disillusioned Inners and Outers, as has been noted in the analysis of Labour leader Jeremy Corbyn in Britain and Democratic primary candidate Bernie Sanders.[288] Populists claim that there is an establishment conspiracy between big business, ethnic and religious minorities and politicians. The Greens commandeer many populist tropes, asserting political leaders are in the pockets of big business or perhaps those dirty foreigners behind the Adani Coal Mine. The Greens talk about 'power to the people.'[289] They say that the political elite represents the 'big end of town' and claim to be anti-corruption crusaders.[290]

The Greens overwhelmingly focus on post-materialist concerns, such as the environment which attracts an ecological base, and other non-economic issues such as asylum seekers, which appeals to liberal cosmopolitan sensibilities. The 'policies' category on the

Greens website lists democracy, ecological sustainability, peace and non-violence, social justice and, lastly, economic justice.[291] There is limited discussion of defence, law and order, or traditional budget management.

Greens voters exhibit post-materialist values (See Table 7). Academic and professional achievement, not national pride or connection to Australia Day, Anzac Day or historical statues, is the basis of their identity. Three-quarters of Greens say that being successful is important to them.[292] They are less supportive of housewives and the breadwinner family model.[293] Greens are also very engaged in the political process, being substantially more likely to contact politicians, express their opinion online and contact the media.[294] Their experience of work itself is also different. Greens are less likely ever to do physical work, think their work contributes more to society and they do not prioritise job security but do feel secure in their jobs.[295] Greens voters are also more open to moving overseas for a job, exhibiting their cosmopolitan attitude.[296]

Greens voters hold fringe views on issues such as immigration, asylum seekers and terrorism (See Table 5). Greens want more spending on the environment and culture and arts, and less spending on defence and law enforcement.[297] They are substantially less concerned about the threat of terrorism and Islamic extremism and less supportive of Australia's border security arrangements.[298]

Monash University academic Nick Economou argues against exaggerating the political importance of the Greens. Greens supporters are 'confined to a very small geographic area in metropolitan Australia where a clustering of the socio-economic cohort likely to vote for the Greens has occurred.'[299] That is, young, public transport using, university educated, single, professionals who rent. Human geography contains the Greens to a small number of seats in parliament. Nevertheless, Economou acknowledges that their 'impact on the political debate has been quite profound' due to media attention, the cultural power of their supporters and their direct power on the Senate crossbench.

Fuelling each other

The Greens claim to be not only the opposite but also the solution to right wing populists. 'We pledge to you that we will act as Australia's antidote to Donald Trump,' the Greens declare.[300] The Greens have even used Trump's election to recruit support. 'The Greens are all in against Trump. Are you with us?' the Greens declare on the 'Reject Trump' page on their website which also asks for contact details.[301] The Greens are unlikely to be the solution. Just like Donald Trump's rise, One Nation and their ilk do not exist in a vacuum. One Nation is a response to precisely what the Greens represent. Authoritarian populists and cosmopolitan post-materialists fuel each other.

In *The Authoritarian Dynamic*, Karen Stenner argues that intolerance, which may appear to come from nowhere, is triggered by the feeling that your family, community and nation are under threat.[302] A latent authoritarian switch in some people's brains is activated when progressive liberals criticise the nation, encourage diversity over unity and allow immigration without limits and integration. The response to a perceived group threat is seeking to protect their tribe with 'closed' policies that are tough on crime, limit immigration and restrict international trade.

Left liberal Mark Lilla wrote shortly after the election of Donald Trump that the 'whitelash' theory of Trump's rise, that he turned economic disadvantage into racial rage, excuses the left's identity obsession which fuelled the backlash.[303] Lilla wrote that 'the whitelash thesis is convenient because it absolves liberals of not recognizing how their own obsession with diversity has encouraged white, rural, religious Americans to think of themselves as a disadvantaged group whose identity is being threatened or ignored.' Lilla concludes that 'Those who play the identity game should be prepared to lose it.'

A backlash *against* the cosmopolitan progressivism epitomised by the Greens, and often embraced by the major parties, explains the original rise and recent re-emergence of One Nation. It is no surprise One Nation voters consistently have the opposite perspective on cultural and identity issues to the Greens (See Table 7). It is also no surprise that the original rise of One Nation came in an era when Labor, under the leadership of Paul Keating, adopted cultural progressivism in the 1990s; and that One Nation's re-rise came when Malcolm Turnbull, who represents cosmopolitan liberalism on the political right, became Prime Minister. Keating and Turnbull activated a vesical response, the authoritarian dynamic that Stenner identified.

One Nation supporters do not perceive themselves as the 'hard right' they are often portrayed. They are concerned about the way the world is functioning; they feel their communities are not secure, that politicians are focused on the wrong issues and failing to address the dangers that Australia is facing. They feel left behind in the modern world. Australian politics is failing to speak to those with traditional values and ways of life, alienating large swaths from the mainstream and making them susceptible to extreme solutions proposed by One Nation.

One Nation voters do not perceive themselves to be particularly *ideological* compared to Greens. When asked on a left-right scale (0 being left and 10 being right), One Nation voters place themselves across the political spectrum. Twenty-six per cent place to the left (0-4), 36 per cent in the centre (5) and 39 per cent to the right (6-10). By comparison, 75 per cent of Greens put themselves on the left (0-4), 18 per cent in the centre (5) and 7 per cent to the right (6-10). The result is consistent with research which indicates those with more education – such as Greens supporters – are more ideological and partisan.[304]

David Marr calls One Nation the 'nostalgia party.'[305] Social researcher Rebecca Huntley told Marr that 'Prosperity is important, but what worries this group is the cultural, social slippage they feel in their life. They imagine their fathers' and grandfathers' lives were better, more certain, easier to navigate. Maybe they were maybe they weren't, but it's loss of that that is worrying them.'

In the 2016 election campaign, Hanson effectively mixed together 'righteous patriotism, authentic rage and blunt message that "ordinary" Australians were being screwed at both ends – by multicultural minorities at the bottom and by the "political elite" at the top,' as explained documentary maker Anna Broinowski who followed Hanson in the year leading up to the election.[306] While many of Hanson's policies should not be welcomed, it is important not completely to dismiss the concerns – as they will only grow and endanger a stronger illiberal backlash if ignored.

David Goodhart discusses the need to be 'tough on populism, tough on the causes of populism.'[307] Goodhart argues that while democracy is unlikely to collapse, we do need to 'make room for a new set of voices pre-occupied with national borders and the pace of change, appealing to people who feel displaced by a more open, ethnically fluid, graduate-favouring economy and society, designed by and for the new elites.' Journalist Margo Kingston, writing about Pauline Hanson's first foray into national politics in the 1990s, concluded that it is 'better to have her in parliament as a token voice representing the rednecks rather than leave them outside the political process and have them grow far more dangerous.'[308] People who hold concerns should have a voice in the political system. It is also essential to decrease alienation and intolerance by avoiding the triggers. Stenner recommends highlighting sameness and building group solidarity to combat the authoritarian dynamic. Stenner writes that:

> 'Ultimately, nothing inspires greater tolerance from the intolerant than an abundance of common and unifying beliefs, practices, rituals, institutions, and processes. And regrettably, nothing is more certain to provoke increased expression of their latent predispositions than the likes of "multicultural education," bilingual policies, and nonassimilation.'[309]

§

Part I of this book establishes that:

(1) a divide has emerged between Inners and Outers in Australian society;

(2) interrelated economic, educational, and sociocultural factors fuelled the rise of the Inners and a substantial political realignment;

(3) the divide between Inners and Outers overlaps the major parties who are struggling to represent an electorate with divergent issue priorities and viewpoints; and

(4) the extremes of the Inners-Outers divide is reflected in the politics of the Greens and One Nation who fuel each other.

Part II explores the impact of the rise of Inners on policymaking in Australia. The following chapter outlines how Australian politics, particularly since the economic reform era of the 1980s, has become a bargain between Inners that often excludes the Outers voice.

PART II:

Governance by Inners

FIVE

Australian Politics:
Inners bargain, Outers hushed

'Australia can no longer afford to go down the path of confrontation and fragmentation,' the then recently elected prime minister Bob Hawke declared to *National Economic Summit Conference* on 11 April 1983, 'This conference itself is part of the process of bringing Australia together.'[310] The Summit included Australia's political, business, finance and union elites and was convened to address economic issues and build 'genuine consensus.'[311] Hawke's goals were lofty, 'this conference has a part to play, not only in the urgent and immediate task of achieving national economic recovery, but in laying foundations for the whole future of this great country of ours.'

Attendees were given the unusual privilege of sitting in the House of Representatives chamber, speeches were transcribed in a Hansard-style publication and dinners were at the Governor-Generals' Government House in Yarralumla and the Prime Minister's Lodge. 'There was a distinct sense that they were given guest status at the policy-making banquet and left intoxicated,' commentator and historian Paul Kelly wrote.[312] Proceedings concluded with a communique agreeing to Hawke's proposals for centralised wage fixing and to addressing high inflation and low employment.

The Summit, and the broader model of consensus policymaking adopted by the Hawke-Keating government, was designed to reduce elite political conflict. (The format was subsequently replicated, with much less success, by Kevin Rudd's Australia 2020 Summit in 2008 and Julia Gillard's Jobs Summit and the Tax Forum in 2011.) The Hawke-Keating Government largely achieved consensus. 'Australia's political debate during the late 1980s saw Labor and Coalition, business and unions, opinion makers and economic institutions, agreed upon the direction,' Kelly surmises.[313]

The consensus-driven model of Australian policymaking, however, excluded most Australians. Those at the table were empowered; everyone else was, physically and metaphorically, locked out of the corridors of power. The Summit is an exemplar of policymaking by Inners.[314] The format was designed to hash out differences among Inners, of the political left and right, and reach policy consensus in the 'national interest' – but only the Inners' interpretation of the national interest which often coincides with their sectional interests.

The consensus only included the elite of Australian society. Historian Frank Bongiorno notes that the Summit attendees, 'businesses, unions and the professions of law, medicine and accountancy,' are hardly a representative sample of Australian society.[315] 'Critics of the summit wondered whether Australia was developing its own brand of corporatism, one in which government, business and unions ran the country as a cosy partnership, the conflicts between them being frozen "by a permanent truce",' Bongiorno writes.

Corporatism emerged from European thinkers of the 19th century and was adopted by Germany, Italy, Spain and

Portugal in the 20th century.[316] Corporatism seeks to compromise capitalism and socialism through cooperation between capital, labour and the state to minimise class conflict. In practice, power is centralised in the hands of the political, corporate and union elite with limited public debate and scrutiny. This dynamic benefits the organised and those who have representatives in Canberra. 'The real decisions are hidden from view. The substantive decisions take place behind closed doors where only the tripartite partners are accorded privileged access,' one commentator noted.[317]

Some criticised Hawke's policymaking method. In 1984, retiring Treasurer secretary, and later Queensland Liberal senator, John Stone condemned the 'industrial philosophies of fascism' in Australia's coordination between unions and government.[318] In 1985, Jeff Kennett, who later became Victorian premier, scathingly labelled the Summit 'Mr Hawke's version of the Grand Council of Fascists.'[319]

Corporatism is the style of politics that Liberal founder Robert Menzies was railing against in his seminal *The Forgotten People* address. Menzies defines the 'forgotten people', the middle class, by process of exclusion. Menzies says that on one end there is the working class, the 'mass of unskilled people, almost invariably well-organised, and with their wages and conditions safeguarded by popular law,' and on the other, the upper class, the 'rich and powerful: those who control great funds and enterprises, and are as a rule able to protect themselves'. Menzies claims to represent the political and financial middle class, the 'salary-earners, shopkeepers, skilled artisans, professional men and women, farmers and so on. These people lack proper representation. They are not sufficiently lacking in individualism to be organised for what in these days we call "pressure politics".'

Australia is in a new era of forgotten people: the Outers. The precise dynamics over time have changed. Today, following the gentrification of the Labor Party, even the unskilled (*The Left Behind*) are lacking in organisation, representation, leadership. The upper segment of the middle class (the Inners) are ably represented by the Greens and Labor (*The New Elite*) and the Liberal Party (*The Old Establishment*).

This dynamic has developed because of electoral re-alignment, in combination with economic and social change. French economist Thomas Piketty found, from analysis of French, British and American voting patterns since 1948 that parties of the left have transformed from attracting 'lower education and lower income voters' to increasingly attracting 'higher education voters.'[320] Piketty writes that 'the "left" has become the party of the intellectual elite (Brahmin left), while the "right" can be viewed as the party of the business elite (Merchant right)'. As a consequence, Piketty argues, there has been an emergence of a '"multiple-elite" party system, in which the two governing coalitions alternating in power represent the views and interests of a different elite (intellectual elite vs business elite)'. Australia's political realignment has followed a similar path, with similar consequences.

The 1980s reform era is the critical turning point. Reform was a technical success and social and cultural change was much-needed. Australia has not only become an extraordinary economic success story – with a quarter century since the last recession – we have also become a more tolerant, interesting and forward-thinking place. It is hard to avoid, however prosperous Australia has become, that policymaking is dominated by the Inners tribe and Outers are sidelined (See Figure 17).

The Inners consensus is driving Australia's policy stalemate; it has created a system of high taxes, red tape and paternalistic and technocratic policy. Inners have the best jobs and can reap the rewards for themselves – such as university research funding and a regulatory state beneficial to corporates – and they are happy for the status quo to continue. Outers have little ability to influence change.

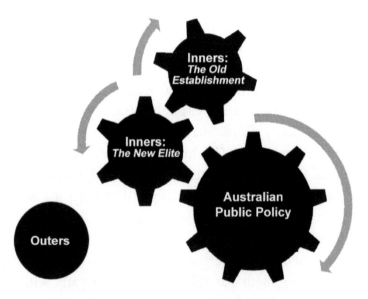

Figure 17. A model Australian politics: Australian public policy has become a debate between two types of Inners, The Old Establishment and The New Elite, and Outers have little say.

More debate about less and less

Australian public debate has not been about the fundamentals since the 1980s. The traditional left-right ideological conflict has largely dissipated. The Labor Party no longer pursues the socialisation of the means of production; the Liberal Party has given up on industrial relations reform and the liberalisations of the *Fightback!* package. The consensus behind policymaking explains why most Australians think the parties are practically the same. Just 27 per cent say that good deal of difference between the parties, down from 44 per cent in 1993.[321]

Australia's elites, Inners of both the economic left or right, are well-represented in policymaking. The economic right Inners are ably represented by the Business Council of Australia, the Australian Chamber of Industry and Commerce and various lobbyist outfits across Canberra; the economic left Inners are well-represented by the Australian Council for Trade Unions (ACTU), GetUp and other activist groups.

Meanwhile, other than the perfunctory nod at election time and the occasional handout, Outers are rarely consulted or actively involved with the way decisions are made.[322] Outers have been locked out of the decision making process since economic reform in the 1980s, which was never as popular with the public as with the political class. The locking out helps explain the widespread dissatisfaction that has led most to disengage from politics altogether. Less than a third of Australians took a good deal of interest in the last election campaign.[323] Australian politics has become the realm of the educated and well-connected.

Australia's major political parties have become 'catch-all' parties, as seminally described by Otto Kirchheimer.[324] He theorised in 1966 that parties would converge in policy because of economic changes which were decreasing traditional class distinctions between workers and capital. Consequently, there would be 'opposition of form rather than of content.'[325] Other factors, such as leadership and media appeal, would become increasingly important. The party's choice of leader would become a key focus of national debate because as it is the only remaining difference between the parties.[326] The public is left with an 'illusory choice.'

'The style and looks of the leader, the impact of a recent event entirely dictated from without, vacation schedules, the weather as it affects crops—factors such as these all enter into the results,' Kirchheimer argues.[327] In an era of 'catch-all' parties, voters have less loyalty leading to an increase in swing voting. The only remaining powerful voices in the political process are organised interest groups. At worst, parties collude among themselves to employ the resources of the state to ensure the survival of themselves and their cronies.[328] The public feels remote and disconnected from the political process. 'Vanishing opposition, cartelisation and professionalisation of politics pits citizens against a powerful state, which increases political cynicism and apathy,' André Krouwel surmises.[329]

The catch-all model is an ideal-type, an exaggeration, a worst-case scenario. Nevertheless, there is evidence across the developed world that parties have converged in policy, particularly since the 1980s and 1990s, and voters are becoming increasingly apathetic.[330] Notably, Imbeau and collaborators meta-analysis of 43 empirical studies, including 693 measures, on the impact of political parties on policy concludes that 'average correlation between the party composition of government and policy outputs is not significantly different from zero.'[331] As Kirchheimer predicted, party identification has fallen, in systems with optional voting turnout has decreased and the public has become less interested in the political process.[332]

Australian politics fits the 'catch-all' model in a variety of ways. In a catch-all party system, experts and professionals rather than 'workers' or 'middle class' dominate the parties. Australia's political parties are directed by a professional class made up of 'staffers,' 'campaign professionals,' or 'machine men' focused on electoral victory rather than ideology.[333] Party membership numbers have substantially shrunk despite a growing population. In the 20 year period from the late 1940s until the late 1960s, approximately 15 per cent of the Australian population was a member of a major political party.[334] Today, rounded to the nearest whole number, approximately 0 per cent of Australians are a member of a major political party. There are 53,550 Labor Party members, about 50,000 Liberal Party members, 15,000 Nationals and 15,000 Greens members – about 0.005% of Australia's population.[335] Meanwhile, the capacity to speak out internally has declined as party discipline has grown.[336] The events have empowered a professional class, the 'machine men', within the parties, who focus less on ideology and more on the popularity of leaders and complex opinion polling and focus groups to find swing voters.[337] Australian politics was not always so elitist.

The Outers Settlement

Historically Australian politics was a contest of Outers, between *The Left Behind* on Labor's side and *The Aspirational* represented by the non-Labor parties. The contest led to the creation, in the first decades of the 20th century, of what Paul Kelly calls the Australian Settlement: White Australia, Industry Protection, Wage Arbitration, State Paternalism and Imperial Benevolence. This was a bipartisan settlement, supported the humanitarian middle class represented by Alfred Deakin on the right and the working class union movement on the left.[338]

The Australian Settlement was precipitated on stability, both culturally and economically, that appeals to Outer sensibilities. It was a system established to deliver 'income, justice, employment and security', long before Inners existed in substantial numbers.[339] The Australian Settlement was not sustainable in the modern world. It ultimately failed to deliver living standards, served sectional interests and could not withstand the rapidly changing world and the rise of the Inners.[340] Its cultural strength, unity and stability, was its economic weakness, preventing change and dynamism.

White Australia, which limited entry to Europeans, was designed to protect Australian unity and minimise competition from outside labour. The idea of a stable multi-racial democracy was beyond the conceptualisation of Australia's early leaders. Prime Minister Alfred Deakin argued that 'The unity of Australia is nothing if it does not imply a united race. Unity of race is an absolute to the unity of Australia.'[341] The union movement supported White Australia to safeguard national unity and restrict lower paid foreign labour undercutting wages. The Australian Workers Union did not withdraw support for White Australia until 1972.[342]

Industry Protection, high tariffs and subsidies, was designed to deliver economic stability and to secure manufacturing jobs. Wage Arbitration aimed to deliver the benefits of protection to employees in higher wages and better working conditions; and sought to minimise class warfare after the recession and industrial conflict of the 1890s. The Harvester Judgement of 1907 explicitly established the 'living wage' – premised on a breadwinner social model in which the man of the household earned enough to support his wife and children.

Imperial Benevolence is the underwriting of Australian foreign policy by the British Empire and later the United States, and the associated respect for the key alliance. State Paternalism refers to extensive government intervention in the economy, including ownership of major enterprises – transport, communications and energy – public provision of education and health, and social regulation to define gender roles, encourage church attendance, restrict alcohol and enforce sexual morality through content censorship.

State Paternalism fits the Australian disposition for the state to provide. Historian Keith Hancock's seminal *Australia*, published in 1930, discusses how Australians depend on the state for individualist ends. 'Australian democracy has come to look upon the State as a vast public utility, whose duty it is to provide the greatest happiness for the greatest number,' Hancock wrote, 'the origins of this are individualistic.'[343] 'To the Australian, the State means collective power at the service of individualistic "rights". Therefore, he sees no opposition between his individualism and his reliance upon Government.'

Combining the themes, political scientist Francis Castles called Australia a 'wage earner welfare state' – defined by high wages and relatively low social spending.[344] Australia had wage control through the arbitration system; protective tariffs to boost wages in manufacturing, urban service industries and fringe rural production; and regulation of manpower through controlled migration to maintain the bargaining power of labour. High wages precipitated high levels of home ownership. Australia was among the lowest welfare spenders in the developed world for much of the second half of the 20th century with relatively limited means-tested age, health and disability support and wage supplements.

The Australian Settlement was maintained with cross-party consensus until the early 1980s (except for the White Australia policy that began to be dismantled under the Holt Government in the late 1960s and the Whitlam Government pursuit of lower tariffs in the 1970s). The economic logic for the abolition of the Australian Settlement is undeniable. The system failed in its core mission: to achieve high living standards.

The Australian economy lacked dynamism and was closed to mutually beneficial international trade in both products and ideas. For much of the 20th century, Australia was in economic decline. As Paul Kelly points out, in 1870 Australia's average income was 40 per cent above any other nation; in the 20th century it was worse than any other developed economy. Australia's economy fell from 1st place to 14th. Nevertheless, it took a domestic economic crisis, the collapse of commodity prices and severe drought, external economic pressure and changing global policy consensus to undo the system.[345]

There was a severe need to address the inefficiency of publicly owned enterprise and 'creative destruction,' letting old inefficient industry collapse and be replaced by new entrepreneurial activity.[346] There was also an emerging international consensus for economic liberalisation, intellectually led by economists Milton Friedman and Friedrich Hayek, politically by Margaret Thatcher in Britain and Ronald Reagan in the United States and institutionally by the International Monetary Fund and the World Bank.[347]

Under the Hawke-Keating Labor government, the Australian economy was opened to international competition, tariffs were substantially reduced, the Australian dollar was floated, foreign banks were allowed in the financial system, government enterprises (including banks, airlines and telecommunications) privatised and competition was introduced in the provision of power, ports and transport. Policymaking also became more technocratic, including increasing Reserve Bank independence and the establishment and empowering of independent regulatory agencies such as ASIC and APRA to set economic rules.[348]

Ironically, it was Labor, the party of the economic left, that atypically pursued liberal economic policies. The Labor Party, to this day, is formally dedicated to the 'socialist objective,' which includes the 'democratic socialisation of industry, production, distribution and exchange.'[349] If the Liberal Party was in government, Labor is unlikely to have resisted the political temptation of siding with interests who benefited from the Australian Settlement. Nevertheless, under Hawke and Keating, the Labor Party changed track, re-modelling Labor as the party of economic management that could usher in the necessary change. Labor found faith in the markets, belief in economic competition and globalisation of the Australian economy. The Liberal Party also transformed in the 1980s, from the 'wet' economic policies supportive of tariffs and state ownership pursued by Malcolm Fraser, to the 'dry' economic policies pursued by John Howard and John Hewson.

The Inners Reform

The economic reforms – however necessary and effective – were an elite project. The Australian Settlement was the consensus for Outers. Economic liberalism is the consensus for Inners. 'The fundamental divide in Australian politics in the late 1980s was no longer Labor versus Liberal' Paul Kelly writes, 'Party differences were real and bitter, but the underlying policy direction was the same.'[350] The major parties broadly agreed on tariff reduction, financial sector reform, immigration and competition. The reform consensus also stretched from politics into business, media and the unions, who worked together to reshape the system.

The consensus of elites meant that politicians did not have to achieve popular support for the details of the change. It was possible to fundamentally alter Australia without the pesky issue of having to convince the electorate. The elite-driven process empowered and encouraged organisation by both unions and businesses. The changes were ultimately accepted; however, most Australians were not part of or consulted in the process.

The preeminent governing approach of the Hawke-Keating era was close cooperation between the government and the 'big end of town,' corporates, finance and trade unions. Hawke pursued a 'cult of consensus' to be achieved by getting the big players on side.[351] Australia adopted a form of corporatism – control of society by large interest groups in collaboration with government in a 'managerial and technocratic' manner.[352] 'An increasingly corporate state is certainly (if not the only) logical extension of Bob Hawke's political personality, value and tactics,' commentators Geoffrey Barker and Max Teichmann noted in 1983.[353]

The corporatist approach to policymaking was epitomised by the Accords. The Accords were a series of agreements between the Labor government and the union movement, represented by the Australian Council of Trade Unions (ACTU). An Accord was first proposed Labor opposition leader Bill Hayden following weak relations between the parliamentary party and the unions under Whitlam. The initial goal of the Accord was to achieve industrial stability and address the wage breakout that was fuelling inflation; however, they became broad agreements that covered a wide range of policy areas, including industrial relations, welfare, foreign investment, health, education, industry and immigration policy. It was an extraordinary way to develop policy: an agreement between the government and one part of the economy.

The central trade-off the Accords, which gave unions the power to set policy direction, was wage stagnation.[354] The unions agreed to 'no extra claims' above inflation. At times, the unions even allowed wages to fall in real terms. The trade union movement explicitly agreed 'that while maintenance of real wages is a key objective, in a period of economic crisis, as now applying, it will be an objective over time' at the National Economic Summit.[355] In 1983 the unions agreed in the Accord to limit wage rises to 3-4 per cent and declared that there should be no 'catch-up', allowing for a real wage reduction.[356]

The result of the Accords was stagnant income growth in the 1980s. Over the decade, real wages grew by just 1.2 per cent.[357] In exchange for wage restraint the government increased the so-called 'social wage,' which included lower taxes and social spending on family payments, education and healthcare including Medicare. There was a substantial political advantage to these cosy agreements. The government averted aggressive political conflict by bringing the union movement into the tent. As one commentator noted, the 'quasi-corporatist arrangements of the Accord' meant that 'political and industrial dissent was muted.'[358]

The Accords have been heavily criticised by Australia's socialist left who reject the acceptance of lower wages and worse working conditions.[359] One writer in the Marxist Left Review recently surmised that 'The Accord entrenched class collaboration with the bosses, pushed aside strikes in favour of arbitration and appeals to the ALP, accelerated the destruction of independent shop floor union organisation and centralised power in the hands of the growing union bureaucracy.'[360] The Accords combined with the changing labour market conditions to hasten union mergers and membership declines that concentrated power in larger unions, the ACTU and the Labor Party.[361]

On the other side of the corporatist ledger, the Accords

stimulated coordination, organisation and mergers of business representatives. Labor's approach to governing, consensus at the top of Australian society, created incentives for businesses to organise in national structures like the trade unions. Hawke's consensus approach required the existence of business leadership with which the government could wheel and deal. Businesses needed to organise themselves to lobby government and provide representatives for 'tripartite committees,' which include government, labour and employer representatives, such as the National Planning and Advisory Council and the National Occupational Health and Safety Commission.[362]

Partly in response to the Accords and the emerging corporatism of the era, the Business Council of Australia (BCA) was established in 1983 to represent Australia's largest businesses; and the Australian Chamber of Commerce and Industry (ACCI), the peak body representing business groups was established in 1992 through mergers.[363] The creation of the BCA and ACCI was hastened by the necessity to have a united and coordinated voice of business in the national debate in response to the organisation of the unions in the ACTU.[364] For the Hawke-Keating Government to achieve 'consensus' they needed business groups who could make deals – they were the third leg of the tripartite corporatist organisation of society.

In the later stages of the Accords the traditional role of industry-wide bargaining was diminished in favour of enterprise bargaining in which deals are made between unions and specific companies. This has led to cosy deals between big businesses and big unions; unions have been caught trading lower wages for union benefits.[365] Coles and Woolworths, for instance, agreed to 'sweetheart' deals with the SDA Union which traded weekend penalty rates for higher hourly pay and supermarkets paying the SDA for 'training.'[366] These deals were ultimately found to be illegal. Fairfax Media estimated that workers were paid $300 million less a year because of deals between retail and fast-food outlets and the SDA.[367]

The Accords also undermined Australia's traditional social model, premised on high wages and relatively low transfers.[368] Labor and the unions, in a reversal of their historic role, allowed the market forces to be unleashed and sought to address inequalities through redistribution and the welfare state rather than wage bargaining.[369] Despite the claims of a 'neoliberal' turn, a decreasing role of the state, the level of social expenditure has substantially increased since the 1980s.[370] Between 1984 and 2004, social expenditure per household grew by 30 per cent, however, the wages of the lowest quintile of Australian households remained stagnant for the entire period.[371]

Success at a cost

Economic reform was largely successful. Australia has not had a recession since 1991 despite the Asian financial crisis, the dotcom bubble and the Global Financial Crisis. Australia has had the longest period of continuous growth of any country in modern history.[372] Since 1990, Australia's economy has grown by 125 per cent, there are 4.6 million additional jobs and inflation has remained stable around the 2-3 per cent target.[373] Meanwhile, the cost of goods has *declined* in fields opened to international competition, including clothing (-4 per cent), household appliances (-18 per cent), motor vehicles (-22 per cent) and TVs and computers (-92 per cent) while wages have grown by 90 per cent since 1997.[374]

Nevertheless, Outers did not have a seat at the table during the elite-driven reform era. As David Kemp writes:

> 'The gathering pace of reform after 1980 was a product of the desire of Australia's political class to establish a process in which expert policy analysis had a key role. This analysis reflected the growing dominance at the level of liberal values shared across the elite political spectrum, but not of public opinion.'[375]

The argument for liberalisation never had to be won among the public because opposition dissipated among elites.

Across a range of topics, the public is less economically liberal than their political leadership. The Outers do not entirely support the consensus reached between *The New Elite* of middle class Labor and *The Old Establishment* of middle class Liberals. This applies to a range of issues including privatisation and globalisation of the economy. Throughout the 1980s and 1990s, a minority of Australians supported privatising public assets such as Telstra (34 per cent support), Commonwealth Bank (25 per cent) and Qantas (36 per cent) – and support declined over the period.[376]

In broad terms, most Australians think that globalisation, especially the increasing connections of our economy, is mostly good for Australia (78 per cent), and a majority of Australians believe free trade improves their standard of living (67 per cent), the Australian economy (67 per cent), Australian companies (61 per cent) and job creation (55 per cent).[377] Nevertheless, there is strong support for restrictions on foreign ownership of Australian agriculture land (80 per cent), limiting imports to protect jobs (65 per cent) and concern that international companies damage local business (75 per cent).[378]

Kemp attributes the public negativity towards liberalism to a 'deep public conservatism and the difficulty of assessing the actual effects of policies.' Kemp notes that even after reform there remained strong support for public ownership, protection of Australian industry and arbitration. The reasons for opposition to the reforms could be even deeper than Kemp suggests. Economics professor Bryan Caplan has argued that the public is systematically biased against economic liberalism because of a psychological tendency to underestimate the benefits of the market mechanism and interaction with foreigners.[379] Caplan notes, for instance, that 'People tend to see profits as a gift to the rich' rather than the reward for providing a useful product, and an economically important incentive to reduce production costs, efficiently allocate resources, and develop new products.[380]

There may have been enthusiasm on pragmatic grounds for change and happiness with the positive outcomes. Nevertheless, the specifics of the Hawke-Keating reform era were defined by the elite. Australia adopted a social and economic model of pluralism, of dynamism and creative destruction. The new system undermined the stable life sought by Outers. Importantly, most Australians do not feel much better off for all the change. Just 5 per cent of Australians think they have personally gained a lot over the last 26 years of uninterrupted growth – compared to 74 per cent who think that large corporations have gained a lot.[381]

Social researcher Hugh Mackay wrote in 1993 that, 'The story of Australia between the early 1970s and the early 1990s is the story of a society which has been trying to cope with too much change too quickly and on too many fronts.'[382] Mackay was commenting broadly of social, cultural and economic transformations of the era – from new divorce laws, to women entering the workplace and increasing immigration and economic reform. Much of the change may have been actively sought, necessary and inevitable, however, that did not make it any less daunting.

'The common cry now being heard around Australia is, "Why does everything have to change so fast?" The common complaint is that individual Australians feel as if they have lost control of their own lives and their own destinies,' Mackay argued, 'Australians are increasingly feeling victimised by the rate and character of the changes which are having such an enormous emotional, cultural and financial impact on their lives.'[383] The sentiment, which Mackay called 'The Big Angst,' could just as easily be expressed today. Change is not only constant and accelerating; it is deeply unsettling.

When the Australian public was given the ability to reject further Inner-driven change, first on the economic front at the 1993 election and subsequently on the cultural front at the 1996 election, they took the opportunities. The Liberal Party's 1993 election platform, *Fightback!*, was the most ambitious liberal reform package taken by any party to an election in Australian history. It included tax reform, spending cuts, industrial relations reform, and privatisations. The public, however, had had enough. Reform fatigue had befallen Australia.

Outers were willing to accept liberal economic reform for as long as it seemed to work. The failure of Liberal leader John Hewson to make the case for further change, in combination with the 1993 recession – which saw unemployment skyrocket to 11 per cent, the highest in 60 years – changed the perception.[384] The recession beset a national pessimism.[385] Paul Keating, after multiple attempts, successfully challenged Bob Hawke for the prime ministership. Keating promised a slower pace of reform and stimulus to combat the recession. Hewson lost the 'unlosable election,' and Keating won the 'sweetest victory of them all.' The win would prove bittersweet.

The Inners' cultural agenda

The fault line that would become the ultimate undoing of Hawke-Keating Labor was disillusionment with the progressive cultural agenda. In an era of declining disagreement on the economic fundamentals divisions emerged between and within the parties on cultural, identity and lifestyle issues. The division was fuelled by the embracing of university educated progressive Inners by the Labor Party.

The seeds of the Hawke-Keating era's undoing were planted decades earlier. Labor came to power in 1972, for the first time in almost a quarter century, on the coattails of stretching the party's appeal beyond their traditional working class industrial base into the growing university educated intelligentsia. These intellectuals, public servants and professionals, were less interested in traditional economic concerns and more focused on cultural and social issues, including Indigenous Australians, multiculturalism, women, arts, Asia and environmentalism.

This younger cohort, disillusioned by the disastrous Vietnam War and the conservatism of the Liberals, was attracted to Gough Whitlam. Whitlam was the first Labor leader from an educated middle class background, his father was a Commonwealth Crown Solicitor and Whitlam himself was a barrister.[386] Whitlam successfully mixed Labor's traditional working class base with the new educated middle class, catapulting the party to power for the first time since the 1940s. Whitlam's tenure, however, was short-lived because of political chaos and scandals, inept economic management, defined by inflation, unemployment and deficits, and a bitter dismissal. Labor came back to power in 1983 by moderating Labor's economic positions while still using the same working class-middle class intelligentsia coalition.

Labor needed to find new constituency and political focus. Across the developed world, the decline in blue collar jobs is a challenge to parties of the left that were established under the mantle of class conflict. Labor in Australia accelerated this process by pursuing market reforms and tariff abolition, cannibalising their traditional base. To borrow the classic Marxist phrasing, if there is a declining class of 'oppressed' proletariats, and a growth in bourgeoisie jobs, who does the left represent?

The Australian Labor Party, as well as (Bill) Clinton's Democrats in the United States, Tony Blair's Labourites in Britain and Gerhard Schroder's Social Democrats in Germany, finding their socialist left economic policies out of fashion began appealing to the new bourgeoisie class.[387] The centre-left in developed nations moved their appeal away from socialist economics and towards liberal positions on social and cultural issues. The new appeal also suited the marked change in the background of Labor politicians. Labor members of parliament with a blue collar background declined from 63 per cent in 1901, to just 12 per cent by 1981.[388]

Labor's new middle class domination was not universally welcomed. In 1972, Arthur Calwell, Whitlam's predecessor as Labor leader, warned about of a new 'faction' asserting itself in the Labor Party which:

> 'consists of aggressive, assertive, philosophical, way-out people whose purpose is certainly not to promote the well-being of the party or of society; it is to create an agnostic, hedonistic society based on Freudian philosophy, even if the philosophy is largely discounted today. These people seek to challenge all accepted vies and standards that govern our society... Nothing that exists is above criticism to them. There are more of them in the Labor Party than any other party. But the newspaper, radio and television have also been the subject of similar penetration.'[389]

Michael Thompson, a lifetime Labor Party member and author of *Labor Without Class: The Gentrification of the ALP*, was 'angered with the hijacking of the Australian Labor Party... by the tertiary educated (with their contempt for the contribution to Labor of the under educated).'[390] Mark Latham, who later became Labor leader, wrote about Labor's 'identity crisis' following Labor's 2001 election loss that, 'We abandoned our dialogue with suburban Australia, while the gentrified Left abandoned us for the Greens and the Democrats. A wedge has been driven through the middle of Labor's ranks. We need to close the gap between our dual constituencies.'[391]

After Keating's success at the 1993 election, promising a semblance of economic stability, his focus strayed away from Outer priorities and towards the cultural agenda of the Inners, Labor's new middle class constituency. On the economic front, Keating did not replicate earlier careful economic management, plunging Australia into substantial debt during the recession that he dismissively declared as 'the recession we had to have.'[392] Australia's national debt grew from $16 billion in 1990 to over $95 billion in 1995.[393] In the face of the debt, Keating pursued privatisations including Qantas and the Commonwealth Bank, prioritising revenue raising over market competition in the process.[394]

On the non-economic front, Keating's post-1993 agenda was dominated by 'big picture issues', related to culture, history and identity. These issues included Aboriginal native title following the Mabo case, relations with Asia and the republic. 'This made him enormously popular among intellectuals,' political scientist Judith Brett remarks.[395] It did not make him politically popular among Outers whose concerns were more traditional – the economy, service delivery and rising living standards.

In response to Labor's abandonment of the working class and posturing on cultural issues under Keating, Labor lost working class voters to the Liberal Party – who, under Howard, came to highlight cultural conservatism as a contrast with Labor.

Keating's cultural agenda was epitomised by his approach to Aboriginal Australians, his number one focus following the 1993 election.[396] Following the Mabo decision of 1992, there was an immediate policymaking necessity to address land rights issues, which came to fruition in the Native Title Act of 1995. However, Keating went much further than the practical. He sought to reshape Australia's understanding of history. This change in approach was marked by Keating's seminal Redfern Address.

Redfern marks the full transformation of the Labor Party; it was the moment the party's focus changed from its traditional working class constituency to its new middle class intelligentsia. The latter, organised, capable, well-spoken and educated, had won; the former had lost. The transformation that began under Whitlam came to its logical conclusion.

On 10 December 1992, Keating addressed Redfern Park in Sydney to launch the International Year of Indigenous Peoples. In the speech, he not only declares a need to 'find just solutions to the problems which beset the first Australians', but he also goes on to blame *all* Australians for these problems. Keating says that 'the starting point might be to recognise that the problem starts with us non-Aboriginal Australians':

> '…it was we who did the dispossessing. We took the traditional lands and smashed the traditional way of life. We brought the diseases. The alcohol. We committed the murders. We took the children from their mothers. We practised discrimination and exclusion. It was our ignorance and our prejudice.'

These comments placed Indigenous Australians at the centre of the emerging history wars. Critics complained that Keating exaggerated the past, inappropriately allocated collective blame for the actions of paternalistic government bureaucrats, undermined Australian identity and turned Indigenous Australians into helpless victims. Meanwhile, Australia has failed to close the achievement and life expectancy gap between Indigenous and non-Indigenous Australians.[397]

Historian Geoffrey Blainey, in the 1993 John Latham Lecture, castigated the Keating view of the past. Blainey described it as the 'The Black Armband view of history' – the view that 'much of Australian history was a disgrace.'[398] Blainey, pointing to Australia's economic prosperity and stable democratic tradition, took a more balanced view of the past:

> 'Some episodes in the past were regrettable, there were many flaws and failures, and yet on the whole it stands out as one of the world's success stories. It is ironical that many of the political and intellectual leaders of the last decade, one of the most complacent and disappointing decades in our history, are so eager to denounce earlier generations and discount their hard-won successes. Most young Australians, irrespective of their background, are quietly proud to be Australian. We deprive them of their inheritance if we claim that they have inherited little to be proud of.'

Putting aside the merits of this debate, the decision by Keating to focus on these issues proved electorally fatal. There was a heavy focus on identity and history issues in Keating's 1996 election campaign launch speech. Keating mentioned Aboriginal Australians twice, women four times, tolerance three times and diversity four times, the Republic four times, Asia eight times and the environment twelve times. Keating's focus empowered the Liberal opposition to claim Labor was captive to minority interests and out of touch with mainstream Australia.

Howard effectively tapped into Outer disillusionment with Labor's cultural agenda. These people became known popularly as 'Howard's Battlers,' former Labor working class voters disillusioned with Keating. 'Voters were angry not only about Labor's new taxes but about the programs the money would be spent,' Pamela William explained in *The Victory*.[399] 'They felt left out of Keating's political agenda as he pushed Mabo, the republic, and relations with Asia to centre stage. And they didn't trust the loud lobby groups that surrounded him or the social goals he seemed to be pushing for.'

Andrew Robb, the Liberal Party campaign manager in 1996, compared this group to the Reagan Democrats – the Republican Party's similar success with the working class. The Liberal Party campaign slogan was 'For All of Us' in 1996. Howard's election campaign launch speech committed to 'represent all Australians', declaring that 'We are owned by nobody. Our only desire is to be given the opportunity to build a better Australia and a better future for all Australians.'[400]

Howard's pitch was designed to contrast with Keating, who was representing only the 'the social progressive, often highly educated, affluent end of middle Australia,' Robb explained. 'Over and over, the blue collar workers and low-earning white-collar workers [that Liberal Party pollster Mark] Textor had polled, articulated the same kind of bitterness. But they harboured special rancour for Paul Keating: "He might have knowledge of what's affecting us, but he just doesn't seem to be interested. He's got no empathy for my problems. After all he's said, in some ways I think he's betrayed us."'

Political scientist Robert Manne linked Howard's cross-class appeal to Menzies' forgotten people mantra: 'Just as Menzies had transformed the forgotten class into the forgotten people, Howard's battlers transcend their class identifies, including both the employed and the self-employed as they struggle to raise a family and make ends meet'. Manne continued, 'The Liberals not only claimed to represent the mainstream, or the whole, but did so in a way that directly challenged Labor's core historical identity.'[401]

In the balance

Following the Liberal success at the Lindsey by-election of 1996, Labor shadow minister Duncan Kerr reportedly told shadow cabinet that 'We must recognise that Howard is talking in code to our supporters, and our view are seen as part of an elite.'[402] Howard's 'code' was an appeal to aspiration combined with national unity and opposition to elitist cultural progressives. Howard appealed to families and small businesses owners who identify with their community and Australian identity; and to people at the individual, family and national level avoiding the 'elite' fascination with distinctions by class, gender, race, region, religion and ethnicity.[403]

Howard built a modest Australian national narrative around the themes of Gallipoli, mateship, egalitarianism by rejecting elitism. Howard declared in his 1997 Australia Day speech that:

'the symbols that we hold very dear as Australians and the beliefs that we have about what it is to be an Australian are not things that can ever be imposed from above by political leaders of any persuasion. They are not things that can be generated by self appointed, cultural elite who seek to tell us what our identity ought to be. Rather they are feelings and attitudes that grow out of the spirit of the people.'[404]

Howard repeatedly asserted that the Liberal Party is a 'broad church' of liberals and conservatives. In the face of a rapidly changing world, the Liberal Party began to appeal, explicitly for the first time, to conservatism. Howard sought to balance economic liberalism with a defence of conservative values such as family support, protecting cultural institutions and national unity. This helped stretch the Liberal Party's appeal beyond its traditional middle class base to include the culturally conservative working class. Howard sought to balance Inners and Outers instincts – change with cultural stability and strength.

A prime example of Howard balancing Inners and Outers pressures is on immigration. The questioning of Australia's level of immigration has remained a consistent feature of Australian politics. The economic effect of migrants by most accounts is positive, particularly for a society with an ageing population such as Australia. Migrants, tend to be younger and higher skilled, they increase productivity and pay higher taxes while using fewer services. A report by Independent Economics for the Migration Council estimates that, through to 2050, migration will increase workforce participation by 16 per cent and wages for low skilled workers by 22 per cent as well as contribute 6 per cent to GDP per capita growth.[405]

Nevertheless, immigration raises a series of issues including infrastructure congestion and planning, identity and social cohesion, as well as social and cultural change that can lead to discomfort.[406] Harvard social scientist Robert Putnam found that increasing ethnic diversity lowers social capital – people trust each other less, are less altruistic and people have fewer friends in areas with new migrants.[407] Putnam concludes that a diverse society provides long term benefits; however, there are inevitable challenges with integrating new arrivals.

The controversy surrounding Australia's immigration policy was reinvigorated in 1984 by the declaration, from Geoffrey Blainey, that the 'slow Asian takeover of Australia' was not inevitable. Blainey argued that Australia must not become a 'cluster of tribes'.[408] The Labor government's 1998 Fitzgerald Report found that public support for immigration was declining. As opposition leader, Howard responded by proposing the 'One Australia' policy, which focused on skilled migration and national unity. In the 1980s, the majority of Australia's immigration intake was family rather than skilled (See Figure 18).

Howard was criticised at the time for suggesting that this implied a decline in Asian migration – which was both not explicitly stated in the opposition's policy and unlikely because increased skilled migration could just as likely lead to increased Asian migration.[409] This was an important lesson for Howard. He subsequently expressed regrets for his earlier remarks.[410] The issue dissipated in the immediate term because of bipartisan elite support for immigration.

The rise of Pauline Hanson's One Nation and Keating's discussion of 'multiculturalism' reinvigorated the immigration question in the late 1990s. Howard initially reduced immigration after 1996 to restore confidence in the immigration system. Following the 2001 *Tampa* controversy, Howard declared that 'we will decide who comes to this country and the circumstances in which they come' and successfully introduced the 'Pacific Solution' to combat illegal boat arrivals.[411]

Howard, nevertheless, committed Australia to a large, non-discriminatory immigration program and explicitly opposed discrimination, bigotry and intolerance. In response to Hanson, Howard declared in May 1997 that:

'She is wrong when she says that Australia is in danger of being
swamped by Asians. She is wrong to seek scapegoats for society's
problems. She is wrong when she denigrates foreign investment,
because its withdrawal would cost jobs. She is wrong when she
claims that Australia is headed for civil war.'[412]

Throughout his time in office Howard sought to highlight
unity in discussions of immigration by appealing to family, hard
work and the small business values of Asian Australians:

'People of Asian communities have contributed very greatly to
the enrichment of our life. They have bought their value of the
extended family, they have bought their values of hard work, they
have bought their values of commitment to small business and
entrepreneurial flair and their infectious vigour in so many other
areas to our shores.'

Australia's immigration intake grew by 45 per cent in the
Howard era (from 0.5 per cent to 0.8 per cent) as a proportion
of the population and has remained at similar levels since (See
Figure 18). Despite increased immigration during the 2000s,
opposition fell over the period compared to the 1980s and 1990s.[413]
Katharine Betts, who has been studying attitudes to immigration
for decades, says the renewed positivity was because of Howard's
effective border management, a strong economy, restricted
access to welfare for new arrivals and less divisive rhetoric about
multiculturalism.[414] Howard's 'tough control' approach 'helped
generate acceptance of legal immigration,' she writes.[415] Howard
was able to both increase immigration *and* deliver community
unity by balancing Inner openness with the Outer instinct for
community and security.

Howard's balancing Inners and Outers instincts proved an
effective strategy. Howard became Australia's second longest
serving prime minister and, with Treasurer Peter Costello,

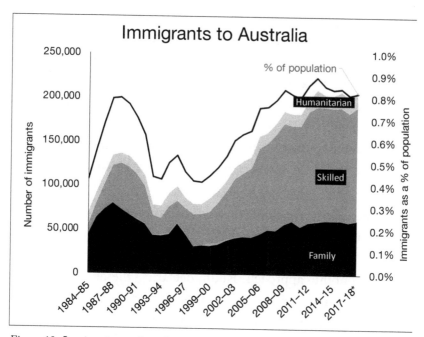

Figure 18. Immigration to Australia since 1984 *Planned (Source: ABS cat. no. 3412.0, Department of Immigration)

undertook tax reform, bought the budget under control, reformed industrial relations and oversaw an era of immense prosperity.[416] Howard was most successful when he took difficult and contested economic reform, such as Goods and Services Tax (GST), to an election, which he did successfully by winning the election in 1998. Howard, however, stepped over the mark with the WorkChoices industrial relations package which was introduced without a specific mandate. WorkChoices allowed Labor and the unions to appeal to their leftist economic roots and win back enough of their former blue collar voters in 2007.

The moderate alternative presented by Kevin Rudd appeared to be unthreatening to Outers. Rudd adopted many Outer positions avoided by modern Labor, including a tough-on-terrorism approach and supporting logging of Tasmanian forests.[417] Rudd also declared himself an 'economic conservative' – 'When it comes to public finance, it's a badge I wear with pride' – and promised a balanced budget, low interest rates, building an 'education revolution' including trades and apprenticeships education and a 'fair and balanced industrial relations system.'[418] Rudd came to power by appealing to Outer interests, promising all the best parts of Howard without the rough edges.

Since 2007, however, Australian politics has become beset by a growing national pessimism and disillusionment. Party leaders from both sides of politics have failed to appeal to Inners and Outers. Rudd in office dramatically reversed course from his steady economic approach. Rudd, declaring the end of 'extreme capitalism and excessive greed,' increased the role of the government in the market and markedly increased the national debt.[419] Rudd also dismantled the Pacific Solution, which led to the arrival of thousands of asylum seeker boats and increased concern about the entire immigration system.[420] Rudd's leadership fell apart because of his hectic leadership style and disillusionment in Labor's caucus.[421] He was successfully challenged by Julia Gillard in 2010.

Gillard, aware of the electoral limits of only appealing to Inners, made a special effort to appeal to Outers, declaring herself to have had a conservative upbringing. 'I had a pro-union, pro-Labor upbringing in a quite conservative family, in a sense of personal values. I mean we believed in lots of things that are old fashioned in the modern age,' Gillard claimed, 'We believed in politeness and thrift and fortitude and doing duty and diligence. These are things that were part of my upbringing. They're part of who I am.'[422] In 2013, in the face of negative polls, Gillard spent a week visiting Western Sydney.[423]

Following the 2010 election which resulted in a hung parliament, Gillard entered into a coalition with the party of Inners, the Greens and broke the 'no carbon tax' pledge. This beset an era of disillusionment and disappointment, that was effectively exploited by the Tony Abbot led opposition. Abbott became party leader in 2009 following internal opposition to Malcolm Turnbull's support for Rudd's carbon emissions trading scheme.[424] Abbott became prime minister in 2013 by appealing to Outer sensibilities on issues such as border protection, fiscal responsibility and opposition to Labor's environmental agenda.

Abbott, however, was unable to shake the perception that his style, persona and social conservatism were out of touch. The government struggled to deliver on pre-election promises and was embarrassed by self-inflicted political wounds.[425] Following successive negative polling results, Abbott was successfully challenged by Turnbull. Turnbull, while initially appealing to Inners, struggled to connect to Outers particularly on the question of energy policy and climate change. Turnbull ultimately lost the leadership during August 2018 in a revolt led by conservative Peter Dutton and taken advantage of by Scott Morrison. Prime Minister Scott Morrison immediately began his leadership with an appeal to Outer sensibilities. 'We're on your side,' Morrison said, 'because we share your beliefs and values.'

§

Australians were comfortable with economic policy directed by Inners for as long as it appeared to worked. The public may have disagreed with specific elements – such as privatisation – however they were happy enough to let their benign leaders take charge.

We do not love our political leaders; we tolerate them for as long as they serve a function. We were founded as a penal colony, not the most authority respecting folk; we attracted free settlers who were sick of the segmented class structures of Great Britain; we have become the home of people seeking a better life for themselves and their families, not a grand ideological experiment.

In recent political history, prime ministers lost office when they failed to balance their appeals to Inners and Outers. This matches the axiom of Australian politics: we vote out governments, not in new governments. Keating fell on his sword by focusing on post-materialist issues; Howard messed up the politics of WorkChoices; Gillard lost the leadership because she pursued a deal with the party of the Inners, the Greens; Abbott alienated Inners; Turnbull struggled to appeal to Outers.

Australians are feeling an increasing disconnect between themselves and those who make decisions on our behalf. Government has become increasing Inners-dominated; which has weakened Australian democracy and created a gap between the governed and their leaders. This is driving frustration.

The following chapter explores the disposition of Inners towards technocratic governance – that is, rule by themselves.

SIX

Inners: Educated, condescending, powerful, technocratic and wrong

Australian Cultural Fields is a research project led by Western Sydney University that correlates cultural tastes – including music, television and books – with income, education, age and gender.[426] The project builds on French sociologist Pierre Bourdieu's theory that power in society is made up of economic, cultural and social capital.[427] Bourdieu argues people who are socialised to value certain culture, including art, food, music and abstract ideas, are more likely to achieve educationally, which they can then convert into social networks, better paying jobs and higher status in society.[428]

Australian Cultural Fields found that cultural tastes diverge by income, education, age and gender. The upper middle class are more likely to own books, read Australian novels, like modern art, visit museums and galleries and attend music events. The working class like country music, watch reality television, are fans of Eddie McGuire, read little and do not visit galleries or museums. The findings could be presented as neutral – there is nothing inherently wrong with Australians having varied tastes, assuming you think cultural tastes are themselves equal.

The research, however, was reported by the ABC with the accompanying headline, 'Good taste, bad taste? What your habits reveal about social class.'[429] The elitist premise of the research was barely hidden. If you enjoy reality television and romance novels you have 'bad taste'; if you like museums and the ABC's *Australian Story*, you have 'good taste'. 'By and large, people with postgraduate degrees have the most distinctively high cultural tastes,' project manager Professor Tony Bennett of Western Sydney University told the *ABC*.

Inners not only have more educational and professional achievements and the associated better incomes; they think they are *better people* in the first place. Their authority is premised on their education, intelligence and tastes. They are confident in their perspective and technocratic in their disposition. Inners think everyone but themselves are dumb and must be forced to make the right decisions. If you think you are better than the masses then surely you should be able to rule over them.

Political scientist Judith Brett, discussing the cohort's first incarnation as the leaders of the middle class protest movements of 1960 and 1970s, writes that 'these people were used to making decisions, were articulate, confident of their opinions and had ideas about how things could be improved.'[430] Their ideas, however, are premised on their biases, overconfidence and methods that restrict liberty. Australia's democratic egalitarian ethos is being undermined by our educated, condescending, powerful, technocratic and wrong Inners governing class.

Educated and condescending

University education has created a new class with a distinctive identity and set of attitudes. They are sure of themselves, condescending towards those who do not share their worldview and lack self-awareness of their difference.

Humans suffer from 'illusory superiority,' the overestimation of one's qualities and abilities compared to others.[431] Psychologically, our egos cannot accept being less talented than those around us. Illusory superiority exists in everything from personality and life circumstances to relationship quality and intellect. Education does not alleviate such arrogance, it can make our superiority complex worse by providing confidence and social status. The educated think they are both better than their educated peers and much better and more moral than those with less education. This belief leads to some laughable consequences, such as 94 per cent of professors rating themselves *above average* relative to their academic peers – a mathematical impossibility.[432]

The feelings of superiority are heightened by the physical and social clustering of graduates in the inner-city, which drives a lack of understanding of their privilege and hostility to those with different ideas and lifestyles.[433] Graduates live in suburbs with other high income professionals and assess their wellbeing and views compared to people like themselves – not Australian society at large.[434] Physical clustering means that graduates do not realise how well-off and politically, culturally and socially different they are to others.[435]

Australia's highly educated go out of their way to avoid interacting with people who come from different backgrounds. In the gentrifying inner-north of Melbourne educated, professional residents are avoiding local schools which contain a high number of immigrants from the nearby public housing and sending their children to distant schools with more prestige.[436]

When you are not exposed to different people with different perspectives it breeds overconfidence, misunderstanding and hostility. The highly educated, the people are most tolerant of different cultures, races and sexualities, are the most partisan and intolerant of those with different ideas and lifestyles. Education is linked to higher levels of polarisation and political prejudice.[437] This is because education provides the cognitive ability to structure thinking and the ability to use motivated reasoning to support bias. In just one example of this tendency, the Labor Party found that inner-city Greens voters 'look down on' people in the suburbs who they think are holding Australia back from being 'tolerant' and 'just'.[438] Educated progressives are more likely than conservatives to block or unfriend someone on Facebook from the opposite political persuasion.[439]

Universities exemplify the lack of exposure to different ideas breeding hostility.[440] In the United States, studies have found that less than 10 per cent of academics are conservative.[441] In some fields it is even more extreme. A study of social psychologists found that just 2.5 per cent are right of centre.[442] The situation among academics in Australia is unlikely to be different. The lack of viewpoint diversity is damaging to research and learning at universities. The existence of only one perspective establishes and strengthens views to the extreme. It is costly to change your mind when you are part of a like-minded group, even in the face of contrary evidence, because you endanger being ostracised from the group.[443]

Because of the monoculture, conservative students and academics who hold a different perspective become too scared to speak up. The reluctance gives the impression to progressives that their perspectives are unchallengeable. Dr Florian Ploeckl, a senior lecturer in economics at the University of Adelaide, warns that academics are ceding the space to 'activists with their fundamentalist convictions' who do not approach topics scientifically. 'Funding is easier and more plentiful if you pick the right topic, publishing is easier if you don't rock the boat, and life in the department is easier if you see the world in the same way your colleagues do.'[444]

Echo chambers decrease tolerance and understanding. University of Queensland student Matthew Blackwell argues, from his experience on campus, the 'heavily left-biased education' is creating a 'Frankenstein generation of fanatical students.'[445] 'The conservative hears the progressive's latest demands and says, "I can see how you might come to that conclusion, but I think you've overlooked the following...", In contrast, the progressive hears the conservative and thinks, "I have *no idea* why you would believe that. You're probably a racist",' Blackwell laments.

The on-campus Inners experience is reinforced by life outside of campus in digital and physical spaces. The internet allows Inners to seek out and consume information that fulfils their pre-existing biases and desirability. Social media shows people information which they are most likely to agree.[446] If you regularly like posts from the Greens you are unlikely to be exposed to conservative ideas on your news feed.

The internet also enables users to self-select agreeable news and minimise exposure to alternative sources. The Reuters Institute's *Digital News Report 2017* found that Australians of the political left are selectively consuming *Buzzfeed*, *The Guardian*, *Huffington Post* and *ABC News*.[447] The self-selection drives a completely different set of knowledge about the world compared to readers of *The Australian* or the *Daily Telegraph* and viewers of *Sky News*.

Yale academic Amy Chua describes American progressives as an exclusionary and arrogant political tribe.[448] 'American elites often like to think of themselves as exact opposite of tribal, as "citizens of the world" who celebrate universal humanity and embrace global, cosmopolitan values,' Chua writes in comments that apply to educated Australian cosmopolitans. 'But what these elites don't see is how tribal their cosmopolitanism is. For well-educated, well-travelled Americans, cosmopolitanism is its own highly exclusionary clan, with clear out-group members and bogeymen – in this case, the flag-waving bumpkins.'

The view was epitomised by Democratic presidential candidate Hilary Clinton's description of Donald Trump supporters as 'deplorables'. 'You know, to just be grossly generalistic, you could put half of Trump's supporters into what I call the basket of deplorables. Right?,' Clinton reportedly told a New York City fundraiser, 'The racist, sexist, homophobic, xenophobic, Islamaphobic – you name it. And unfortunately there are people like that. And he has lifted them up.'[449] These comments backfired on Clinton. The 'Deplorables' mantle was proudly adopted by Trump supporters. Donald Trump tweeted 'Wow, Hillary Clinton was SO INSULTING to my supporters, millions of amazing, hardworking people. I think it will cost her at the polls!'[450] After the election Clinton admitted that the 'Deplorables' label was a 'political gift' to Trump and one of the reasons for her loss.[451]

Gillian Triggs, the former president of the Australian Human Rights Commission, has expressed a similar attitude in the context of free speech. 'There has never been a more important time to stand up for laws which prohibit racial abuse in the public arena,' Triggs said, implicitly defending Section 18C of the Racial Discrimination Act to a Hobart fundraiser for Greens founder Bob Brown's foundation. In the next breath, Triggs said that 'Sadly you can say what you like around the kitchen table at home' while dismissively waving her hand. Triggs paints Outers as the enemy, responsible for injustice and suggests that they cannot be trusted to express themselves.

Section 18C has been used to silence political debate in the Andrew Bolt case and dragged innocent students through years of painstaking process in the QUT students' case.[452] Nevertheless, Triggs' comment goes one step further by scorning the ability to have uncensored discussions in the sanctity of one's home. Triggs is effectively saying that Australians cannot be trusted enough to think and express themselves without unleashing the worst of human behaviour. The patronising sentiment comes not from an undergraduate student activist, but the highly paid leader of a prominent government institution, the Human Rights Commission, that is responsible for mediating disputes about racially discriminatory speech.

Condescending and powerful

In 1971, when Ronald Inglehart first raised the prospect of post-materialist values, he noted that 'the post-bourgeois types tend to be highly educated, they are likely to be better organised and politically more active than the acquisitive oriented group. In terms of political effectiveness, the two groups might reach parity within, say, the next 15 years.'[453] The Frankenstein students have become Frankenstein adults and come to hold influential positions across society.

Angelo M. Codevilla of Boston University has written about how education has created a new elitist class at the centre of power. 'Today's ruling class, from Boston to San Diego, was formed by an educational system that exposed them to the same ideas and gave them remarkably uniform guidance, as well as tastes and habits,' Codevilla said in 2010.[454] 'These amount to a social canon of judgments about good and evil, complete with secular sacred history, sins (against minorities and the environment), and saints. Using the right words and avoiding the wrong ones when referring to such matters – speaking the "in" language – serves as a badge of identity.'

Australia's Inners cluster in the centre of Australia's cities, the location of economic, cultural and political power, and hold influential positions in society across government, media, trade unions, not-for-profits and even corporates. Their position in society empowers them to set the public agenda. This leads to a disproportionate focus on post-materialist concerns such as the environment and identity politics and minimises the attention received for Outer concerns. Crikey journalist Guy Rundle argues that, following the 1990s, 'the progressive class became not a group external to the economy, but at the centre of economic and state power. They ceased to advance their values through argument and petitioning, but through embedding them in cultural and institutional power.'[455]

Armed with the confidence and knowledge from their education, Inners are substantially more engaged and active in the political process. Graduates are more likely to be interested in politics, donate, organise politically, sign petitions, contact politicians, engage online and vote even if it were optional (See Table 8).

Author Nassim Nicholas Taleb warns that a small, motivated and intolerant minority can impose their preferences on everyone else.[456] Activism requires substantial time and effort. This dynamic is advantageous to a highly engaged minority, Inners, and disadvantages to the disengaged, Outers, for whom the costs

Political engagement	Education	
	Graduate	No post-school
A good deal of interest in what's going on in politics#	48%	28%
Donated money or raised funds for a social or political activity*	53%	25%
Worked together with people who shared the same concern#	30%	14%
Signed a written petition#	51%	31%
Signed an online or e-petition#	47%	21%
Contacted a politician or government official by email#	30%	10%
Expressed political views on the internet*	26%	10%
Definitely would vote if it were not compulsory*	75%	60%

*Table 8. Political engagement by education level (Source: *Australian Social Studies Survey 2014, #Australian Election Study 2016)*

of political activism in time and effort are too high. Taleb writes that 'it is the most intolerant person who imposes virtue on others precisely because of that intolerance.'

Outers are physically on the periphery of Australian life and practically have less influence on policymaking. The *Grattan Institute* found feelings of powerlessness grow stronger further from city centres. Regional Australians feel that policy choices – such as banning live animal exports – are being made without considering the 'history, social context, and future' of regional communities.[457] Report authors Danielle Wood and John

Daley theorise that this is driving minority party voting. 'A concern that regional Australia is left out of politics was more consistent throughout *Grattan*'s consultations than concern about immigration, worries about the expansion of social liberalism, or anxiety about the economy.'

Graduates, the people most likely to have influence, express more confidence in the political system. When asked whether Australia's system of 'the system of government we have in Australia … needs major change', just 31 per cent of graduates agree, compared to 48 per cent of those with a trade qualification and 50 per cent of those who did not finish year 12.[458]

There are several important conduits for Inners influence, including the media, bureaucracy and corporate Australia.

Inners use the media to set the public agenda. Political scientist Robert Dahl classically described 'power' as the ability of A to force B to do something that they would otherwise not be willing to do.[459] This, however, is only the first face of power. Just as important, if not more important, is the capacity to decide what issues come up in public debate in the first place. Political scientists Peter Bachrach and Morton S. Baratz call this the 'second face' of power.[460] They stress the importance of 'creating or reinforcing social and political values and institutional practices that limit the scope of the political process to public consideration of only those issues which are comparatively innocuous to A.'

The key player that decides what issues receive public attention is the media – who shape the political debate by how they present issues, the choice of issues they present and the relative weight of importance through positions in newspapers, websites and bulletins.[461] Authoritarian regimes keep their citizens docile by using the state-controlled media to direct attention to issues that the regime deems to be non-threatening – rather than trying to manipulate opinions on threatening topics, such as democracy or human rights.[462]

The public agenda, the issues that people are concerned about at any particular time, is inherently limited – we have time constraints and attention spans, so we can only focus on a small set of issues.[463] At any time, the public agenda is said to include no more than about five to seven issues.[464] The public agenda is a zero-sum game, increasing concern about one issue comes at the expense of others.[465] This provides the media with substantial power to decide what policy, cultural and social issues are addressed by drawing attention to them in their coverage.

The rise of the Inners has diversified the public agenda. Education has established an influential cohort interested in post-materialist issues that are reflected in the issues covered by the media, at the cost of less coverage of traditional economic concerns.[466] Journalists mostly come from the highly educated cosmopolitan liberal cohort – ABC journalists, for example, are five times more likely to vote for the Greens.[467] Journalists are predisposed to write and present on the issue that they think are important. Consequently, public debate and policymaking has become less focused on the materialist concerns of Outers and disproportionately focused on post-materialist concerns of Inners. This perhaps helps explain why Australians have among the lowest trust of the media in the developed world.[468]

Former ABC chairman Jim Spigelman has warned that the bias expressed by journalists is:

> 'more often a function of the topics chosen for reporting, than of the content. Journalists – all of you, not just those at the ABC – tend to have a social and educational background, perhaps

particularly in Canberra, Sydney and Melbourne, that may make them more interested in, say, gay marriage than, say, electricity prices.'[469]

This was confirmed by a 2018 internal audit of ABC reporting, designed to investigate claims of elitist story selection, which found that the national broadcaster showed a lack of concern with issues that affect 'average citizens'.[470] The report concluded that the ABC should spend 'more time talking to ordinary Australians' about hip pocket issues.'

The bureaucracy is an additional conduit for Inners influence. Bureaucrats are humans with preferences, which include both a concept of the public interest and their self-interest in improving their salary, work conditions and power.[471] To the extent that bureaucrats are public spirited they are inclined to pursue their conception of the public good. Bureaucrats' idea of the public good is limited to an Inners conceptualisation of what is and is not important.

Mark Higgie, former Australian ambassador to the European Union, NATO, Belgium and Luxembourg, highlights the bureaucratic bias in foreign policy – but the same logic applies across policy areas. Higgie argues that the dominant culture in the Department of Foreign Affairs is 'leftish groupthink':[472]

> 'Most of our diplomats dream of an Australia less aligned with the US and have an often unqualified enthusiasm for the United Nations. They prefer Greens/Labor approaches to climate change to those of the Coalition. They're deeply uncomfortable with recent Coalition governments' border protection policies and like the 1970s version of multiculturalism which 'celebrates diversity' without much concern for common values and integration. They want us unshackled, as they see it, from our symbolic linkages with the UK.'

Beyond media and government, corporate Australia has

become dominated by individuals from a cosmopolitan liberal perspective. The liberal political right, *The Old Establishment*, has acquiesced if not come to support to the cultural domination of *The New Elite*. The professionals that work at corporates went to the same universities, are in the same social circles and have similar lifestyles and cultural perspectives to liberal progressive activists, bureaucrats and journalists. While they may disagree on economic policy, in identity, culture and lifestyle they are all Inners.

The corporate leadership have actively adopted the progressive agenda, from gender quotas on company boards to not providing loans to coal projects. Corporates do not want to be seen to be anti-progressive and labelled racist, sexist or homophobic. In response they are increasingly adopting social justice causes. *The Australian* columnist Janet Albrechtsen writes that corporate Australia is dominated by people who 'proselytise about gender targets, diversity, social values,' those who support the efforts, and those who are too scared to speak out against 'corporate fads.'[473] This 'virtue signalling' was exemplified by the same-sex marriage campaign. Australian Marriage Equality was formally backed by more corporates (851) than local business (508) and regional businesses (224) combined.[474] This is despite there being substantially more small businesses than larger businesses in Australia.[475]

Ross Douthat of *The New York Times* has labelled the adoption of the progressive agenda by businesses 'the rise of woke capital'.[476] Douthat argues that this alienates large swaths of the working class. 'It confirms the blue collar suspicion that liberalism is no longer organised around working class economic interests,' Douthat writes, 'and it encourages cultural conservatives in their feeling of general besiegement, their sense that all the major institutions of American life, corporate as well as intellectual and cultural, are arrayed against their mores and values and traditions.' Inners have captured practically all the major institutions in Australian society, from politics and civil society through to the media, bureaucracy and corporates.

Powerful and technocratic

In a 1946 book review, British author George Orwell scathingly describes the type of person who supports the Soviet Union in the West. 'If one examines the people who, having some idea of what the Russian régime is like, are strongly russophile, one finds that, on the whole, they belong to the 'managerial' class,' Orwell wrote:

> 'That is, they are not managers in the narrow sense, but scientists, technicians, teachers, journalists, broadcasters, bureaucrats, professional politicians: in general, middling people who feel themselves cramped by a system that is still partly aristocratic, and are hungry for more power and more prestige. These people look towards the USSR and see in it, or think they see, a system which eliminates the upper class, keeps the working class in its place, and hands unlimited power to people very similar to themselves.'[477]

The Inners use their dominant position to exercise disproportionate influence and control. This accords with their disposition towards rule by educated elites – that is, rule by themselves. Graduates think they are both better informed and have a better understanding of politics.[478] They think they know best and have a responsibility to lead. Moreover, through their positions in society, they have the power to do so.

Inners are what economist Adam Smith describes as 'the man of system' in the *Theory of Moral Sentiments*.[479] 'He seems to imagine that he can arrange the different members of a great society with as much ease as the hand arranges the different pieces upon a chess–board,' Smith writes. They ignore that 'every single piece has a principle of motion of its own,' that people have their own principles and preferences that might be different from the views of the technocrats.

It is not uncommon for Australia's Inners to express explicit support for technocracy. Former Greens candidate Clive Hamilton called for a 'suspension of democratic processes' to tackle climate change.[480] He has also criticised 'personal freedoms, democracy, material advance, technological power,' which are, he claims, 'paving the way to [our] destruction.'[481] Gillian Triggs told *The Saturday Paper* that 'Australians don't even understand their own democratic system' and asserted that 'Our parliamentarians are usually ill-informed and uneducated.'[482] Triggs subsequently claimed that these comments were taken out of context; however, she recanted the next day when a recording of the interview confirmed the remarks.[483]

Similar sentiments have been expressed on the political right. Liberal-leaning Melbourne talkback radio host Tom Elliott declared in 2015 that 'It's time we temporarily suspended the democratic process and installed a benign dictatorship to make tough but necessary decisions.'[484] Elliott proposed governance by an elite committee. 'This committee would consist of experts in their fields without political axes to grind. It'd need at least five years to complete its tasks during which time elected governments could administrate, but take no major decisions,' Elliott wrote. According to Pew, over half of young Australians aged 19 to 29 say that a technocratic form of government would be acceptable – this is unsurprisingly the age group who are most likely to experience higher education.[485]

Even elected politicians appeal to rule by experts. Former Prime Minister Kevin Rudd, in the early days of his reign, called for of 'evidence-based policy,' that is, policymaking directed by experts. 'Policy innovation and evidence-based policy-making is at the heart of being a reformist government,' Rudd declared in a lecture to Australia's 900 most senior public servants.[486] Commentators often call for an increased role for experts in policymaking, including non-politician expert appointments to the cabinet – 'the idea would see experts - not politicians - leading policy development and delivery,' an anonymous 'Public Sector Informant' declared in the *Canberra Times*.[487]

This idea that an educated elite should rule is by no means new. Ancient Greek philosopher Plato, the founder of the first higher education institute in the Western world, was a strident critic of democracy. Plato argued that people like himself, so-called 'philosopher-kings' with the most intelligence and knowledge, should be in charge.[488] Future president of the United States Woodrow Wilson described the majority of people as 'selfish, ignorant, timid, stubborn, or foolish' and argued that benevolent bureaucrats should govern on behalf of the populous.[489]

American commentator Michael Lind calls technocratic rule by the best and brightest university graduates the 'Insider Nation' phenomenon.[490] Within Insider Nation it is thought that domestic and foreign policy is simply a set of problems that require unemotional evidence-based solutions. 'Voters are ignorant and dangerous, from the insider perspective, and legislatures are too much under the influence of the voters,' Lind writes:

> 'The political project of Insider Nation is to remove decision making from legislatures to non-legislative bodies — bureaucracies, courts, trans-national agencies, treaty arrangements — or, failing

that, to nullify the will of the voters by persuading elected officials to support the nonpartisan elite consensus, whatever they may have said during the campaign.'

Harvard University academic Yascha Mounk calls this the rise of 'undemocratic liberalism.'[491] The modern state has been designed by elites in their interests and the vast majority have been locked out of the decision making process. The growth of the size and regulatory functions of the state in the late 20th and early 21st century has empowered a small set of individuals with extraordinary and largely unaccountable political and bureaucratic power.[492]

Mounk argues that:

'A lot of important issues are taken out of political contestation by trade treaties and independent agencies. When the popular will strays beyond the bounds of the acceptable, it is constrained by technocratic institutions, from the US Supreme Court to the European Central Bank... Even in areas in which the people are formally remain a master of their own fate, the mechanisms for translating popular views into public policy are so attuned to the interest of social or economic elites that the people's influence over their own government is severely restricted.'

Technocratic and wrong

Nassim Nicholas Taleb scathingly describes the 'Intellectual Yet Idiot' (IYI) as the highly educated 'who are telling the rest of us 1) what to do, 2) what to eat, 3) how to speak, 4) how to think... and 5) who to vote for.'[493] Taleb continues:

'The IYI pathologizes others for doing things he doesn't understand without ever realizing it is his understanding that may be limited. He thinks people should act according to their best interests *and* he knows their interests, particularly if they are "red necks" or English non-crisp-vowel class who voted for Brexit.

When plebeians do something that makes sense to them, but not to him, the IYI uses the term "uneducated".'

Technocracy, empowering experts to rule over everyone else, not only undermines democracy, it is the path to bad public policy. Technocracy is based on a series of false assumptions: all that is needed in policymaking is expertise, the preferences of experts are the same as everyone else and experts are not flawed like everyone else.

Experts have an important role, but policymaking requires more than expertise. Evidence alone does not answer fundamental questions about principles, values and goals. These decisions should be made by elected officials responsible to the public who are impacted by the policy – the people who have 'skin in the game' for the outcome of their decisions.[494] It is the role of experts to *advise*, within the confines of their knowledge and with awareness of their biases, on how to achieve the democratically selected outcomes. It is not the role of experts to re-shape society towards their biased interpretation of utopia. Classicist Moses Finley writes that 'When I charter a vessel or buy a passage on one, I leave it to the captain, the expert, to navigate it – but I decide where I want to go, not the captain.'[495]

The balance between taxing and spending, for example, is not just a technical question; it should reflect society's preferences. Increasing taxes may grow government revenue in the short-run. However, it can also mean less money for business investment and individual spending.[496] It is the public's role, through who they elect, to decide the level of taxation and spending; it is the role of experts to design a collection system that is the least burdensome on taxpayers. If the 'experts' are the ones not only implementing the popular will but also deciding on the outcomes of policymaking they will inevitably, intentionally or otherwise, prioritise their own preferences. This creates an expertocracy, in which most people have limited say over policies that impact their lives.

The notion that experts working in the public interest is all that is necessary for successful policymaking was prominent in the post-war period. The idea was exemplified by the American Political Science Association president Harold D. Lasswell's 1956 address which discussed the fully rational and objective 'policy scientist of democracy'.[497] Lasswell claimed that political science expertise could be used to guide society effectively.

Lasswell's high hopes overlook the inherent limitations of humankind. As American economist Thomas Sowell writes, 'Intellect is not wisdom'.[498] Sowell argues that throughout the twentieth century supposed intellectuals made terrible decisions and were apologists for mass-murdering tyrants.

Education and intelligence provides the ability to analyse information to support preconceptions. Dan Kahan of Yale University undertook an experiment to test how people with different levels of education respond to information about a partisan issue.[499] Kahan found that individuals with better numeracy skills were *more* polarised after seeing the data about gun control. The more educated individuals used their 'quantitative-reasoning capacity selectively to conform their interpretation of the data to the result most consistent with their political outlooks'. The better informed an individual, the more skilled they are at manipulating information about the world to favour their ideological perspective and accordingly are more likely to become polarised. Being smart does not reduce bias – smart people use their intelligence to be more confident in their views. Therefore smart people are dangerous precisely because they can confidently guide society in the wrong direction.

There are serious dangers that stem from this over-confidence. Even the best expert is not fully rational and does not have access to the knowledge necessary to understand and control every facet of society. Political scientist Herbert Simon argues humans suffer from 'bounded rationality,' we lack the brain capacity to weigh all costs and benefits of all policy options and instead, due to limited time, cognitive ability and information, we must select from a limited range of options.[500] We do not know what we do not know. We cannot conceptualise or calculate the probability of many outcomes because of our experience is limited. The limitation leads to what Nassim Nicholas Taleb calls black swans: events that deviate completely from what one would expect.[501]

The dispersion of knowledge means that we cannot fully understand the world. Knowledge is not wholly held by experts, intellectuals, or central planners. Knowledge is located throughout society in billions of minds. We each understand our own patch and preferences better than anyone else. Economist Frederick Hayek argues that even the smartest, best-intentioned experts cannot possibly have the knowledge to manage an economy effectively.[502] The failure of expertise is why the centrally planned economies of the Soviet Union and Eastern bloc could not keep up with the free market driven West. The market system uses disperse knowledge, through the price mechanism, to direct the allocation of resources towards their best use.[503] The socialist system is flawed because it depends on an all knowing central planner to direct society.

The dispersion of knowledge helps explain why experts are terrible at predictions. Political scientist Philip E. Tetlock found, from a 20 year study of 284 experts across a variety of fields, that experts are no better at predicting the future than anyone else. However, they are over-confident and rarely held to account for their wrong predictions.[504] The American foreign policy establishment failed to forecast the disastrous conflict which followed the 2003 invasion of Iraq and almost all economists did not predict the global financial crisis of 2008.

The difficulty of prediction demonstrates the danger of over-reliance on experts in public policy. Predicting outcomes is a core tenet of policymaking. Policy recommendations are predictions. The suggestion that Y is a solution to X is a prediction that Y will have the intended effect on X. However, predicting the impact of an intervention is extremely difficult because of uncertainty in the social world.[505] The unknowns lead to policies which do not achieve their stated aims and have unintended consequences.

Bent Flyvbjerg of Oxford University describes the 'iron-law of megaprojects': major projects are 'Over budget, over time, over and over again.'[506] Despite the best hopes of expert policymakers, nine out of ten mega projects have cost overruns – the Sydney Opera House was 1,400% over budget. Australia's most expensive building, Adelaide Hospital, was both 17 months delayed and $640m over-budget, ultimately costing $2.4 billion (it is among the most expensive buildings in the world).[507] 'Front-end planning is scant, bad projects are not stopped; implementation phases and delays are long; costs soar, and benefits and revenue realization recedes into the future,' Flyvbjerg writes. He estimates that just one in a thousand projects are on time, on budget and deliver the promised benefits. The consistent failure of major projects is an exemplar of expert wishful thinking and difficulty of full comprehension.

Even if experts were fully rational and fully knowledgeable they are not immune to biases from their interests and worldview.[508] Bias is why gathering more data from more experts does not reduce uncertainty. Science is often uncertain. There is conflicting evidence, divergent viewpoints and the ability to cherry pick data and hide assumptions. Consequently, the gathering of more evidence leads to 'endless technical bickering' between groups with pre-existing interests, according to David Collingridge and Colin Reeve.[509] Even ostensibly technical questions – such as the approval of new drugs – can be influenced by political considerations. A study of drug approval by the US Food and Drug Administration found that drugs which receive more media attention are approved quicker, showing how even 'independent' regulatory bodies with technical mandates are influenced by reputational pressures.[510]

Experts also have a bias at the individual level which stems from their position in the world. Experts are people too. Experts take their kids to school, watch the nightly news and vote at elections. They exist in a social world that helps shape their perspectives. Australia's experts have been socialised into Inners culture, lifestyle and identity. Experts are socially and professionally surrounded by likeminded individuals who reinforce their views. This socialisation process provides a perspective on how society should work that is often divorced from or against the interests of Outers.

A prominent example of bias policymaking by Inners is paternalistic public health policies, including advertising bans, plain packaging and sin taxes. The highly educated exercise more, smoke less and eat healthier food.[511] Inners within public health organisations seek to force other people to live in the same way as themselves by restricting individual choice.[512] The introduction of a sin tax, for example, is an effective prohibition on the product for those without the means to pay. The intervention removes the choice to purchase, or not purchase, the product.

The merchants of paternalism rarely acknowledge the condescending and authoritarian premises of their advocacy. As Chris Berg writes, 'If we don't believe our fellow citizens are intellectually capable of deciding what and how much to eat, whether to drink, or how to arrange their financial affairs, then why do we think they are capable of voting?'[513] They also ignore the people who feel the brunt of their policies. Paternalistic policies created by Inners impact Outers who have less influence in policy-making. Sin taxes on tobacco, alcohol and sugar disproportionally impact those on lower incomes who both consume more of these products and have less capacity to pay.[514]

An increasingly popular outlet for expertise is applying the insights from behavioural psychology, the flaws in human decision making, to policymaking. This was popularised by *Nudge* theory, which advocates 'soft paternalism,' modifying the options presented in the 'choice architecture' to help improve decision making.[515] These interventions, such as moving healthier food to more prominent places on shelves, have benign intentions. However, the interventions are still premised on the preferences and rationality of those who design the 'nudges.'

Chris Berg and Sinclair Davidson argue that it is contradictory to assert that while public rationality is limited, and therefore requires 'nudges', that somehow experts' rationality is limitless.[516] Experts, like everyone else, have biases in their decision making and goals. There is an ever-expanding list of alleged behavioural failures that are used to justify interventions on individual behaviour.

These failures are premised on the underlying preferences of the policymakers and not necessarily the preferences of those who are impacted.[517]

During the campaign for Britain to leave the European Union Conservative minister and Vote Leave campaigner Michael Gove infamously remarked that 'the people of this country have had enough of experts.'[518] This remark was scolded as scolded as 'anti-intellectualism' and the 'road back to the cave.'[519] Gove, however, was interrupted by the presenter and consequently many reports did not include the full remarks:

> 'I think that the people of this country have had enough of experts from organisations with acronyms saying that they know what is best and getting it consistently wrong, because these people - these people - are the same ones who got consistently wrong.'

Proving Gove's point, the experts were wrong after the Brexit vote.[520] The UK Treasury, the International Monetary Fund and banks predicted that, because of a dive in confidence immediately after the *vote* to leave, there would be an immediate economic downturn. The Treasury, for example, predicted that voting for Brexit could lead to 500,000 job losses. Employment has, in fact, *risen* by 560,000 since the Brexit vote.

'It is a case study of unconscious bias in forecasts,' *Spectator* editor Fraser Nelson explained in the *Wall Street Journal*.[521] 'Too many economists assumed that the public would react to a Brexit vote in the same way that they themselves would: Run for the hills and wait for the sky to fall. So they made guesses – about consumer spending, investment, productivity – and entered them into computer models that came up with nonsense figures.'

The danger of experts is not simply that they are incapable of making perfect predictions and decisions – we are all flawed in some way – it is that they have been given status by their achievements which leads to *overconfidence*. This is known as the 'Dunning–Kruger effect,' our lack of awareness of our incompetence and our ego-driven inflated self-assessment.[522]

§

Inners' educational achievements drive arrogance; their professional positions give them the power to rule and their power is used to impose technocratic policy solutions onto the Australian people. Their underlying claim, that expertise alone can solve every problem is dangerously wrong and fundamentally undemocratic.

The following chapter explores how this plays out in the practice of regulatory decision making.

SEVEN

The Regulatory State: Big Government, Big Business and Big Unions

'The unions and the government are driving me and other truck drivers out of business,' owner-operator truck driver Craig Prosser of Murray Bridge, South Australia, told the IPA.[523] Prosser's comments were in response to an independent regulatory agency, the Road Safety Remuneration Tribunal (RSPT), introducing minimum prices for road haulage that was set to put up to 60,000 owner-drivers out of work.[524]

The RSPT is a product of big government, big business and big unions. The trade unions advocated for the tribunal. The Gillard Government introduced the legislation. The corporates supported the effort. The RSPT was an Inners project designed to hurt Outers, the small operators in the trucking industry.

The Gillard Government established the RSPT in 2012 following extensive lobbying by the Transport Workers Union (TWU). The Australian Road Transport Industrial Organisation, the industry body for multi-national transport companies, supported the introduction of the tribunal.[525] Jennifer Acton, a former industrial advocate for the ACTU, led the RSPT.[526] The tribunal membership also included Steve Hutchins, a former Labor senator and representatives from large trucking businesses. There was no owner-operator representation.

The system was two tiered. The RSPT only set prices for owner-drivers. Larger operators were allowed to charge whatever they please. In practice, the smaller owner-operators would be forced to charge higher prices that would make their business uncompetitive and threaten their livelihood. Subsequently, the trucking corporates could charge higher prices after the smaller, non-unionised operators went out of business. Higher transport prices would be costly to farmers, producers, manufacturers and ultimately consumers.

The 'public interest' justification for the RSPT was that it would improve road safety by determining haulage rates in the sector.[527] Multiple reviews, however, failed to find a link between remuneration and road safety.[528] Michael Wong, the former media officer of the TWU, admitted that 'The practical effect of the RSRT is to push owner-drivers out of the market... The unique success of the TWU's achievement in the establishment of the RSRT was that it framed a marginal issue – the link between rates of pay and safety – as the central issue and then drove legislative change through its political mates.'[529] The RSPT was set to cost the economy $2 billion over fifteen years, according to a review by consultancy PWC.

The RSRT was abolished following public outrage in April 2016.[530] This was an all too rare victory against the encroaching force of the regulatory state. Big government, big business and big unions went a step too far and were unsuccessful. Nevertheless, it is just one of the thousands of cases of the regulatory state undermining human flourishing and democracy.

In the seminal Gettysburg Address delivered amid the US Civil War, President Abraham Lincoln provided the quintessential definition of democracy: 'government of the people, by the people, for the people.' Today this has largely disappeared. As Arthur Seldon of the Institute for Economic Affairs has written, 'It is government of the Busy (political activists), by the Bossy (government managers), for the Bully (lobbying activists).'[531]

Modern government has become dominated by the few, the elite subset of *Governing Inners*. Governing Inners pull the levers of power on behalf of the tribe they represent. The domination by Inners at the top of society damages the prospects of Outers. Australians are aware of this power dynamic. Two-thirds of Australians believe that big business has too much power and almost half think that unions have too much power.[532] They are right. Across the economy, big government, big business and big unions work in tandem to undermine policymaking and democracy.

The growing role and complexity of the state has provided ample opportunity for the organised to receive special advantages. Coalitions for regulation have formed; both the Bootleggers and the Baptists support regulation.[533] Bootleggers profit from market restrictions and work with the Baptists who have a moral justification for state intervention. Both Bootleggers *and* Baptists are Inners. They seek to further the interests of their tribe, material and non-material, to the detriment of the majority.

For the few, not the many

It is often asserted, following the presidency of Ronald Reagan in the United States, prime ministership of Margaret Thatcher in Britain and the Hawke-Keating era in Australia, that the role of government has substantially shrunk since the 1980s.[534] A so-called move from 'big government' to 'small government,' from Keynesianism to laissez faire. The assertion is demonstrably false.

There has not been a decline in spending despite the oft-repeated claims of a 'neo-liberal' era.[535] In Britain, expenditure on social services such as welfare, healthcare and housing *increased* under Thatcher as a proportion of GDP.[536] In the United States, the national debt grew by 190 per cent during Reagan's presidency.[537] In Australia, the federal government has grown substantially under governments of both political stripes – in the early years of the Howard Government spending per person increased at about double the rate of spending in the final years of the Keating Government.[538]

The most significant change in governance since the 1980s is the privatisation of public utilities such as electricity, communications, banks and airlines.[539] It is, however, a common misconception that privatisation led to a reduction in the power of the state.[540] Across Western nations government power was not reduced, the role *changed* and *grew*. Governments did not simply leave control to market forces when public functions were privatised. They have introduced extensive regulation to control the privatised industry, even more.

Political scientist Giandomenico Majone describes the situation as a shift from a 'positive state', in which the government exercised control through public ownership, to a 'regulatory state', in which the government exercises more power than ever before through competition, health, safety, consumer, environment and technical standards.[541] The introduction of this extensive array of regulation has 'greatly widened the range of social and economic life that was subject to public power'.[542]

Regulation is preferred over public ownership by politicians and bureaucrats because it allows them to exercise power – by directing business activity – without the less glamorous and often fraught task of actually providing the services directly.[543] As Seidman and Gilmour write, 'government by regulation is the inevitable concomitant of government by proxy.'[544]

Regulation enables the state to transfer costs from the explicit public pursue to private operators.[545] Politicians can mandate the delivery of a service in a particular manner rather than fund specific services, shifting the cost from the state onto businesses and, by stealth, consumers. Regulations, for example that requires energy companies to provide financial assistance to low income households, hide and spread the cost of a social goal.[546] Providing lower prices to poorer families may be an admirable aim. Nevertheless, enacting this through regulation is a hidden redistributive tax that forces energy users to subsidise other people through higher prices without their knowledge – hiding the actual costs of government policy.

Australia's regulatory state is for the few, not the many. The creation of thousands of pages of regulation and 'independent' agencies provides an ideal opportunity for Inners across corporates, trade unions, the bureaucracy, civil society and politics, to seek advantages.[547] The Inners who lead corporates and trade unions are the same tribe as politicians, bureaucrats and regulators who make the decisions. They live in the same suburbs, come from a similar cultural background and send their children to the same schools. Politicians, journalists, lobbyists, regulators and bureaucrats spend so much time together, from their university days to the bars of Canberra, that they come to share similar views. The dynamic provides access and synergy, creating a comfy relationship between the regulators and the regulated.

The relationships lead to the seeking of special privileges

which drive political frustrations. Australians feel disconnected from the levers of political power. A mere 12 per cent of Australians believe that government is run for all the people.[548] Three-quarters of Australians think that people in government look after themselves.[549] Australians are annoyed with politicians that make decisions under the influence of *selected* stakeholders behind closed doors. The kind of people who make, influence, publicise and implement the decisions are different from those who feel the brunt of the policies.

A study of influence on policymaking in the United States by Martin Gilens and Benjamin Page thoroughly tested four potential theories: average citizens, mass-based interest groups, narrow interests and economic elites. They found that the only groups that have a substantial independent influence on policymaking are the last two, narrow interests and economic elites – who succeed more often in getting their way and blocking legislation that they dislike. There was little evidence that the views of citizens or mass based interest group have an effect. There are similar trends in Australian politics. Societal elites have a disproportionate impact on policymaking.

The cost of regulation is most strongly felt by those who have the least capacity to pay. Dustin Chambers and collaborators of the Mercatus Centre at George Mason University found that regulations increase consumer prices – as regulations are costly for businesses to implement and limit competition.[550] Prices increase by almost 1 per cent for every 10 per cent increase in regulation in a sector. Poorer households are the worst off because of regulation, because they spend the largest proportions of their incomes on highly regulated goods and services which are prone to sharp price increases.

An Australian exemplar of insidious influence and high costs is the childcare industry. Big government, big business and big unions teamed up to create red tape, demand government subsidies, hurt small providers and increase the cost of childcare. In 2012, the Gillard Government introduced the *National Quality Framework* which replaced previous state-based systems. The Framework mandates qualification requirements for childcare workers, higher staff to child ratios and increased physical space at centres. These changes were a result of successful lobbying by United Voice, the childcare sector's union and came with the support of larger providers.[551] The regulatory changes have contributed to higher prices – since 2012, the cost of childcare has increased by almost 40 per cent.[552] Meanwhile, taxpayer subsidies for childcare are expected to reach over $10 billion in the coming years.

The qualification requirements are particularly heinous. It now takes 300 hours of study to care for children – an activity that parents have been doing for thousands of years without a certificate.[553] These requirements benefit the unions and larger providers of childcare. United Voice has used the qualification requirements to demand wage increases.[554] Bigger providers, who can use their economies of scale to absorb the costs and lobby for more government subsidies, supported the requirements.[555]

Smaller providers, however, are struggling. Mark Sperling, the owner and operator of two childcare centres in Queensland, told the *Productivity Commission* that the government's changes were a 'serious threat' to his business.[556] 'As soon as government determined that staff should all hold certifications, wages started spiralling,' Sperling said. Furthermore, according to Sperling: 'Certification alone does not provide better staff. I have never been asked by a parent, and I am in centres seeing parents every day, about a staff member's qualifications... You do not need a 4 year university educated teacher to teach early childhood to preschoolers.' In the childcare industry, as in many others, unions, government, large business and lobbyists have made regulation for their benefit that is hurting small business, parents, and taxpayers. Vested interests have captured the regulatory state.

Non-democratic institutions

Democracy is severely threatened by the regulatory state. Power has increasingly been removed from democratic contestation and handed to unaccountable regulators. There has been an extraordinary rise in 'non-majoritarian institutions', organisations with the power to make decisions disconnected from traditional democratic power structures.[557] The expansion includes independent regulatory agencies, such as competition authorities, utility regulators and financial market regulators; private organisations with the power to set industry standards, such as accounting and legal industry bodies; and global institutions that set cross national standards. These institutions have provided substantial benefits at times. There is no denying, however, that non-majoritarian institutions curtail the power of elected politicians and disempower the public. These bodies are powerful, unelected and highly political.

The IPA's Chris Berg has catalogued the substantial expansion undemocratic institutions in Australia, including dozens of regulatory bodies and ministerial councils and tens of thousands employed by regulators costing the budget billions of dollars.[558] Berg writes that 'the shape of modern Australian government resembles a spider's web of autonomous and independent bureaucratic agencies whose relationship to democratically elected politicians ranges from tenuous to non-existent.'[559] The Australian government now has hundreds of agencies, from the Australian Egg Corporation to the Australian Financial Security Authority, the Australian Fisheries Management Authority and the Foreign Investment Review Board.[560]

Independent organisations are responsible for issues ranging from the money supply to energy markets, competition and GST distribution, airline routes, banking and insurance and telecommunications. They have delegated power, protocols, budget and staffing and claim to be undertaking 'technical' tasks using their expert knowledge. In practice, their remit goes beyond the purely technical and often includes politically contested decision making. Occasionally their leaders are required to attend parliamentary committee hearings; however, they largely operate independently without direct government control.

There are substantial political benefits to regulating. In the regulatory state, politicians can play it both ways. Politicians can take advantage of perceived neutrality, objectivity and appeals to expertise and take credit for positive outcomes by claiming they are the result of effective regulation. Politicians can also distance themselves from unpopular actions by the 'independent' agencies and heavily regulated businesses, even when regulation is ultimately responsible for undesirable outcomes.[561] This buck-passing leaves the public with their head's scratching wondering where responsibility lays in the myriad of complex relations between businesses, regulators, legislators and bureaucrats.

Buck passing is the recent experience in Australia's embattled energy market. Energy providers have been mandated by reliability standards and targets to spend substantially on infrastructure upgrades and renewable energy. The operators have spent billions 'gold-plating' the networks which, in turn, has led to price rises.[562] There is an incentive to spend as much as possible on upgrades which can then be used as a justification for higher prices and profits in the cartel-like captive energy market.

The cost of electricity has increased by 215 per cent in Australia over the past twenty years – twice as fast as wages because of overspending on the network and other government interventions.[563] Politicians have blamed energy companies instead of taking responsibility for the creation of a flawed regulatory regime. Prime Minister Malcolm Turnbull has blamed 'energy network companies gaming the system at the expense of Australian families' for the higher costs.[564]

The regulatory state, once established, is difficult to dismantle because it locks in future decision makers.[565] Inherited policies, organisations and bodies bound decision makers to the status quo. The creation of agencies and regulation creates a normative precedent for government intervention and supportive constituencies who will lobby for the maintenance of the status quo – as they have adapted to the regulation that keeps out new entrants.[566] Consequently, even if democratically elected politicians with a mandate to reduce red tape came to power, it is difficult to undo past regulatory decisions.

The end of small

Powerful independent regulatory agencies provide an ideal platform for special interests to focus their attention.[567] Regulators are mandated to consult with, and are dependent on information from, the entities that they regulate. These close relationships facilitate the seeking of special privileges such as monopoly status, special zoning, quotas and protective tariffs. Rent seeking, manipulating public policy to increase profits, is extremely costly to society. There are both the direct costs of lobbying, campaign contributions, voting distortion and the waste of human capital, as well as the costs of regulation itself including higher product costs, lower incomes, fewer jobs, less productivity and slower technological progress.[568] Red tape is costing the Australia's economy $176 billion a year.[569]

The rule of law, the consistent application of the law in all cases, is undermined by the regulatory state. Elected officials provide vague delegations of authority to independent organisations. Unclear instructions can lead to 'bureaucratic drift', agencies implementing policy in a different way to what was intended.[570] In practice, regulation is created through a process of negotiation between the regulated and the regulators; it is often made up on the fly and implemented inconsistently. This looseness empowers Inners across businesses, industry bodies and trade unions to spend millions advocating for regulation that is too their taste. As the benefits of regulation are often concentrated among a small number of businesses, and the costs disperse among millions of consumers who pay higher prices for worse service, it difficult to organise against rent seeking.[571]

Despite the common belief that businesses are against regulation, in many cases existing market operators lobby for benefits from regulation. Ideally, for an existing business, regulations would impose a substantial cost of entry to discourage potential competition.[572] Australia's 'Four Pillars' banking regulations, for example, ostensibly exists to deliver stability in the system. It includes benefits such as the implicit bank deposit guarantees and the low cost of temporary borrowing from the reserve bank. The banks, in exchange, are expected to follow a complex array of regulations that have very high compliance costs which reduces the likelihood of new challengers against the banks.[573] The lack of competition in the market ultimately lowers the quality of service for consumers, as the recent Royal Commission into the finance sector has revealed.

The regulatory state is detrimental to small businesses. The cost of complying with government regulation is easier for big business.[574] Older, larger firms have the economies of scale to comply with the increasingly complex array of regulations. Big businesses can afford large regulatory compliance teams. Newer, smaller firms cannot. Regulation is a barrier to entry. Coles and Woolworths, for example, can afford to analyse and comply with thousands of food regulations by spreading the costs among their hundreds of stores – this is difficult for a corner store grocery. Accordingly, existing firms are often sympathetic to the status quo regulation: they have adjusted to the cost and it prevents competitors from entering the market.

A smaller number of larger firms increasingly dominate. Since 2007, the number of Australians employed in small businesses, with fewer than 20 employees, has *declined* by 7 per cent, compared to the number who work for medium and large businesses which have grown by 25 per cent.[575] Australia is full of large, ancient companies. In the United States, 88 per cent of the largest 500 companies did not exist 50 years ago; by contrast, nine of Australia's top ten companies were founded before 1925.[576]

The declining number of small businesses endangers Australia's social fabric. Small businesses are more reflective of their local communities and provide character to neighbourhoods. They provide opportunities for social mobility and immigrant integration.[577] Entrepreneurs are also essential to long run economic prosperity, jobs and economic growth, productivity.[578] Newer, smaller firms challenge existing businesses, improving methods and process, providing new and interesting products and creating jobs. Joseph Schumpeter called this process 'creative destruction,' an implicit benefit of a free market economy, in which old firms are destroyed to free up resources for new endeavours.[579] The lack of entrepreneurial small business ultimately reduces innovation and competition which means higher prices, fewer jobs and lower incomes.

Undercutting democracy

Even to the extent that independent agencies are effective, they undermine democracy by design.[580] These agencies are often created with the best intentions and, in many cases, fulfil their mandate. Independent central banks, for instance, have proven effective at keeping inflation low. Nevertheless, independence creates barriers between the people and those who have the power to make decisions on their behalf. This rift creates a 'democratic deficit', an inaccessibility to the public, and even elected officials, to important decisions.

The independence of regulatory agencies is justified by 'output legitimacy', doing a good job with regards to their mandate. However, mandates are often unspecific, leaving substantial discretionary power to the regulators.[581] The decisions are often not purely technical. They have distributive consequences. In the case of central banks it may be appropriate to aim for low inflation; however, there are winners and losers created by their decisions.[582] Interest rate setting is a redistributive decision. In the most immediate sense, higher interest rates curb inflationary pressures and are beneficial to savers but costly to mortgage holders.

Democracy is the control of policymaking by individuals who are accountable to the public. The Westminster parliamentary system is supposed to establish democratic governance through a 'chain of accountability'.[583] Voters elect representatives who make legislation and hold government ministers to account. Ministers lead the executive branch and hold the bureaucracy, who implement the decisions, to account. In practice, modern democracies have stretched this chain of accountability to breaking point.

In the first instance, citizens have a limited choice of policy bundles at election time (the Labor bundle or the Liberal bundle, or perhaps a Greens or One Nation bundle). Governance has become extremely complex and wide ranging. It is impossible, in both the options presented at elections and the number of activities taking place, to have a say over the millions of decisions that could impact one's life.

Furthermore, Australia's parliament struggles from an accountability deficit. Parliamentarians do not adequately hold the executive to account. Australia's parliamentarians, most of whom are on the frontbench or would like to be in future, are highly disciplined.[584] This dynamic empowers the executive, who are rarely, if ever, unable to pass legislation through the House of Representatives. There is more opposition in the Senate, where the government of the day rarely has a majority. However, most legislation attracts little debate.[585]

Meanwhile, democratically elected ministers struggle to hold their bureaucracies to account.[586] As the role, size and complexity of governance has grown so have government departments. It is near impossible for a minister to direct the millions of decisions made by their department. This challenge was the underlying theme of the British comedy *Yes Minister*, which humorously shows how the bureaucracy uses their informational advantages to *control* the minister.[587] The power of bureaucrats is substantial across all levels, from the policy bureaucrats who write the laws, to bureaucrats at the street level who decide on the delivery of policies.[588] This situation leaves much decision making power in the hands of the unelected.

Furthermore, many governing functions are no longer directly accountable to ministers. Executive power has been delegated to independent agencies that are, by design, not directly accountable to elected representatives in government. As Majone states, 'Regulators wield enormous power, yet they are neither elected nor directly responsible to elected officials.'[589] Majone claims this leads to a welcome 'diffusing power' away from elected officials which prevents the 'tyranny of the majority,' a danger of democracy flagged by American founding father James Maiden in Federalist 10.[590]

Majone, however, overlooks *who* has the power to regulate. It is humans who make decisions within regulatory agencies.[591] It is naive to think the staff of regulatory organisations simply leave their values and prejudices the door – like all humans they have likes and dislikes, political and policy views and an identity and lifestyle. Regulators are not neutral, nor are their decisions purely technical and rationale. As American economist George Hilton writes, 'regulators are not automatons, but men and women who go to baseball games, advocate their political philosophies, have their gall bladders removed, take their cats to the veterinarian, and otherwise behave like the rest of us.'[592] When decisions are made by elected officials it is at least possible for the public to have a say at election time – this ultimate accountability does not exist for regulators.

Regulatory agencies justify their power by claiming to act in the 'public interest.' Their concept of the public interest, however, is inherently limited by the people they are. It has been found that the background of decision makers in independent organisations influences their conclusions. American political scientist Christopher Adolph found, for example, that the career path of a central banker has a significant influence on their attitude to interest rates and inflation.[593] Adolph found a link between lower inflation and more conservative backgrounds of the central bank governors.

In addition to regulating directly, agency staff have become part of the political process. They use their information advantage, and the prestige of the positions they hold, to make public pronouncements that manipulate the public, bureaucrats, parliament and ministers in their chosen direction. As Chris Berg has written, 'Regulators are increasingly political actors, using their statutory powers to influence and conduct public policy, which, in a democratic society, should be the domain of elected representatives.'[594] The agencies, such as the Australian Prudential Regulation Authority, Australian Competition and Consumer Commission (ACCC) and the Australian Human Rights Commission (AHRC), have become active participants in public debates.

In September 2017, the head of the ACCC, Rod Sims, used a 'hard-hitting' speech at the National Press Club to call for a changing of electricity pricing rules.[595] Tim Soutphommasane, the former Race Discrimination Commissioner at the AHRC, has delivered and written dozens of speeches and articles in support of 18C of the Racial Discrimination Act.[596] Soutphommasane's role at the AHRC means he not only implements race discrimination law – complaints are made to and mediated by the commission – but he is also actively partaking in defending the existence of the law using the taxpayer provided resources of the organisation. While this advocacy is likely heartfelt, it is questionable whether taxpayers should be footing the bill for political pronouncements.

Independent agencies may not lead to majoritarian tyranny, nevertheless they further one the Federalist's other major sins: the tyranny of faction. The delegation to regulatory agencies gives power to one faction, with limited democratic oversight and accountability. The faction, in contemporary Australia, are the Inners. Inners dominate the staff and leadership of powerful organisations disconnected from democratic mandates. Lawyers, economists and other professionals staff independent agencies – they are not a representative sample of the Australian population.[597] While the Inners who staff regulatory agencies may consciously believe that they are acting in the public good, their worldview and social bubble inherently impact their perspective.

Independent agencies are used to further the interests and issue priorities of the Inners tribe. For example, ASIC Commissioner John Price has declared that companies may be legally liable to disclose climate change risks.[598] Price also announced that ASIC is probing climate related disclosures by hundreds of Australia's largest companies. ASIC is pressuring companies to respond to an environmental issue which is of particular concern to Inners.

This intervention is arguably outside the mandate of a company regulator.

Democracy is further undermined by the internationalisation of regulation. Many regulatory decisions have now been taken out of the domestic regulatory sphere altogether. Decisions are made through negotiation at a global level and then thrust onto Australia at a substantial cost.

Legal scholars John Braithwaite and Peter Drahos have written that Australia has become 'rule-takers rather than rule-makers... because when government announce new regulatory laws they are somewhat embarrassed to disclose that the national legislature voted for those laws without having any say in shaping them':[599]

> 'For years some of Australia's air safety standards have been written by the Boeing Corporation in Seattle, or if not by that corporation, by the US Federal Aviation Administration in Washington. Australia's ship safety laws have been written by the International Maritime Organization in London, its motor vehicle safety standards by Working Party 29 of the Economic Commission for Europe and its food standards by the Codex Alimentarius Commission in Rome. Many of Australia's pharmaceutical standards have been set by a joint collaboration of the Japanese, European and US industries and their regulators, called the International Conference on Harmonization. Its telecommunications standards have been substantially set in Geneva by the ITU. The Chair (and often the Vice-Chair) of most of the expert committees that effectively set those standards in Geneva are Americans.'

The rise of 'global governance' erodes national sovereignty and undermines democratic principles by outsourcing decision making to compromises with foreign governments, many of whom are authoritarian regimes.[600] Eric A. Posner of the University of Chicago has written about the 'Invisible College of International Lawyers' who have undermined the

'Westphalia' notion of sovereign states in favour of international law that binds states without the consent of the populace.[601] The European Union, domestic courts taking into account foreign and international law, the proliferation of treaties and the creation of international organisations typify the internationalisation of policymaking.

The Invisible College asserts that the public has 'internalised' international law, however, 'there was never much evidence for this view'.[602] This, Posner argues, has left open a genuine criticism, which is now being exploited by authoritarian populists, that 'global elites' are dominating policymaking at arm's length from the people. Global Inners are now making policy. Posner writes 'that elites in all countries supported forms of international cooperation that benefited them and harmed the masses or were perceived to harm the masses.'

§

The state has become the regulatory state. Regulation is the primary and growing tool of power used by the state. The regulatory state is disconnected from democratic accountability at both the national and international level. Independent bodies wield an enormous level of mostly unaccountable power across practically every field of human activity.

Australians are frustrated in democracy and feel like they do not have a say in the governance of society. This complaint is, to a much greater extent than in the past, demonstrably true. The state's role has substantially increased and democratic decision making is outsourced to 'expert' independent organisations. This delegation of authority has empowered a relatively small few – a selected cohort of Inners – who are making decisions that impact millions. Decision making has been captured by inners. The pronouncements reflect the values of the few, not the many.

Part II of this book establishes that:

(5) since the 1980s liberal reform era Australian politics has become a bargain between Inners which often excludes Outer voices;

(6) Inners have substantial political, social, cultural and economic power which they wield in a technocratic manner often to the detriment of Outers; and

(7) the rise of the regulatory state has empowered Inners to wheel and deal in their own interests.

Part III explores how to balance the demands of Inners and Outers, return power back to the people and improve democratic decision making in the process.

PART III:

A path forward

The Five Pillars of Liberal Populism

1. **Egalitarianism:** All voices should be heard in national debate.
2. **Localism:** Embrace difference and decentralise decision making.
3. **Freedom:** Let individuals make decisions about their own lives.
4. **Dignity:** Treat everyone with equal respect.
5. **Unity:** Australian identity should unite, not divide us.

EIGHT

A Liberal Populism?

'And show to the minions of tyranny, Bold Britons are we, who dare to be free, And die for our rights and liberty,' *The Great Confederated Anti-Dray and Land Tax League of South Australia* declared in 1850.[603] The South Australians settlers came to Australia seeking a better life for themselves and their families. However, they had found 'a system of oppression and misrule, unparalleled in the history of British legislation.' The Great Confederated League was formed after meetings across South Australia to oppose the colonial administrator's taxation of drays (a horse drawn wagon) and land.

The League considered the tax design to be both unfair and undemocratic. The elites designed a tax that disproportionally burdened those who had no say in creating it. The dray tax required the workers, who owned larger drays to move produce, to pay higher taxes than the aristocrats, who had smaller drays. Worse still, a legislature which only represented propertied aristocrats designed the 'obnoxious, odious, and detestable impositions'.[604] The League's slogan was 'No Taxation Without Representation' – explicitly borrowed from the American revolutionaries.[605]

Following the substantial opposition, the tax was repealed within months and those who paid were refunded. The capitulation by the governor was in the same era as South Australia's adoption of self-government and democracy.[606] South Australia was granted self-government in 1850 and became the first to Australian colony to introduce universal suffrage for men aged over 21 in 1857 – as was advocated for by the League years earlier.[607]

The historic revolts for liberal values, from the English Civil War and the American Revolution through to the Chartists and Eureka Stockade, were deeply populist. They channelled the populist concern that there is an elite governing in their own interest against the majority into a positive force for liberal change. They were liberal populists. Today, however, populism is most often associated with authoritarian forces for illiberal change.

Authoritarian populists are a serious threat to liberal democracy.[608] Authoritarian populists, such as Marine Le Pen in France, Pauline Hanson in Australia and Donald Trump in the United States, use vulgar, dehumanising rhetoric that defines 'the people' narrowly in competition with an elite linked to a racial, ethnic, or religious minority.[609] They fuel bigotry and hatred and undermine the liberal notion of treating people as individuals and not members of a group. They propose an array of counterproductive policy responses, such as trade protectionism. In opposition, authoritarian populists appeal to democracy and notions of representing 'the people.' Once in power, however, authoritarian populists undermine democracy by dismissing the legitimacy of opposition and taking steps to silence dissent and prevent free and fair elections.

The authoritarian populists, however, have identified genuine and widely felt disillusionment. Liberal democrats ignore these frustrations at their peril. Pretending that they do not exist, or are simply bigotry, fuels the problem. Authoritarian attitudes are activated when people feel threatened and a loss of control of their communities and destinies. Liberals are often at fault for activating these concerns.[610] As Jonathan Haidt writes, 'globalization and rising prosperity have changed the values and behaviour of the urban elite, leading them to talk and act in ways that unwittingly activate authoritarian tendencies in a subset of the nationalists.'[611]

The Economist's Bagehot column argues that the liberal project has become too elitist, top-down and globalist – and in the face of populism, liberals have double-downed on 'technocratic elite' decision making and painted the public as 'too stupid (aka short-sighted, racist, sexist, transphobic, nationalistic, bigoted).'[612] The more liberals entrench themselves in unpopular causes, 'the more furious the populists get'. Bagehot recommends rebalancing in favour of democracy, self-organisation and localism.

It is essential to understand and effectively respond to frustrations – not to allow them to fester and grow. The alternative is not some progressive nirvana; it is a more divided, unstable and illiberal society. Liberal democracy can only survive if we accept that many feel they have little say in the system. Democracy has been undermined by institutions and a governing clique that are unresponsive and unrepresentative of the public. We must harness these widespread frustrations into a *positive* force. In doing so, we can stitch liberalism and democracy back together.

In a divided Australia, in the face of a disillusioned public and competing tribes, we must rethink the way we govern ourselves. Australia's challenge is to ensure that *both* Inners and Outers are heard in a pluralist manner. We must acknowledge the equal moral worth of all individuals. We must not allow one tribe to govern over the other. We should nurture differences and allow individuals and communities to pursue their own ends – and strengthen our representative democratic institutions, checks and balances and separation of powers to make it difficult for one faction to dominate another. People should have a greater say in the governance of their lives, family and community. I call these principles Liberal Populism.[613]

Liberal Populism has five pillars: Egalitarianism, Localism, Freedom, Unity and Dignity. This is not an all encompassing political philosophy; nor is it not a perfect solution to all of society's ills. These pillars are designed to begin a debate about the appropriate cultural, political and institutional response to a divided Australia.

Liberal Populism seeks to strike an appropriate balance between Inners and Outers which enables a divided Australia to function as one political unit. It treats all individuals with equal moral worth and deserving of representation – rejecting the elitist tendency for one group to govern over another and the authoritarian populist tendency to split society into an in-group and out-group. Decisions are taken out of national contestation and control given back to local communities to minimise conflict between Inners and Outers. Individuals are freer to enable both Inners and Outers to pursue their chosen purpose.

These principles necessitate substantial compromise on behalf of both Inners and Outers. The aim is to utility maximise on average, not for Inners or Outers to be better off than the other. In practice, Inners are unlikely to give up their power easily. However, it is essential that Inners acknowledge the limits of their knowledge and ability to shape society towards their values – or otherwise risk an authoritarian backlash from angry Outers. On the other side, Outers will continue to feel uncomfortable in a society that does not fully reflect their values. Outers must resist the temptation to impose their values onto Inners because it encourages Inners to impose their values onto Outers.[614] Both sides must learn to compromise.

1. Egalitarianism

Liberalism and populism are premised on egalitarian notions: that the people deserve a say in society. A core tenet of liberalism is that all humans are of equal moral worth and therefore should be equally represented in how society is governed.[615] Populists advocate for returning power to the people from distant elites.[616]

This liberal notion of equal worth is succinctly stated in the American Declaration of Independence. In the context of opposing foreign rule, the Americans declared that 'that all men are created equal' with 'certain unalienable Rights, that among these are Life, Liberty and the pursuit of Happiness' and that 'to secure these rights, Governments are instituted among Men, deriving their just powers from the consent of the governed.'[617] This revolutionary concept, which derived from English enlightenment thinkers such as John Locke, is the basic premise of any democratic society.[618] Those who make decisions on our behalf, that can change our lives, must only do so with our consent.

Populism also appeals to people power.[619] This is not necessarily associated with a particular ideological agenda. The notion that the people should have a say does not suggest what the people want. Accordingly, there is a history of populists on both the left and the right. Liberalism can and has in the past given meaning to populist frustrations. Today, however, liberalism has become elitist, both in the way decisions are made and who is making them.

Liberals argue that representatives must have limited power to protect the sovereignty of individuals.[620] Democracy, particularly of a representative nature, has a natural tendency towards oligarchy, it can empower a governing clique who infringe individual liberty.[621] In response, liberals support checks and balances, such as multiple legislative chambers and an independent judiciary, to prevent representatives from becoming tyrants. Liberal Populism entails equal representation in decision making while the power of the state is limited to safeguard individual rights.

Australian democracy is becoming less egalitarian. A new elite is governing for themselves and in their interests. Inners are dominating society. Inners have done much good. In global terms, Australia is a prosperous and successful society. Their instincts on some issues, such as tolerance for different races and sexualities, have been widely adopted. Nevertheless, Inners also use the levers of power for their own benefit. They have created a society in their own image. Status is based on educational and professional success. Decisions are made by unaccountable bureaucrats and independent regulatory bodies. Outers feel increasingly alienated and frustrated.

The Economist's Bagehot outlines the managerial turn of liberalism. 'The biggest problem with managerialism', the author writes:

> 'is not that it is inefficient but that it divides humanity into two classes of people: the rulers and the ruled, the doers and the done to, the thinkers and the hod-carriers. It recreates the very division that liberals, in their salad days, set out to destroy—though this time the people at the top are a global elite of educated citizens, wearing their MBAs like modern coats of arms, and the people at the bottom are the uneducated masses, condemned to spend their lives on the receiving end of orders.'[622]

This is not sustainable. The backlash is furious when people feel like they have lost control and that their values, culture and identity are under threat. The success of authoritarian populists is premised on the failure of liberals to be egalitarian. Liberals have failed to include the people in decision making. They have created a functional society, however not one in which everyone is worthy of equal moral worth.

The solution to the gap is to find ways to increase democratic accountability and to give the people a greater say in how their society is governed. In *Why Nations Fail*, Daron Acemoglu and James Robinson argue that 'inclusive' institutions, as opposed to 'exclusive' institutions, are necessary for a country to succeed.[623] Exclusive institutions are ones controlled by a small group of people; inclusive institutions give everyone a say, providing room for engagement and participation and human flourishing by unleashing talents and creativity. A core feature of democracy is the ability to self correct: when governments are acting against the popular will it must be possible to change course.

Australia should make our institutions more inclusive by removing limits on democratic accountability. The proliferation of independent regulatory agencies, for instance, has provided substantial administrative benefits. However, they, by design, limit democratic accountability. The agencies operate separately from elected officials and have limited oversight. At the very least, efforts must be made to increase democratic accountability of these organisations and if not bought into traditional accountability structures of representative democracy.

It is also essential that all voices can be freely expressed. A liberal society depends on the freedom of expression for egalitarian reasons: to ensure that all voices are part of political debate. This often leads to uncomfortable situations. Some ideas are bad. These ideas should be debated against, not allowed to fester. Banning speech does not make bad ideas go away; it pushes them underground. When Inners seek to censor certain types of speech – such as so-called 'hate speech' – they are presuming that their own ideas are infallible and prioritising hurt feelings over a free debate. This prevents the contest of ideas that is necessary to discover the truth. It also increases frustrations and disillusionment when people see that not only are their ideas ignored but they cannot even express them in the first place.

2. Localism

Australian politics is becoming a zero-sum game. Inners and Outers not only fight for economic spoils but, more fundamentally, for the ability to define the nation's identity. Inners and Outers have a different set of preferences in policymaking driven by their identity, culture and lifestyle. People want different things from their government. Compromise is difficult. Neither side feels like they are getting their way. Both Inners and Outers are frustrated and disillusioned.

The situation raises a serious democratic dilemma – how can both sides be accommodated? The existence of division is an opportunity for radical governance reform. Australia should harness diversity of opinion into local decision making and participation to reduce political conflict at the national and state level.

The century long consolidation of power in the federal government must come to an immediate halt.[624] Centralisation has undermined Australian democracy and good governance. It has disconnected the people from decisions made on their behalf. It has empowered Inners of the Canberra bureaucracy to ignore the wishes of Outers.

Local decisions are more reflective of local wants and needs and are more responsive and accountable.[625] Those who use a service should decide how the service is provided.[626] Localism is uplifting; it gives people a greater say in their lives and community. It enables participation that is impossible when decisions are made far away. Localism allows for the preferences of both Inners and Outers, who are interested in their local communities, to be accommodated to a much greater extent.

A politician that is responsible for representing tens or hundreds of thousands can ignore the preferences of many. A politician that has just thousands of constituents must be more responsive to each. The smaller the constituency, the more powerful each voice is within. People can also vote with their feet by moving to the community that is more agreeable to their preferences.[627]

Local decision making also improves the quality of governance. Advisory organisations, including the International Monetary Fund and World Bank, have encouraged countries to decentralise to improve governance.[628] Australia is an exception to global trends for more decentralisation over the past twenty five years.[629]

Local decision making encourages competition and innovation that improves outcomes.[630] Decentralisation, particularly fiscal decentralisation, is associated with higher economic growth and improved health and education outcomes.[631] It prevents central governments acting like monopolists and the never ending expansion of state power.[632] Citizens, civil society and media can more easily scrutinise governments that are smaller and closer to them, leading to less rent seeking and corruption.[633]

In practice, localism must empower local councils and communities, not just state governments. States should be able to raise the revenue to fund their services, ending the blame game between federal and state politicians. Responsibilities should be devolved. Australia does not need a federal department of education which does not employ teachers and nor do we need a department of health that does not employ doctors. The states should be responsible for health and education oversight. Boards elected from the community could manage schools and hospitals.

Local councils should have a larger role, including infrastructure, transport and policing responsibilities. More power and prestige could potentially attract a higher calibre of local representatives. Local council decision making should not just include regular elections, but also regular surveys of public opinions, town hall meetings, public hearings and, in some cases, local referenda.

Decentralising many specific decisions is also possible. Australia could end polarising national debates about the curriculum and educational programs such as 'safe schools' by leaving decisions about curriculum to each school in consultation with their community.[634] Planning decisions, instead of being made at a council and state level, could be made at a street level. Each street could propose a development plan and decide themselves on the appropriate level of development with two-thirds support of residents.

Australia could also adopt the Swiss model of citizenship, which empowers cantons and towns to decide who can join their community.[635] While federal authorities must authorise all citizenships, naturalisation is a regional responsibility and each region sets specific requirements for familiarity with Swiss habits, customs and traditions.

The process of decentralising would not be easy or straightforward; there are vested interests in the status quo. It is rare for any bureaucracy to want to give up power. It could also be costly and require time consuming local engagement to be successful. Nevertheless, in a divided Australia it is essential to take steps to defuse political conflict by allowing for more decision making at a local level.

3. Freedom

Inners are predisposed to paternalism and technocracy. Education, status and confidence have created an elite that thinks they know best. Often with the best of intentions, Inners use the levers of state power to manipulate the behaviour of the Outers. They fail to realise, however, that their preferences are not universally held – people can and do choose to live different lives and should be free to pursue their own vision of the good life.

Inners have, for instance, introduced sin taxes on goods such as alcohol and tobacco with the explicit intent of changing the behaviour of Outers. These taxes are both paternalistic and have a deeply regressive impact on Outers – who are more likely to smoke and drink and spend a higher proportion of their income on these goods.[636]

Egalitarianism gives everyone a say and localism ensures that Inners and Outers do not govern the other. Freedom devolves power directly to the individual. As a general principle, individuals should be free to pursue their preferences when it does not harm others and within the rules of the political community.[637] Beyond these restrictions, nobody else should interfere with an individual's ends and their definition of virtue. The point was elegantly made by J.S. Mill, who argues that because humans are imperfect and we cannot be certain of the existence of a perfect way of life, 'there should be different experiments of living'.[638] Individual differences are a virtue, not a vice.

Inners and Outers express different preferences. They can each be satisfied through freedom in the market and society. Inners can purchase electricity from renewable energy providers; Outers can prioritise cheaper options. Inners can eat vegan tofu curry; Outers can throw a shrimp on the barbeque. Inners can attend the Opera; Outers can watch Oprah.

Not only does freedom let people get what they want, it also works. Economic freedom leads to prosperity and human flourishing. In a meta-study of 52 separate studies, Chris Doucouliagos and Mehmet Ali of Deakin University in Melbourne found a strong, independent positive relationship between economic freedom on economic growth.[639] The adoption of the free market and free trade has lifted over a billion people out of poverty in the developing world over the past 30 years.[640] Empowering individuals is the path to human flourishing.

There has, nevertheless, been a consistent trend towards an ever-bigger state, in both expenditure and role.[641] The expansion of the state inevitably diminishes the individual. Before the industrial revolution people lived their entire lives among in their family and tribe – who were responsible for work, social welfare, education, defence, law and order.[642] This all changed with the agricultural and then industrial revolution, which provided the state with the resources, communications and technology to expand. The state now guarantees law and order, food, shelter, education, health and welfare. The unintended consequence of the expanding state is that it has both empowered the tribe that controls the state, the Inners, and diminished individual freedom and family and community bonds.

Once the government establishes a justification for intervention in one field, it is used to provide a precedent for further intervention.[643] This is difficult to reverse. American founding father Thomas Jefferson warned that 'The natural progress of things is for liberty to yield, government to gain ground.'[644] French intellectual Alexis de Tocqueville said that while individuals generally do not want the state to get too big, they do, nevertheless, want 'the government to take action in his domain.'[645] Consequently 'the sphere of the central government insensibly spreads in every direction, although every individual wants to restrict it.'

We must place greater faith in ourselves. Individuals and communities have been spontaneously ordering without outside interference throughout human history.[646] Civil society organisations, such as Rotary and volunteer fire brigades, workplace rules and cultural norms, come from the bottom up, not the top down. It does not take the cohesion of the state to get things done. Cultural norms and institutions, rules for action, develop and spread without the state. We have not become more tolerant of different races, for instance, because the government told people what to think – we have learned to be more accepting by interacting with different people.

As government power has expanded our capacity for self-organisation has shrunk.[647] Fewer Australians are getting involved with social, community, civic and sports groups.[648] Australians have become less self-reliant. There is a greater expectation for government to fix every problem. This has weakened local communities and families. For instance, the welfare state provision of unemployment support has without-a-doubt helped many in their times of need. It, nevertheless, displaced pre-existing private, charity and family sources of unemployment support. People have become reliant on the state, limiting the role of civil society and personal responsibility.

Australia's history establishes the ethic of individual freedom. As David Kemp argues, Australia has an 'individualist culture,' the defining element of which is 'the pursuit of purposes identified by individuals – whether selfish or altruistic – rather than purposes enforced by some external source – a church or religion, a paternalistic aristocracy, an ideological movement or an empire.'[649] The divisions within Australian society are a justification for more freedom. Communities of interest should be able to organise freely. Individuals should be free to make decisions that are best for themselves and their families. A freedom agenda, which encompasses less role for government, is essential to reduce divisiveness and polarisation that comes with one tribe governing over another.

4. Dignity

The premise of liberal democratic society is the equal moral worth of all citizens. Every individual has a vote worth the same value and is entitled to the same rights. Australian society, however, has become increasingly dominated by a single idea of value: the test passing, university attending, professional managerial person. The expansion of higher education has created extraordinary opportunities for many Australians from a variety of backgrounds. For others, however, a university degree and a professional job is neither appropriate nor is it necessary to find meaning. Not everyone can do work in genetic algorithms and genetically modifying food. This is difficult for university-attending Inners to comprehend.

The promotion of one idea of success is damaging to society. It raises a certain class of people above all others. It gives them access to the 'best jobs,' and immense wealth. It has led to the creation of occupational licensing with educational requirements, which limits the entry of outsiders to the best careers.[650] It gives a class of people the authority and legitimacy to make decisions on behalf of everyone else. It creates a permanent underclass, who have lower incomes and status.

The creation of one idea of success and the associated lower status for those who do not make it, breeds frustrations. These issues will only grow in the future. Artificial intelligence is unlikely to cause mass unemployment any time soon; however, it is likely to intensify the rewards from knowledge economy jobs and displace many menial or semi-skilled roles.

Society functions best when every individual feels as if they have a purpose. American Enterprise Institute president Arthur Brooks explains that everyone must feel needed. 'At its core, to be treated with dignity means being considered worthy of respect,' Brooks writes:

> 'Certain situations bring out a clear, conscious sense of our own dignity: when we receive praise or promotions at work, when we see our children succeed, when we see a volunteer effort pay off and change our neighbourhood for the better. We feel a sense of dignity when our own lives produce value for ourselves and others. Put simply, to feel dignified, one must be needed by others.'[651]

Brooks argues that the establishment of the welfare state, while alleviating material poverty, has combined with technological change and social pathologies to create a 'dignity deficit', a loss of meaning and purpose in many people's lives – and these people voted for Trump in high numbers. Brooks advocates for a *neediness agenda* that gets people into jobs. Work not only provides material wealth it also provides meaning, a day-to-day purpose and a feeling of being needed.

There should be no pre-determined path. Australian society should embrace a diversity of life choices. Just because Inners found that attending university was their path to accomplishment does not mean that this is the only path. There are many fruitful life and career paths. People should be encouraged to pursue their desires. To make this possible, Australian society must culturally embrace the acceptability of diversity of life choices.

Service, caring, technical and menial careers should be on equal social standing to graduate roles. Contemporary society requires a good measure of both. The knowledge economy office worker needs the sparkie to install and maintain the lights and electricity for their computer and tablet to function. Moreover, ironically, many of these sparkies will be earning more than office workers.

The Australian Government's Skill Shortage list is dominated by trades fields, including panel beaters, sheet metal workers, metal fitters, locksmiths, bricklayers, stonemasons, joiners, glaziers, roof tilers and plumbers.[652] In 2017, the Commonwealth government assessed a shortage in every construction trade role and found only half of the vacancies are filled.[653] 'New supply has not kept up with labour market demand, with a reduction in completions from related apprenticeships and traineeships in recent years,' the report surmises.

The achievement society rhetoric, that the only pathway to success is a university degree, is putting off many students whose interests and academic ability are well-suited to technical options. Students are put off by the lack of prestige and financial cost of non-graduate education in comparison to the high status and generous taxpayer support for university students.[654] Students are more interested in technical *jobs* than they are in technical *education*.[655]

Meanwhile, 15 per cent of school leavers are neither in work or education, creating a high risk of long term idleness and loss of dignity.[656] A young person is twice as likely to be unemployed and yet there are thousands of job openings in technical trades.[657] There is a mismatch between what many young people are being encouraged to pursue and the available job opportunities. We need an education system that fits our needs and allows people to reach their potential.

It is impossible to allocate prestige and enforce cultural change centrally. Nevertheless, there are concrete normative steps that governments can take to put technical education on an equal standing to university education. The prioritisation of university students, who are more likely to come from middle class backgrounds, is regressive, unfair and culturally problematic. In 2015-16, universities received $25.9 billion in funding compared to VET which received just $5.7 billion.[658] Technical options should be given equal public support as university students. If governments are going to provide state-subsidised loans, grants, allowances and no up-front fees to university students, they should offer the same support to technical students.

We should treat a wide variety of lifestyles, education, families and life choices and work with equal dignity.

5. Unity

Humans are groupish.[659] We desire belonging, attachments and bonds. The need to belong comes with the simultaneous need to be different and exclude.[660] We want to belong to a group which is distinctive.[661] The universalist, cosmopolitan attitude of Inners, in combination with the rise of identity politics, is undermining Australia's national bonds and increasing political conflict.

Both Inners and Outers feel isolated and under attack by the other. We are not talking to each other. From social media echo chambers to separate schools, suburbs and community groups, Inners and Outers live in bubbles. The lack of contact builds misunderstanding and resentment. It fuels bitter political debate that makes Australia less wholesome.

Cosmopolitanism, the notion that every human belongs to a single community, is supposed to build respect and tolerance. However, in recent history, cosmopolitans have aligned with efforts to delegitimise Australian identity, history, culture. There are many genuine injustices in Australia's history which are having an ongoing human impact. Consequently, for many Inners, patriotic sentiment is suspicious and backwards.

The undermining of national identity is making us less tolerant of difference. The need to belong has not disappeared. Identity primarily based on politics, gender, race and sexuality is replacing a unified national identity. The focus on group membership not only undermines individual humanity, it also increases tribalism and creates intolerance of difference.

Asserting that Australia is a racist country with a terrible history does not make people less bigoted. The opposite is true. Threatening the identity of the alleged bigots unites them against the minorities that identity politics is supposed to protect. Psychology research has found that perceived threats against the dominant group, as pursued by identity politics, threaten identity and culture.[662] This triggers a defensive tribal response that increases racial prejudice, dislike of minorities and anti-immigrant sentiment. [663] When progressives claim all white people are racist it becomes, to an extent, a self-fulfilling prophecy. This is because calling people bigots increases threat perception and defensive tribalism of the dominant group.

This leads to a downward spiral. Identity politics creates hierarchical competition for victimhood, an 'oppression Olympics' that every group in society competes. White conservatives feel threatened, and a need to organise against minorities, when they are told their national identity is racist, sexist and homophobic. The minority groups, and their supporters, then feel under threat and respond by fighting back against the bigotry. Both sides fuel each other.

Australia needs an identity that can unite us; an identity that creates a cohesive, tolerant and inclusive society. Thankfully we already have one. We are Australian.

Australians are patriotic – 66 per cent of Australians are very proud to be Australian and a further 28 per cent are somewhat proud. [664] Just 1 per cent are not proud at all. Most Australians believe that patriotic feelings strengthen Australia's position in the world and are needed to keep Australia united. [665]

Australians are patriotic without widespread prejudice. Just 5 per cent of Australians would not like to have someone of a different race as a neighbour. [666] Just 4 per cent of Australians would refuse to mix with people from other cultures if they could. [667] Australia is one of the most culturally and racially diverse countries on the planet. An astonishing 28 per cent of Australians are foreign born – the third highest in the developed world. [668]

Australian patriotism is also inclusive. Australian identity is not based on immutable characteristics like 'blood and soil' nationalism common in Asia and Europe. The *Pew Research Centre* found that Australians do not believe that you must be of a single ethnicity, religion or creed, or even born in Australia, to be a 'true Australian'.[669] What Australians consider to be important, speaking English and sharing our national customs and traditions, can be learnt and adopted no matter one's background.

A nation unites people. National identity has bought people from separate tribes, races, cultures and religions into a single social unit for hundreds of years. Nationalism is a key tool to expand our circle of sympathy beyond immediate family and tribal surroundings.[670] We are in a so-called 'imagined community,' we feel connections with millions of people we have never met and an associated responsibility and empathy with those people.[671] Nationalism has also been a force for evil, a justification exclusion, war, ethnic cleansing and genocide. However, because our tribal instincts do not simply disappear, the alternative to nationalism is not cosmopolitanism; it is ugly divisions within society.

Liberal nationalists, also known as civic nationalists, argue for a nationalism based on cultural and identity, not religion or race like illiberal nationalists or nativists.[672] Conservative philosopher Roger Scruton argues that our identity, sense of belonging and loyalty is attached to a territory that is ours, as well as history, customs, and national myths of glory, sacrifice and emancipation.[673] This attachment is necessary for a shared political identity, citizenship and the rule of law. A united identity encourages people to take responsibility for their welfare in combination with the general welfare of society.

British sociologist Frank Furedi argues about cosmopolitanism undermines bonds across generations and a sense of commonality.[674] 'Citizens possess important political rights, and also have responsibilities and duties towards other members of their community,' Furedi writes. 'Narrow nationalism is a scourge on public life. But identification with people born into a common world is the main way that solidarity between people can acquire a dynamic political character.'

Opponents of nationalism assert that it is a racial construct – this does the bidding of actual bigots who want nationalism to serve their racial prejudices. It is important not to allow the nation to be associated with a single ethnic or religious group because this inevitably excludes and disadvantages others.[675] Positive, inclusive nationalism built on a set of values, not immutable characteristics, is a force for unity.

I Am Australian by musicians Bruce Woodley and Dobe Newton surmises Australia's unity among difference. Each verse of the song discusses a different group of Australians and the chorus brings the groups together: 'We are one, but we are many. And from all the lands on earth we come. We share a dream and sing with one voice. I am, you are, we are Australian.'

A confident, united nation is a more welcoming one. Furedi writes that 'Paradoxically, the best protection for refugees is provided by nation states where citizens feel confident about their role and where, as a result, they can extend their solidarity to those beyond their national borders.'[676]

A national identity creates solidarity among diverse citizens and establishes support for public institutions and brings people together.

§

In the face of a divided and changing Australia we have a responsibility to rethink the structure of society. Liberal Populism is a work in progress, not a fully formed political philosophy. It is a framework designed to begin a discussion about how an increasingly divided Australia governs itself in the future. Liberal Populism has five pillars:

(1) egalitarianism, listening to all voices;

(2) localism, reducing conflict by decentralising;

(3) freedom, letting individuals be sovereign;

(4) dignity, creating a society of equal respect; and

(5) unity, finding what brings us together.

CONCLUSION

Uniting a divided Australia

Australia's challenge in the years ahead is to rediscover and bolster what unites us.

Inners will not disappear. The continuing growth of university education, and demographic and technological change that is favourable to graduates, is likely to make Inners more sizeable and powerful. Outers are also unlikely to disappear. The majority of Australians will continue not to have a graduate degree. Post-materialists will continue to be a minority. Australians will continue to value cultural institutions, be it the footy and rugby or Anzac Day and Australia Day.

In *The Righteous Mind*, Jonathan Haidt concludes that society needs *both* conservative and progressive voices in public debate. They are complementary, yin and yang, forces. Conservatives protect the community from potential danger; progressives push the envelope and advocate for necessary change.

Inners' impatience and campaigning for social progress have bought many benefits. Australia has become a more welcoming, prosperous and interesting place. Nevertheless, Outers, who want to protect the community from potential dangers and threatening change, must form a part of Australia's national debate. The Outer voice is not heard because Australia's centres of power – government, universities, media, unions, civil society and corporates – are dominated by change-seeking Inners.

Inners and Outers must learn to live together in one society. We must learn how to agree more strongly about less, accepting the differences and emphasising what unites us. The cardinal sin, which intolerant Inners have been committing for decades, is to assert the values, identity and culture of Outers is illegitimate. Inners have said, or acted, as if Outers' love of country and concern about change is driven by bigotry and backwardness. This view is not only untrue, but it is also counterproductive.

Hillary Clinton learnt that calling your opponent's supporters 'deplorables' strengthens their bonds and alienation. Telling Australians that they are racist, sexist homophobes will not make anyone less racist, sexist or homophobic. The more you talk about 'multiculturalism', celebrating 'diversity,' and embracing 'difference,' the less united, accepting and tolerant people become.[677] The backlash against liberal values will appear to come from nowhere; however, it will be ugly and dangerous.

A nation cannot survive without a uniting identity. We must acknowledge the dark parts of our history while embracing the success we have created. Australia is on a never-ending journey of self-improvement. Over the last 117 years we have made plenty of mistakes along the way to a more perfect nation. It is difficult to conclude, however, that we have been anything but successful. We live in one of the most successful nations on earth. Despite our small size and geographic isolation, we consistently punch above our weight, from our incomes and health to the sports field and the United Nations.

The alternative path, to focus on the darkness in the past, will leave us divided and with no future. British commentator Douglas Murray, in *The Strange Death of Europe*, points to the importance of acknowledging the good and bad in history. 'A country that believes it has never done any wrong is a country that could do wrong at any time,' Murray discerns, 'But a country that believes it has only done wrong, or done such a terrible, unalleviated amount of wrong in the past, is likely to become a country that is inclined to doubt its ability to do good in the future.'[678]

Too often our schools – using a national curriculum designed by Inners – and universities are failing to teach Australia's successes, the rule of law and the development of liberal democracy.[679] Without a proper understanding of our history and essential institutions they are bound to rot. Considering the lack of civics education, it is no surprise that young Australians are less supportive of democracy.[680]

A nation requires a uniting vision, a culture that people want to be apart. A confident nation is also a more welcoming one. In the context of integrating immigrants, Murray points to the work of Syrian immigrant to Germany, Bassam Tibi, who, in 1962, wrote about the need for a 'leitkuktur,' a 'core culture.' We must find values we can agree upon – ideally, our core liberal democratic values, such as free speech, the rule of law and equal moral worth of all citizens. Beyond that, individuals, families and communities should be free to live as they please.

Some might consider this a 'melting pot' approach, in which differences disappear and everyone becomes the same. A better metaphor, however, may be a 'salad bowl' in which many ways of life are successfully bought together like salad ingredients. Not everyone should be expected to live the same lifestyle; within the confines of the whole, every sub-culture should be able to keep their distinct qualities.[681] To extend the metaphor, certain ingredients can spoil a salad, but there are also lots of tasty mixes.

Our society is stronger when there is a mixture of cultures and ideas. Our politics is more effective with conservatives challenging progressives and vice versa. Our businesses are more successful with expertise from a wide array of fields. Our universities can more effectively research and teach with debate between competing perspectives. Our streets are more vibrant when they contain shops selling products from London to Rio De Janeiro. Our diets are more interesting when we have a choice between Italian, Vietnamese, American and Lebanese food.

We should celebrate, or at least tolerate, political, cultural, social, religious, racial, ethnic, gender and sexual preference differences. Every group contributes something to the Australian salad. We should also acknowledge that Australia can only function as an connected nation. What we share is more than what divides us. We will only be able to live together and integrate new arrivals if we are comfortable and relaxed with who we are.

People from across the globe have come to Australia to join something that is great – a prosperous liberal democratic nation where opportunity is aplenty, class hierarchy is shunned and where, with a mixture of blood, sweat and tears, anyone can get ahead. In *The Australian Legend*, historian Russel Ward traces the cultural roots of Australian identity through bushman, convicts, Irish immigrants and pastoral workers and ultimately spread by 19th century literature.

Ward writes that the archetypal Australian is the 'practical man, rough and ready in his manners and quick to decry any appearance of affection in others':

'He is a great improviser, ever willing 'to have a go' at anything, but willing to be content in a task done in a way that is 'near enough.' Though capable of great exertion in an emergency, he normally feels no impulse to work hard without good cause. He is a fiercely independent person who hates officiousness and authority, especially when these qualities are embodied in military officers and policemen.'

Australia is a tough country. We are an isolated island. Most of our interior is uninhabitable. We are sparsely populated. And yet millions have chosen to make this country home, to raise families, to muddle through life and do their small part to improve their community.

The ultimate arbiter of a nation's success is what we bequeath our children. Frighteningly, Australians are losing faith in the future. Just a quarter of Australians think that their children will have a better life than themselves.[682] This pessimistic attitude is seeping through our culture and into our politics. Our optimism, that tomorrow will be better than yesterday and the day after tomorrow will be even better, is disappearing. We are losing our sunny disposition.

Australians are frustrated by their lack of capacity to influence decisions which impact their lives. We are divided in lifestyle, identity and culture. One group designed and manage the key institutions and direct the popular culture. The other group are frustrated and disgruntled about the state of modern Australia. The system designed by the Inners has, for the most part, worked. It has not, however, garnered popular support. People have remained sceptical about the way politics operates and feel locked out; they feel that their perspective is not heard. We have entered an era of political malaise.

We must regain our belief in progress. We can only create a better future if we believe it to be possible. This requires purpose, a national mission of sorts. This is impossible in a divided nation with clashing tribes and when anger replaces dialogue.

We share a single land mass. Like it or not, we must learn to live together.

Appendix 1: Note on quantitative data

This appendix outlines the background to the data used in graphs and tables.

Study	Year	Response rate		Fieldwork date	Researchers	Data collection method
Australian Election Study	1987- 2016	Year 1987 1990 1993 1996 1998 2001 2004 2007 2010 2013 2016	Rate 1,825 2,020 3,023 1,795 1,896 2,010 1,769 1,873 2,061 3,955 2,818	Various, years of elections	Clive Bean, Ian McAllister, Juliet Pietsch and Rachel Gibson	Post-election self-completion surveys with the sample draw randomly from the electoral register including offline and online completion options since 2010
Australian Candidate Study	2016	182		2016	Clive Bean, Ian McAllister, Juliet Pietsch and Rachel Gibson	Questionnaires maile to candidates a week after the election
ISSP 2015: Work Orientations IV		1,211		08/2015- 04/2016		Mail survey selected randomly from the Australian Electoral Commission data, questionnaire bookle and reply paid envelope.
World Values Survey	1984 & 2014	Year 1984 2014	Rate 1,228 1,477	1981 & 2012 (Australia)	Inglehart, R., C. Haerpfer, A. Moreno, C. Welzel, K. Kizilova, J. Diez-Medrano, M. Lagos, P. Norris, E. Ponarin & B. Puranen et al.	Sponsored by the ANU in Australia, completed by Social Research Centre Pty Ltd.
Australian Social Science Survey	2014	1,435		2014	Australian Consortium for Social and Political Research	Mail survey selected randomly from the Australian Electoral Commission data, questionnaire bookle and reply paid envelope.

Study	Year	Response rate	Fieldwork date	Researchers	Data collection method
Newspoll (Australia Day)	2018	1,616	Feb 1-4, 2018		Online interviews of voters weighed for population (age, gender and location)
Newspoll (Statue)	2017	?	Aug 31 – Sep 3, 2018		Online interviews of voters weighed for population (age, gender and location)
Scanlon Foundation	2017	1,500	June 21 – July 18, 2017	Andrew Markus	Randomly generated landline telephone and mobile numbers
Australian Population Research Institute	2017	2,067	July 31 – August 17, 2017	Katharine Betts & Bob Birrell	Online research panel, by The Online Research Unit, of voters, weighed for population (age, gender and location)
What It Takes to Truly Be 'One of Us', Pew 2017	2017	1,000	Apr 6 - 28, 2016		Randomly generated landline telephone and mobile numbers weighed for population (gender, age, education, region, urbanity, phone use and respondent selection probability).
ABS census 2016	2016	23,401,892	9 August, 2016		Postal and online survey of every Australian household.
ANU Australian Socio-economic Index 2006	2006	N/A	N/A		An occupational status scale developed by the Australian National University.

Notes

Introduction

1 See Ian McAllister et al., "Australian Election Study," 2016.

2 For example, since 1990, just 28 pieces of legislation have attracted more than 20 hours of debate in the Senate, and less than 40 per cent of time is spent debating legislation, most legislation is 'non-controversial' and attracts minimal debate, see Parliament of Australia, "Senate StatsNet," text, 2018.

3 Mark Evans, Max Halupka, and Gerry Stoker, "How Australians Imagine Their Democracy: The 'Power of Us'" (Canberra, ACT: Governance Institute, 2017).

4 James Grubel and Jill Sheppard, "Voter Interest Hits Record Low in 2016 - ANU Election Study," ANU, December 20, 2016.

5 McAllister et al., "Australian Election Study."

6 Essential Research, "Satisfaction with Democracy in Australia," The Essential Report, November 20, 2017.

7 Ipsos Global Trends, "Government Prioritising Concerns," 2016.

8 There has been a pronounced downwards trend in Australians' trust of institutions, which is low by global standards, see Edelman Trust, "Barometer Global Report" (Edelman Trust, 2018).

9 Andrew Markus, "Mapping Social Cohesion 2017: The Scanlon Foundation Surveys Report" (Melbourne, VIC: Scanlon Foundation, 2017).

10 David Crowe, "Major Parties Warned on Need to Win Back Angry Voters," The Sydney Morning Herald, May 14, 2018.

11 Paul Kelly, Triumph and Demise: The Broken Promise of a Labor Generation (Carlton, Vic: Melbourne University Publishing, 2014).

12 The Treasury, "2015 Intergenerational Report: Australia in 2055" (Canberra, ACT: Australian Government, March 5, 2015).

13 For promises to return to surplus see AAP, "Joe Hockey Commits to First-Year Surplus," News.com.au, March 7, 2012; Colin Brinsden, "Budget on Course for Surplus in 2012-13: Treasurer Wayne Swan," May 10, 2011.

14 The Treasury, 84.

15 Australian Bureau of Statistics, "6523.0 - Household Income and Wealth, Australia," September 13, 2017.

16 Edmund Burke described society as a partnership 'not only between those who are living, but between those who are living, those who are dead, and those who are to be born,' see Edmund Burke, Reflections on the Revolution in France (Adelaide, SA: eBooks@ Adelaide, The University of Adelaide Library, 1790).

17 Mikayla Novak, "The $176 Billion Tax on Our Prosperity" (Melbourne, VIC: Institute of Public Affairs, May 2016).

18 Roy Morgan, a market research firm, estimates 1.32 are unemployed, almost double the official number released by the Australian Bureau of Statistics, see Roy Morgan, "Employment at Record High but over 2.5 Million Australians Looking for 'More' Work," April 9, 2018; Gideon Rozner, "Australia's Silent Crisis In Male Employment"

(Melbourne, VIC: Institute of Public Affairs, August 19, 2017).

19 Daniel Wild, "Business Investment In Australia Now Lower Than Under Whitlam," Parliamentary Research Brief (Melbourne, VIC: Institute of Public Affairs, March 8, 2017).

20 Matthew Lesh, "Reigniting Australia's Entrepreneurial Flame: Finding The Missing 275,000 Businesses" (Melbourne, VIC: Institute of Public Affairs, November 5, 2017).

21 Gareth Hutchens, "Australian Wages Growing More Slowly than Cost of Living," *The Guardian*, May 17, 2017, sec. Business.

22 World Economic Forum, "The Global Competitiveness Index 2017-2018 Edition: Australia" (Cologny, Switzerland: World Economic Forum, September 27, 2017).

23 See Ch. 5.

24 See Ch. 6.

25 See Ch. 7.

26 David Goodhart, *The Road to Somewhere: The Populist Revolt and the Future of Politics* (London: C Hurst & Co Publishers Ltd, 2017).

27 Historic discussion of the stability Australian politics is common, see Dean Jeansch, *The Australian Party System* (Sydney, NSW: George Allen & Unwin, 1983), 43; Don Aitkin, *Stability and Change in Australian Politics* (Canberra, ACT: Australian National University Press, 1977).

28 See Ch 2.

29 In addition to the growth of non-major parties, there is evidence of movements in self-identity show an increase in polarisation, See Luke Mansillo and Nick Evershed, "Australian Politics Becoming More Polarised," the Guardian, August 7, 2014.

30 McAllister et al., "Australian Election Study."

31 McAllister et al.; Katie Burgess and Clare Sibthorpe, "Australians' Trust in Politicians Hits Two-Decade Low," *Sydney Morning Herald*, June 28, 2016.

32 Crowe, "Major Parties Warned on Need to Win Back Angry Voters."

33 The number of Australians who say that the government has no difference to the country's economy in a year's time has grown from 51 per cent in 1990 to 67 per cent in 2016, see McAllister et al., "Australian Election Study."

34 This calculation does not include Harold Holt and 22-day prime ministership of John McEwen because of the uniqueness of their shortened leaderships.

Chapter 1

35 Malcolm Turnbull, "This Has Been a Very Important Day in the Life of the Nation...," September 15, 2015.

36 Bevan Shields, "Government to Launch $28 Million Taxpayer-Funded Ad Campaign to Sell Innovation Policies," *The Sydney Morning Herald*, January 6, 2016.

37 See Steven Pinker, *Enlightenment Now: The Case for Reason, Science, Humanism, and Progress* (Viking, 2018); Johan Norberg, *Progress: Ten Reasons to Look Forward to the Future* (Oneworld Publications, 2016); Matt Ridley, *The Rational Optimist: How Prosperity Evolves* (New York: Harper, 2010).

38 See the variety of statistics on Cato Institute, "Human Progress," 2017.

39 Tom McIlroy, "Election Slogans: Voters Disagree 'There's Never Been a More Exciting Time to Be an Australian'," *The Sydney Morning Herald*, June 26, 2016.

40 Michael Koziol, "How Malcolm Turnbull's Innovation Agenda Failed to Take Flight," *The Sydney Morning Herald*, July 18, 2016.

41 Koziol.

42 The growth, demographics, and geography of this tribe is discussed in Ch 2.

43 The advantages of the highly educated in the future are discussed by Tyler Cowen, see Tyler Cowan, *Average Is Over: Powering America Beyond the Age of the Great Stagnation*, First Edition edition (New York, New York: Dutton, 2013).

44 McIlroy, "Election Slogans."

45 The political attitudes of Inners and Outers discussed in Ch 3.

46 Research has consistently found links between education and higher levels of tolerance of difference, see, for example, Norman Holt and C. E. Tygart, "Political Tolerance and Higher Education," *The Pacific Sociological Review* 12, no. 1 (1969): 27–33; Lawrence Bobo and Frederick C. Licari, "Education and Political Tolerance Testing the Effects of Cognitive Sophistication and Target Group Affect," *Public Opinion Quarterly* 53, no. 3 (January 1, 1989): 285–308; Ewa A. Golebiowska, "Individual Value Priorities, Education, and Political Tolerance," *Political Behavior* 17, no. 1 (1995): 23–48.

47 The work disposition of Inners is discussed in Ch 2.

48 Socioeconomic status, which interlinks closely to education level, has been linked to openness to try unfamiliar foods, see Ingrid Flight, Phillip Leppard, and David N Cox, "Food Neophobia and Associations with Cultural Diversity and Socio-Economic Status amongst Rural and Urban Australian Adolescents," *Appetite* 41, no. 1 (August 1, 2003): 51–59.

49 Australian Electoral Commission, "2016 Federal Election," Australian Electoral Commission, 2016.

50 See, for example, Paula Matthewson, "The Crashing Disappointment That Is Malcolm Turnbull," *The New Daily*, September 15, 2017; Peter Hartcher, "Fairfax-Ipsos Poll: Voters Feel the Seven-Month Itch," *The Sydney Morning Herald*, March 13, 2016; Paula Matthewson, "Turnbull Looks More Dodgy than Decisive These Days," *ABC News*, March 14, 2016.

51 The concept of 'achieved' and 'ascribed' status was first developed by anthropologist Ralph Linton, see Ralph Linton, *The Study of Man: An Introduction* (D. Appleton-Century Company, 1936).

52 Those with higher education are more likely to identity with being creative, see question V70 in "World Values Survey" (World Values Survey Association, 2012), worldvaluessurvey.org.

53 Those with higher education are less likely to identity with the importance of tradition, see question V79 in "World Values Survey."

54 This is inspired by Bernard Salt's infamous column, see Bernard Salt, "Evils of the Hipster Cafe," *The Weekend Australian Magazine*, October 16, 2016.

55 For discussion of divergent cultural activities by socioeconomic groupings, see Inga Ting et al., "Good Taste, Bad Taste? What Your Habits Reveal about Social Class," *ABC News*, April 13, 2018.

56 This issue is discussed further in Ch 6., extensive literature suggests that education is correlated with political engagement, see Alexander K. Mayer, "Does Education Increase Political Participation?," *The Journal of Politics* 73, no. 3 (2011): 633–45.

57 Dalton discusses how growing education decreases partisanship as people can deal with the cognitive complexities of politics and make their own decisions, and are therefore less likely to follow partisan cues to guide voting behaviour, he calls this a move from

"partisan" party alignment to "cognitive alignment," see Russell J. Dalton, "Cognitive Mobilization and Partisan Dealignment in Advanced Industrial Democracies," *The Journal of Politics* 46, no. 1 (1984): 264–84.

58 This phenomenon is discussed further in Ch. 2 and Ch. 7.

59 Outers do pull some levers of power, or at the very least some individuals with Outer sympathies, however, this is much less common than Inners.

60 The lack of self-awareness of the new highly educated elite is discussed in Matthew Stewart, "The 9.9 Percent Is the New American Aristocracy," *The Atlantic*, June 2018.

61 These are inner-city areas with high incomes, education levels, and a high Liberal vote.

62 Australian Bureau of Statistics, "1800.0 - Australian Marriage Law Postal Survey," November 15, 2017.

63 Liberal voters are most likely to select economic management as their most important issue at an election time, see McAllister et al., "Australian Election Study."

64 This group is epitomised by the Greens-voting demographic, for further discussion and citation see Ch 4.

65 Divergent media patterns by political bias are discussed in Nic Newman, David A. L. Levy, and Rasmus Kleis Nielsen, "Reuters Institute Digital News Report 2017" (Oxford, UK: Reuters Institute, University of Oxford, 2017).

66 McAllister et al., "Australian Election Study."

67 These are inner-city seats with a high Greens vote.

68 The socioeconomic, geographic, and professional tendencies of the Outers are explored in Ch 2.

69 There has been a long term trend towards 'credential inflation' or 'credentialism' in Australia and across the developed world, see Dean Ashenden, "The Australian Skills Agenda: Productivity versus Credentialism?," *Educational and Training Technology International* 29, no. 3 (August 1, 1992): 240–48; Joseph Zajda, "Globalisation, Credentialism and Human Capital," Text, 2012.

70 For divergent work patterns, see International Social Survey Programme, "ZA6770: Work Orientations IV," 2015.

71 For divergent attitudes to work, see International Social Survey Programme.

72 Those with lower education are less likely to be satisfied with their financial situation (question V59), and more likely to aspire towards wealth (question V71), see "World Values Survey.".

73 While church attendance has shrunk, a majority of Australians still identity with a religion, which is more common among individuals who are older, see ABS census 2016.

74 The different readerships of the Fairfax and News Ltd. papers is discussed in Wendy Bacon, "Sceptical Climate Part 2: Climate Science in Australian Newspapers" (Australian Centre for Independent Journalism, 2013), 123–24. Also see Tak Wing Chan and John H. Goldthorpe, "Social Status and Newspaper Readership," *American Journal of Sociology* 112, no. 4 (January 1, 2007).

75 The higher nationalistic tendencies of those with less education is discussed here John Brennan et al., "The Effect of Higher Education on Graduates' Attitudes: Secondary Analysis of the British Social Attitudes Survey," BIS RESEARCH PAPER NO. 200 (London, UK: Department of Business innovation and Skills, November 2015).

76 Individuals with lower levels of education are more likely to be 'very proud' of being Australian, see "World Values Survey."

77 Divergent attitudes to physical security concerns can be seen in Jill Sheppard, "ANUPoll:

Attitudes to National Security" (Australian National University, October 2016).

78 Despite skills shortage, there is less spending in real terms on vocational education than a decade ago, see Sarah Pilcher and Kate Torii, "Expenditure on Education and Training in Australia 2017" (Melbourne, VIC: Mitchell Institute, December 13, 2017).

79 The divergence in attitudes to work is discussed further in Ch 2., also see International Social Survey Programme, "ZA6770: Work Orientations IV."

80 See Katharine Betts and Bob Birrell, "Australian Voters' Views on Immigration Policy" (Middle Camberwell,VIC: The Australian Population Research Institute, October 2017).

81 Those with lower education are less likely to identity as adventurous and want an exciting life, see question V76 in "World Values Survey."

82 Parliamentary Library of Australia, "Part 5 - Referendums and Plebiscites," in *Parliamentary Handbook of the 44th Parliament* (Canberra, ACT: Parliament of Australia, 2014).

83 Public attitudes to immigration have most strongly been linked to 'sociotropic concerns about its cultural impacts—and to a lesser extent its economic impacts—on the nation,' see Jens Hainmueller and Daniel J. Hopkins, "Public Attitudes Toward Immigration," *Annual Review of Political Science* 17, no. 1 (2014): 225–49.

84 Greg Brown, "Green Voters Snobs: Research," *The Australian*, November 20, 2017.

85 See "World Values Survey."

86 If Inners were the only ones who supported same-sex marriage it could never have received 62% support in the 2017 plebiscite. Outers were split on the issue. Nevertheless, small and decreasing numbers of Australians think that homosexuality is itself immoral. The World Values Survey has found that those who say that homosexuality to be 'never justifiable' to have decreased from 39% in 1981 to 13% in 2012, and perhaps further since. Just 13% of Australians would not want a homosexual as a neighbour, compared to 15% of New Zealanders, 20% of Americans, 22% of Germans, 40% of Poles, 66% of Russians, 80% of Iraqis and 94% of Azerbaijanis. There have been similar liberalisations in attitudes towards other social questions such as contraceptives, sex outside of marriage, abortion, and euthanasia.

87 For divergence on political engagement, see Table 8.

88 Australians with lower incomes and less education are less likely to interested in news, and particularly less likely to use online news sources, see Jerry Watkins et al., "Digital News Report Australia 2016" (University of Canberra: News & Media Research Centre, 2017), 13.

89 It could be argued that it is positive that people can disengage from politics and live their lives.

90 The issue priority question is discussed in Ch 3.

91 Individuals with education, likely due to less political sophistication, express less ideological partisanship, and are more likely change between parties between elections, see Dalton, "Cognitive Mobilization and Partisan Dealignment in Advanced Industrial Democracies"; William G. Jacoby, "The Sources of Liberal-Conservative Thinking: Education and Conceptualization," *Political Behavior* 10, no. 4 (December 1, 1988): 316–32; "Floating Voters in US Presidential Elections, 1948-2000," *Studies in Public Opinion: Attitudes, Non Attitudes, Measurement Error, and Change* 166 (January 1, 2004).

92 McAllister et al., "Australian Election Study."

93 Global Scan, "Global Citizenship A Growing Sentiment Among Citizens Of Emerging Economies" (BBC World Service, April 27, 2016).

94 Betts and Birrell, "Australian Voters' Views on Immigration Policy".

95 Jacob Poushter, "As Elections Near, Most Australians Trust Turnbull's Handling of World Affairs," *Pew Research Center's Global Attitudes Project* (blog), June 20, 2016; Australian Consortium for Social & Political Research Inc., "Australian Survey of Social Attitudes 2013," 2013.

96 Bruce Stokes, "What It Takes to Truly Be 'One of Us,'" *Pew Research Center's Global Attitudes Project* (blog), February 1, 2017.

97 Australian Consortium for Social & Political Research Inc., "Australian Survey of Social Attitudes 2013."

98 David Crowe and Paige Taylor, "Newspoll Finds Overwhelming Support to Leave Statues Alone," *The Australian*, September 4, 2017.

99 "World Values Survey."

100 Sheppard, "ANUPoll: Attitudes to National Security".

101 McAllister et al., "Australian Election Study".

102 Essential Polling, "Energy Policy," The Essential Report, December 11, 2017.

103 Wood and Daley also note that the rise of the minor parties cannot be explained by social conservatism, see Danielle Wood and John Daley, "A Crisis of Trust: The Rise of Protest Politics in Australia" (Melbourne, VIC: Grattan Institute, March 12, 2018).

104 Katharine Betts, *The Great Divide: Immigration Politics in Australia* (Sydney, NSW: Duffy and Snellgrove, 1999).

105 Katharine Betts, "Cosmopolitans and Patriots: Australia's Cultural Divide and Attitudes to Immigration," *People and Place* 13, no. 2 (2005): 29.

106 Betts, *The Great Divide: Immigration Politics in Australia*, 320.

107 Mark Latham, "Insiders and Outsiders" (September 17, 2002).

108 Nick Cater, *The Lucky Culture* (HarperCollins Australia, 2013).

109 Guy Rundle, "Rundle: Trump Is the End of the Left as We Know It," *Cirkey*, November 30, 2016.

110 Jill Sheppard and Nicholas Biddle, "Class, Capital, and Identity in Australian Society," *Australian Journal of Political Science*, August 14, 2017.

111 Fairfax Media, "How the Political Persona Project Works," *The Sydney Morning Herald*, February 6, 2017; Inga Ting, "Melbourne's Political Geography Revealed in Seven Maps," *The Age*, February 19, 2017; Inga Ting, "Sydney's Political Geography Revealed in Seven Maps," *The Sydney Morning Herald*, February 18, 2017.

112 This did not include the Greens, see Wood and Daley, "A Crisis of Trust: The Rise of Protest Politics in Australia."

113 McAllister et al., "Australian Election Study."

114 In the past, McAllister has argued that it is in both major parties' interest to avoid divisive social issues and keep debate focused on economic issues, see Ian McAllister, *Political Behaviour: Citizens, Parties and Elites in Australia* (Melbourne, VIC: Longman Cheshire, 1992).

115 Monash University academic Nick Economou points out that most marginal seat contests are Liberal-Labor, meaning the Greens (The New Elite) are of relatively limited importance in electoral politics, see Nick Economou, "From the Inner Cities to the Outer Suburbs: Voting, Parties, Politics and A Post-Industrial Australia," *Journal of Australian Studies* 29 (2016): 50–61.

Chapter 2

116 The Socialist Alternative were founded in 1995 following a split from the International

Socialist Organisation. In previous decades Maoist and Trotskyist groups were common on campus.

117 For further discussion of the dignity of work, see Institute of Public Affairs, "Dignity of Work," IPA - The Voice For Freedom; Arthur C. Brooks, *The Conservative Heart: How to Build a Fairer, Happier, and More Prosperous America* (HarperCollins, 2017), 19–20, 91–97.

118 The Socialist Alternative newspaper, Red Flag, displays this propensity, see Socialist Alternative, "Red Flag Newspaper," n.d., http://redflag.org.au/.

119 There are of course complexities to this generalisation. The parties have been divided throughout their history. For example, during the 1950s, Labor was split between anti-communist elements of the right, and elements more sympathetic to the Soviet Union on the left. However, this divide, like historic divides within the Liberal Party, did not reflect trying to appeal across class divides. Whether anti-communist or Marxist in their thinking, Labor was still largely appealing to the working class vote.

120 This is the Downs model of elections, see Anthony Downs, "An Economic Theory of Political Action in a Democracy," *Journal of Political Economy* 65, no. 2 (1957): 135–50.

121 Robert R. Alford, *Party and Society: The Anglo-American Democracies* (Westport, Conn.: Greenwood Press, 1963), 173.

122 Solomon Encel, *Equality and Authority: A Study of Class Status and Power in Australia* (Melbourne, VIC: Cheshire, 1970), 96.

123 Seymour Martin Lipset, *Political Man: The Social Bases of Politics* (Baltimore: Johns Hopkins University Press, 1960), 254.

124 Political scientist Judith Brett contends that there was a moral dimension to the class-religious dynamic. That is, it was not just that protestants were middle class, they also adopted the protestant work ethnic which appealed to the Liberal Party, and Catholics a social justice framework that led to appeal for the Labor Party. See, Judith Brett, "Class, Religion and the Foundation of the Australian Party System: A Revisionist Interpretation," *Australian Journal of Political Science* 37, no. 1 (March 1, 2002): 39–56.

125 D. A. Kemp, *Society and Electoral Behaviour in Australia: A Study of Three Decades* (St. Lucia, Qld: University of Queensland Press, 1978).

126 See also Simon Jackman, "Political Parties and Electoral Behavior," in *The Cambridge Handbook of Social Sciences in Australia*, ed. Riaz Hassan, Ian McAllister, and Steve Dowrick (Cambridge, England: Cambridge University Press, 2003).

127 Clive Bean and Ian McAllister, "Documenting the Inevitable: Voting Behaviour at the 2013 Australian Election," in *Abbott's Gambit*, ed. Carol Johnson, Hsu-Ann Lee, and John Wanna (ANU Press), accessed April 16, 2018; Robert J. Stimson and Tung-Kai Shyy, "A Socio-Spatial Analysis of Voting for Political Parties at the 2007 Federal Election," *People and Place* 17, no. 1 (2009); Andrew Leigh, "Economic Voting and Electoral Behavior: How Do Individual, Local, and National Factors Affect the Partisan Choice?," *Economics & Politics* 17, no. 2 (July 1, 2005): 265–96; Shaun Ratcliff, "Do Economic Cleavagesstill Matterin Australian Politics?" (2015).

128 Andrew Leigh, "How Do Unionists Vote? Estimating the Causal Impact of Union Membership on Voting Behaviour from 1966 to 2004," *Australian Journal of Political Science* 41, no. 4 (December 1, 2006): 537–52.

129 ABS, "6333.0 - Characteristics of Employment, Australia, August 2016," May 2, 2017.

130 International Social Survey Programme, "ZA6670: Citizenship II," 2014, 2014.

131 Mark N Franklin, Thomas T Mackie, and Henry Valen, *Electoral Change: Responses to Evolving Social and Attitudinal Structures in Western Countries* (New York, NY: Cambridge University Press, 1992); Professor Russell J. Dalton and Steven A. Weldon, "Public Images of Political Parties: A Necessary Evil?," *West European Politics* 28, no. 5

(November 1, 2005): 931–51; Peter Mair, "The Challenge to Party Government," *West European Politics* 31, no. 1–2 (January 1, 2008): 211–34.

132 Terry Nichols Clark, Seymour Martin Lipset, and Michael Rempel, "The Declining Political Significance of Social Class," *International Sociology* 8, no. 3 (September 1, 1993): 293–316; Terry Nichols Clark and Seymour Martin Lipset, *The Breakdown of Class Politics: A Debate on Post-Industrial Stratification* (Woodrow Wilson Center Press, 2001); Giedo Jansen, Geoffrey Evans, and Nan De Graaf, "Class Voting and Left-Right Party Positions: A Comparative Study of 15 Western Democracies, 1960-2005," *Social Science Research* 42 (March 1, 2013): 376-400.

133 Mark N. Franklin, *The Decline of Class Voting in Britain: Changes in the Basis of Electoral Choice, 1964-1983* (Oxford : New York: Oxford University Press, 1985).

134 These became known in the 1980s as 'Reagan Democrats', see Michael Hout, Clem Brooks, and Jeff Manza, "The Democratic Class Struggle in the United States, 1948-1992," *American Sociological Review* 60, no. 6 (1995): 805–28; Thomas Frank, *What's the Matter with Kansas?: How Conservatives Won the Heart of America* (New York: Holt Paperbacks, 2005).

135 Kemp, *Society and Electoral Behaviour in Australia*, 358.

136 Paul Karp, "Too Many Graduates: Universities Chief Warns against Degrees for All," *The Guardian*, August 1, 2016.

137 See Gwilym Croucher et al., *The Dawkins Revolution: 25 Years on* (Melbourne, VIC: Melbourne University Press, 2014).

138 Department of Education, "Higher Education Statistics," 2018.

139 Brett, "Class, Religion and the Foundation of the Australian Party System," 141.

140 Occupation prestige has been measured by ANU's Australian Socioeconomic Index 2006 (AUSEI06), which measures occupations on a scale from 0 to 100 by age, sex, education, labour force status, and hours worked, see Julie McMillan, Adrian Beavis, and Frank L. Jones, "The AUSEI06: A New Socioeconomic Index for Australia," *Journal of Sociology* 45, no. 2 (June 1, 2009): 123–49.

141 This issue is discussed further in Ch 6.

142 Australian Bureau of Statistics, "4159.0 - General Social Survey," June 29, 2015.

143 Andrew Norton, "Mapping Australian Higher Education 2016" (Melbourne, VIC: Grattan Institute, August 7, 2016).

144 Andrew Norton, "Was Higher Education Ever Likely to Reduce Inequality?," *Andrew Norton* (blog), February 21, 2018.

145 Ellis Connolly and Christine Lewis, "Structural Change in the Australian Economy" (Sydney, NSW: Reserve Bank of Australia, September 2010).

146 Cowan, *Average Is Over*.

147 Peter Temin, *The Vanishing Middle Class: Prejudice and Power in a Dual Economy* (Cambridge, Massachusetts: The MIT Press, 2017).

148 Jeff Borland and Michael Coelli, "Are Robots Taking Our Jobs?," *Australian Economic Review* 50, no. 4 (December 1, 2017): 385.

149 Rozner discusses a range of reasons for this change, see Rozner, "Australia's Silent Crisis In Male Employment."

150 Melanie Arntz, Terry Gregory, and Ulrich Zierahn, "The Risk of Automation for Jobs in OECD Countries," May 14, 2016.

151 Christine R. Schwartz and Robert D. Mare, "Trends in Educational Assortative Marriage from 1940 to 2003," *Demography* 42, no. 4 (November 1, 2005); Rich Morin, "New Academic Study Links Rising Income Inequality to 'assortative Mating,'" *Pew Research Center* (blog), January 29, 2014.

152 There are both nature and nurture determinations of this intergenerational advantage, for discussion of this issue, see Toby Young, "The Fall of the Meritocracy," *Quadrant*, September 7, 2015; Toby Young, "The Rise and Fall of the Meritocracy" (April 12, 2017).

153 Jennings Will and Stoker Gerry, "The Bifurcation of Politics: Two Englands," *The Political Quarterly* 87, no. 3 (September 9, 2016): 372–82.

154 McKinney have noted growing congestion and rising house prices driving homelessness as a negative consequence of the growth of cities.

155 This is discussed in Department of Infrastructure and Regional Development, "State of Australian Cities 2014–2015" (Canberra, ACT: Commonwealth of Australia, 2015), 2014–2015.

156 This is calculated based from the 2016 Census by the Australian Bureau of Statistics

157 This is discussed in Department of Infrastructure and Regional Development, "State of Australian Cities 2014–2015," 2014–2015.

158 My calculation based on data from the ABS census 2016.

159 My calculation based on data from the ABS census 2016.

160 Charles Murray, *Coming Apart: The State of White America, 1960-2010* (New York, N.Y: Crown Forum, 2013).

161 Bernard Salt, "Australia's Great Tribal Retreat," *The Australian*, April 20, 2018.

162 Ref to Inquiry into the indicators of, and impact of, regional inequality in Australia

163 See Geoffrey West, *Scale: The Universal Laws of Life and Death in Organisms, Cities and Companies* (London, UK: Hachette, 2017). British physicist Geoffrey West writes that 'Cities are the crucible of civilisation, the hubs of innovation, the engines of wealth creation and centres of power, the magnets that attract creative individuals, and the stimulant for ideas, growth and innovation.' Building from the universal laws of physiology, West argues that cities deliver economies of scale due to network effects. The larger the city, the less infrastructure is required per capita and the higher the incomes and innovation.

164 Michael Young, "Comment: Down with Meritocracy," *The Guardian*, June 29, 2001.

165 Norton, "Was Higher Education Ever Likely to Reduce Inequality?"

166 Goodhart, *The Road to Somewhere*.

167 Over-focus on metrics is discussed by Jerry Z. Muller, *The Tyranny of Metrics* (Princeton: Princeton University Press, 2018).

168 Greg Thompson and Allen G. Harbaugh, "A Preliminary Analysis of Teacher Perceptions of the Effects of NAPLAN on Pedagogy and Curriculum," *The Australian Educational Researcher* 40, no. 3 (August 1, 2013): 299–314.

169 Australian Bureau of Statistics, "6227.0 - Education and Work, Australia, May 2017," November 6, 2017.

170 The Australian, "Top Unis Tell Students That Vocational Education Is Fine," *The Australian*, June 4, 2018.

171 Jennifer Gore et al., "Choosing VET: Investigating the VET Aspirations of School Students" (National Centre for Vocational Education Research, October 23, 2017).

172 Gore et al., 26.

173 Gore et al., 28.

174 Mission Australia, "Youth Survey Report 2015" (Sydney, Australia: Mission Australia, June 29, 2016).

175 Andrew Norton, "To Avoid Uni Drop Outs, Vocational Ed Needs a Boost," *The Sydney Morning Herald*, May 11, 2018.

176 Though less dramatic decline for traineeships, see NCVER, "Apprentices and Trainees" (National Centre for Vocational Education Research, 2016).

177 Andrew Norton, "Universities and the Evolving Graduate Labour Market" (Melbourne, VIC: Grattan Institute, February 28, 2017); Ittima Cherastidtham and Andrew Norton, "University Attrition: What Helps and What Hinders University Completion?" (Grattan Institute, April 29, 2018).

178 Richard Di Natale, "The Trickle Down Hoax & the Need for Government to Step In" (April 4, 2018).

179 See my argument, Matthew Lesh, "A Universal Basic Income Would Create a Permanent Underclass," *The Sydney Morning Herald*, April 4, 2018.

180 For divergent work patterns, see International Social Survey Programme, "ZA6770: Work Orientations IV."

181 See Brooks, *The Conservative Heart*.

182 Terry Nichols Clark and Vincent Hoffmann-martinot, eds., *The New Political Culture* (Boulder, Colo.: Routledge, 1998).

183 Russell J. Dalton, "Economics, Environmentalism and Party Alignments: A Note on Partisan Change in Advanced Industrial Democracies," *European Journal of Political Research* 48, no. 2 (March 1, 2009): 161–75; Guy Rundle, *Quarterly Essay 3, The Opportunist: John Howard and the Triumph of Reaction* (Black Inc., 2001).

184 Murray Goot and Ian Watson, "Explaining Howard's Success: Social Structure, Issue Agendas and Party Support, 1993–2004," *Australian Journal of Political Science* 42, no. 2 (June 1, 2007).

185 For this line of argument see, Rick Kuhn, "Xenophobic Racism and Class During the Howard Years," *Marxist Interventions*, no. 1 (2009): 53–82; Marian Sawer and David Laycock, "Down with Elites and Up with Inequality: Market Populism in Australia and Canada," *Commonwealth & Comparative Politics* 47, no. 2 (April 1, 2009): 133–50.

186 Jonathan Haidt, *The Righteous Mind: Why Good People Are Divided by Politics and Religion* (New York: Vintage, 2013).

187 David Goodhart discusses this well in the British context, see David Goodhart, "Last Hope for the Left," *Prospect Magazine*, March 19, 2012.

188 Jonathan Haidt, "When and Why Nationalism Beats Globalism," *The American Interest* (blog), July 10, 2016.

189 Jonathan Haidt, "Why Working class People Vote Conservative," *The Guardian*, June 5, 2012.

190 Judith Brett, *Australian Liberals and the Moral Middle Class: From Alfred Deakin to John Howard* (Cambridge University Press, 2003), 211.

Chapter 3

191 It was also subsequently revealed that Shorten promised to revoke Adani's mine licence, see Rhian Deutrom and Sarah Elks, "Shorten 'vowed to Kill Adani,'" *The Australian*, February 27, 2018; John Ferguson and Simon Benson, "Labor in Fast Retreat over Adani," *The Australian*, February 2, 2018.

192 For further discussion of Labor's declining support in Batman, see Jake Niall, "Labor Fiddled with Factions While the Land of Tofu Burned," *The Age*, March 10, 2018.

193 Yiani Petroulias Romios, "Opinion: Why Can't the Greens Gain Mass Appeal?," *Farrago*, March 17, 2018.

194 Annika Smethurst, "Labor Declares Batman Victory, Greens Stunned," *Herald Sun*, March 17, 2018.

195 Simon Benson and Ben Packham, "Labor Warns Shorten over Adani," *The Australian*, February 6, 2018.
196 Katharine Murphy, "Bill Shorten Says There's a 'Role for Coal' and Adani Mine Just 'Another Project,'" *The Guardian*, February 19, 2018.
197 Ronald Inglehart, "The Silent Revolution in Europe: Intergenerational Change in Post-Industrial Societies," *The American Political Science Review* 65, no. 4 (1971): 991–1017.
198 See Maslow A. H., "A Theory of Human Motivation," *Psychological Review* 50, no.4 (1943).
199 Christian Welzel, *Freedom Rising: Human Empowerment and the Quest for Emancipation* (Cambridge University Press, 2013), xxiii.
200 Ronald F. Inglehart, "Changing Values among Western Publics from 1970 to 2006," *West European Politics* 31, no. 1–2 (January 1, 2008): 130–46.
201 Developed western countries, which have had this mixture of increasing education, prosperity, liberal social movements, have experienced the greatest level of cultural attitude change and rise of post-materialism, see Inglehart.
202 Flanagan separates the trend towards concern for noneconomic issues (which is generally lacking in Australia) from the trend towards more liberal attitudes (which is generally happening in Australia), see Scott C. Flanagan, "Changing Values in Advanced Industrial Societies: Inglehart's Silent Revolution from the Perspective of Japanese Findings," *Comparative Political Studies* 14, no. 4 (January 1, 1982): 403–44.
203 There has even been a decline in post-materialism in Australia since the late 1990s, despite Australia's strong economic group in that period, see Ian McAllister, *The Australian Voter: 50 Years of Change* (University of New South Wales Press, 2011), 210.
204 Joseph Henrich, Steven J. Heine, and Ara Norenzayan, "The Weirdest People in the World?," *Behavioral and Brain Sciences* 33, no. 2–3 (June 2010): 61–83; Jonathan Schulz et al., "The Origins of WEIRD Psychology," *PsyArXiv*, June 22, 2018.
205 Raymond M. Duch and Michaell A. Taylor, "Postmaterialism and the Economic Condition," *American Journal of Political Science* 37, no. 3 (1993): 747–79; Philip Curry and Michael F. O'connell, "Post-Materialist Values and Political Preference: Some Unlikely Findings from Northern Ireland," *European Journal of Political Research* 37, no. 1 (January 1, 2000): 19–30. This has remained a contested topic, see Inglehart's response: Paul R. Abramson and Ronald Inglehart, "Education, Security, and Postmaterialism: A Comment on Duch and Taylor's 'Postmaterialism and the Economic Condition,'" *American Journal of Political Science* 38, no. 3 (1994): 797–814.
206 See, for example, Bella d'Abrera, "The Rise Of Identity Politics History In Australian Universities" (Melbourne, VIC: Institute of Public Affairs, October 17, 2017).
207 "World Values Survey."; also see, Tranter who found a lack of a link between post-materialism and age group in the Australian context, see Bruce Tranter, "The Impact of Political Context on the Measurement of Postmaterial Values," *SAGE Open* 5, no. 2 (June 19, 2015).
208 McAllister et al., "Australian Election Study."
209 See Ch 2.
210 Jonathan Hair, "Victorian Liberals May Not Run in Inner-City Seats, State Director Says," *ABC News*, November 19, 2017.
211 See Ch 6.
212 Charles Darwin, *The Voyage of the Beagle* (Murray, 1876), 444.
213 Donald Horne, *The Lucky Country: Australia in the Sixties*, 2nd ed. (Melbourne: Penguin, 1964).
214 Matthew Lesh, "A Regulatory Culture?," in *Australia's Red Tape Crisis: The Costs and*

Consequences of Over-Regulation, ed. Darcy WE Allen and Chris Berg (Australia: Connor Court, 2018); David Geoffrey Matthew Llewellyn, "Australia Felix: Jeremy Bentham and Australian Colonial Democracy" (University of Melbourne, 2016); Hugh Collins, "Political Ideology in Australia: The Distinctiveness of a Benthamite Society," *Daedalus* 114, no. 1 (January 1, 1985): 147–69.

215 David Kemp, "Liberalism, Conservatism and the Growth of Government in Australia," in *Liberalism and Conservatism,* ed. Greg Melleuish (Ballarat: Connor Court, 2015).

216 McAllister et al., "Australian Election Study."

217 McAllister et al.

218 Aaron Zitner and Gabriel Gianordoli, "Divisions Among the Republicans," *Wall Street Journal,* May 1, 2018.

219 Aaron Zitner and Gabriel Gianordoli, "Divisions Among the Democrats," *Wall Street Journal,* May 1, 2018.

220 This instinctual divides are discussed by Haidt, *The Righteous Mind.*

221 Haidt, "When and Why Nationalism Beats Globalism."

222 The level of commentary was extraordinary, see Emily Watkins, "More than 200,000 Words Published about Yassmin Abdel-Magied since Last Anzac Day," *Crikey,* April 26, 2018.

223 Nino Bucci and Anthony Colangelo, "'It Felt like a War Zone': Party-Goers at Werribee Airbnb House Pelt Police with Rocks," *The Age,* December 20, 2017.

224 Rebecca Urban, "Plea to PM: Smash the Gangs," *The Australian,* accessed April 27, 2018.

225 John Pesutto, "Weaker Laws Unleashed Gangs," *The Australian,* January 7, 2018.

226 Richard Ferguson, "'No Ethnic Gang Link to Crime,'" *The Australian,* December 27, 2017; Genevieve Alison, "Youth Crime, Gang Violence a 'failure' of Andrews: PM," *Herald Sun,* January 1, 2018.

227 Calla Wahlquist, "Is Melbourne in the Grip of African Crime Gangs? The Facts behind the Lurid Headlines," *The Guardian,* January 2, 2018, sec. Australia news.

228 Cassie Zervos, "Police Vow to Target out-of-Control African Teen 'street Gangs,'" *Herald Sun,* January 2, 2018.

229 McAllister et al., "Australian Election Study."

230 Scanlan: Concern "about becoming a victim of crime in your local area" increased by a large margin, from 26% in 2015 to 35% in 2017, see Markus, "Mapping Social Cohesion 2017: The Scanlon Foundation Surveys Report."

231 Matt Johnson, "Victorians Give Andrews a Whack," *Herald Sun,* November 20, 2016.

232 Clay Lucas, "Poll Shows African Youth Crime a Key Issue, and Andrews Better to Deal with It," *The Age,* January 7, 2018.

233 This is from the ABS Census 2016

234 Dean Jaensch, *The Hawke-Keating Hijack : The ALP in Transition* (Sydney, NSW: Allen & Unwin, 1989); John Warhurst and Andrew Parkin, eds., *The Machine: Labor Confronts the Future* (St Leonards, NSW: Allen & Unwin, 2000).

235 Barry's solution is for Australian politics to become *more* technocratic, and the establishment of a 'Courage Party' of graduates, see Barry Jones, "The need for a new political party," *The Saturday Paper,* February 11, 2017.

236 Adam Creighton, "Labor's Elitist Obsessions," *The Australian,* April 29, 2018.

237 James Madison, "The Federalist Papers No. 10," November 23, 1787, 10.

238 F. A. Hayek, *The Road to Serfdom* (Routledge, 1976), 68.

239 John O'Sullivan, "Hungary Embraces National Conservatism," *National Review,* April

9, 2018.

240 Australian Electoral Commission, "Tally Room" (Canberra, ACT: Australian Electoral Commission, 2016).

Chapter 4

241 Australian Greens, "Change the Date," Australian Greens, January 25, 2017.

242 News.com.au, "Yarra Council Cancels Australia Day out of Respect to Aboriginal Australians," August 16, 2017.

243 Paul Donoughue, "Hottest 100 Will No Longer Be Held on Australia Day," *ABC News*, November 27, 2017.

244 Chip Le Grand and Samantha Hutchinson, "Invasion Rally Exposes Left's Split," *The Australian*, January 26, 2018.

245 Yassmin Abdel-Magied, "I Tried to Fight Racism by Being a 'Model Minority' — and Then It Backfired," *Teen Vogue*, September 28, 2017.

246 Hannah McGlade, "Australia Is Still Fighting Racism and It's Time We Faced up to It," *ABC News*, November 27, 2017.

247 Stan Grant, *IQ2 Racism Debate: Stan Grant* (The Ethics Centre, 2016), "Face Up 2 Racism," accessed April 27, 2018.

248 Paul Karp, "Australia Day's Date Will Not Change While I'm Prime Minister, Turnbull Says," *The Guardian*, January 29, 2018, sec. Australia news.

249 Pauline Hanson, "Pauline Hanson's Please Explain," Facebook, January 14, 2018.

250 Simon Benson, "Two-Thirds Reject Push for Australia Day Switch: Newspoll," *The Australian*, February 6, 2018.

251 This could be considered a manifestation, at least along the Inners-Outers dividing line of the Downs median voter theory in which most voters are in the centre but there are extreme tails on either side; see Downs, "An Economic Theory of Political Action in a Democracy."

252 The Greens have proven themselves a more permanent force in Australian politics than One Nation, who could collapse rapidly like the Palmer United Party in a short time, however, the party manifestation of these values tribes is less import than the people that they represent.

253 Personal conversation.

254 Dani Rodrik, "Populism and the Economics of Globalization," *Journal of International Business Policy*, February 22, 2018, 1–22.

255 See Shadi Hamid, "The Rise of Anti-Liberalism," *The Atlantic*, February 20, 2018; Steven Levitsky and Daniel Ziblatt, *How Democracies Die* (New York: Crown, 2018); Patrick J. Deneen, *Why Liberalism Failed* (New Haven, CT: Yale University Press, 2018).

256 For this argument see Dimitris Ballas, Danny Dorling, and Benjamin Hennig, "Analysing the Regional Geography of Poverty, Austerity and Inequality in Europe: A Human Cartographic Perspective," *Regional Studies* 51, no. 1 (January 2, 2017): 174–85; Tim Vlandas and Daphne Halikiopoulou, "Does Unemployment Matter? Economic Insecurity, Labour Market Policies and the Far Right Vote in Europe," *European Political Science*, January 8, 2018; Simon Bornschier, *Cleavage Politics and the Populist Right: The New Cultural Conflict in Western Europe* (Temple University Press, 2010); Rodrik, "Populism and the Economics of Globalization."

257 Di Natale, "The Trickle Down Hoax & the Need for Government to Step In."

258 For further discussion of the political left and analysis of populism, see Paris Aslanidis, "Avoiding Bias in the Study of Populism," *Chinese Political Science Review* 2, no. 3 (September 1, 2017): 266–87.

259 Goodhart, *The Road to Somewhere*, 52.

260 Ronald Inglehart and Pippa Norris, "Trump, Brexit, and the Rise of Populism: Economic Have-Nots and Cultural Backlash," SSRN Scholarly Paper (Rochester, NY: Social Science Research Network, July 29, 2016).

261 Pippa Norris, "Authoritarian Populist Vote and GINI," Tweet, @PippaN15, April 25, 2018.

262 Diana C. Mutz, "Status Threat, Not Economic Hardship, Explains the 2016 Presidential Vote," *Proceedings of the National Academy of Sciences of the United States of America* 115, no. 19 (May 8, 2018): E4330–39.

263 Nicholas Carnes and Noam Lupu, "It's Time to Bust the Myth: Most Trump Voters Were Not Working Class.," *Washington Post*, June 5, 2017, sec. Monkey Cage   Analysis Analysis Interpretation of the news based on evidence, including data, as well as anticipating how events might unfold based on past events.

264 Eric Kaufmann, "Trump and Brexit: Why It's Again NOT the Economy, Stupid," *British Politics and Policy at LSE* (blog), November 9, 2016; Matt Singh, "Two Years On, Many Still Don't Understand Why the UK Voted for Brexit," *CapX*, June 21, 2018.

265 Wood and Daley, "A Crisis of Trust: The Rise of Protest Politics in Australia."

266 Each one of these parties has different background and policy set, however, they all attract a similar disaffected electoral base.

267 One Nation faces substantial internal political turmoil like many minor populist parties in Australia. This was highlighted by the registration of Senator Brian Burston in 2018. Even if One Nation itself fails to sustain itself in Australian politics, the underlying values group that One Nation represents is unlikely to disappear, leaving open the likelihood of other political leaders and parties seeking to appeal to disaffected Outers. For polling results, see The Australian, "Newspoll," n.d., https://www.theaustralian. com.au/national-affairs/newspoll.

268 In the American context, Chua argues, 'being antiestablishment is *not* the same as being antirich.' 'What these elites don't see is that Trump, in terms of taste, sensibilities, and values, actually *is* similar to the white working class.' See Amy Chua, *Political Tribes: Group Instinct and the Fate of Nations* (New York: Penguin Press, 2018).

269 McAllister et al., "Australian Election Study."

270 Dalibor Rohac, Sahana Kumar, and Andreas Johansson Heinö, "The Wisdom of Demagogues: Institutions, Corruption and Support for Authoritarian Populists," *Economic Affairs* 37, no. 3 (October 1, 2017): 382–96.

271 McAllister et al., "Australian Election Study."

272 Markus, "Mapping Social Cohesion 2017: The Scanlon Foundation Surveys Report."

273 David Marr, *The White Queen: One Nation and the Politics of Race* (Quarterly Essay, 2017).

274 The lack of relationship with income has been established both in relation to One Nation voters in the late 1990s, and in 2016, see Frank Mols and Jolanda Jetten, "One Nation's Support: Why 'Income' Is a Poor Predictor," *Australasian Parliamentary Review* 32, no. 1 (Autumn/Winter 2017): 92; Murray Goot and Ian Watson, "One Nation's Electoral Support: Where Does It Come From, What Makes It Different and How Does It Fit?," *Australian Journal of Politics & History* 47, no. 2 (June 1, 2001): 159–91.

275 Markus, "Mapping Social Cohesion 2017: The Scanlon Foundation Surveys Report."

276 See, for example, Andrew Blyberg, "Old Parties Fail to Protect Australian Athletes: Greens," Australian Greens, July 23, 2013.

277 Kemp, *Society and Electoral Behaviour in Australia*, 16.

278 Kemp, 338.

279 Kemp, 338.

280 A number of former Australia Party member subsequently entered parliament as Democrats.

281 See Gary N. Marks and Clive S. Bean, "Sources of Electoral Support for Minor Parties: The Case of the Australian Democrats," *Electoral Studies* 11, no. 4 (December 1, 1992): 311–33; Ian McAllister, "The Australian Democrats: Protest Vote or Portent of Realignment?," *Politics* 17, no. 1 (May 1, 1982): 68–73.

282 Robert Simms, "The Australian Greens and the Moral Middle Class" (APSA Conference 2013, Perth, WA: Australian Political Studies Association, 2013).

283 "World Values Survey"; McAllister et al., "Australian Election Study." Before the Greens, the Australian Democrats attracted the post-materialist vote, see Mark Western and Bruce Tranter, "Postmaterialist and Economic Voting in Australia, 1990-98," *Australian Journal of Political Science* 36, no. 3 (November 1, 2001): 439–58.

284 International Social Survey Programme, "ZA5900: Family and Changing Gender Roles IV," 2012.

285 Anika Gauja and Stewart Jackson, "Australian Greens Party Members and Supporters: Their Profiles and Activities," *Environmental Politics* 25, no. 2 (March 3, 2016): 359–79.

286 McAllister et al., "Australian Election Study."

287 Nick Fredman, "Watermelons or Tomatoes? Social Democracy, Class and the Australian Greens," *Capitalism Nature Socialism* 24, no. 4 (December 1, 2013): 86–104.

288 See, for example, Freddy Gray, "Corbyn Copy: Why Jeremy and Trump Are (Almost) the Same," *The Spectator*, June 17, 2017.

289 Holly Hammond, "Power to the People," *Greens Magazine*, February 23, 2014.

290 Richard Di Natale, "2016 Federal Policy Initiatives: National Anti-Corruption Commission" (The Greens, 2016).

291 "Australian Greens," Australian Greens, accessed April 9, 2018.

292 "World Values Survey."

293 International Social Survey Programme, "ZA5900: Family and Changing Gender Roles IV."

294 International Social Survey Programme, "ZA6670: Citizenship II."

295 International Social Survey Programme, "ZA6770: Work Orientations IV."

296 International Social Survey Programme.

297 International Social Survey Programme, "ZA4700: Role of Government IV," 2015.

298 Sheppard, "ANUPoll: Attitudes to National Security."

299 Economou, "From the Inner Cities to the Outer Suburbs."

300 Australian Greens, "Reject Trump," Australian Greens, December 21, 2016.

301 Australian Greens.

302 Karen Stenner, *The Authoritarian Dynamic* (New York: Cambridge University Press, 2005).

303 Mark Lilla, "Opinion | The End of Identity Liberalism," *The New York Times*, November 18, 2016.

304 On the relationship between education and self-partisanship, see Jacoby, "The Sources of Liberal-Conservative Thinking."

305 Marr, *The White Queen: One Nation and the Politics of Race.*

306 Anna Broinowski, *Please Explain: The Rise, Fall and Rise Again of Pauline Hanson* (Penguin Books Limited, 2017), 302.

307 Goodhart, *The Road to Somewhere*, 49.

308 Margo Kingston, *Off the Rails: The Pauline Hanson Trip* (Allen & Unwin, 2001).

309 Stenner, *The Authoritarian Dynamic*, 330.

Chapter 5

310 Robert Hawke, "Address by the Prime Minister" (April 11, 1983).

311 Australian Government, *Proceedings: National Economic Summit Conference April 1983, Canberra* (Canberra, ACT: Australian Government Publishing Service, 1983).

312 Paul Kelly, *The End of Certainty: Power, Politics & Business in Australia* (St. Leonards, NSW: Allen & Unwin, 1994), 64.

313 Kelly, 271.

314 Kemp notes that the summit 'reasserted traditional and widely shared Australian beliefs about the beneficial effects which may be achieved by central authority on the working of the economic system,' and committed to 'rejection of (class) conflict,' see Kemp D. A., "The National Economic Summit: Authority, Persuasion and Exchange*," *Economic Record* 59, no. 3 (October 22, 2007): 209–19.

315 Frank Bongiorno, *The Eighties: The Decade That Transformed Australia* (Black Inc., 2015), 23.

316 For discussion of the history and nature of corporatism see F. H. Gruen, "Australia's Long-Term Economic Strategy," *Economic Papers: A Journal of Applied Economics and Policy* 3, no. 2 (June 1, 1984): 40–50; Howard J. Wiarda, *Corporatism and Comparative Politics: The Other Great "Ism"* (Routledge, 2016).

317 Quoted in Ann Capling and Brian Galligan, *Beyond the Protective State* (CUP Archive, 1992), 50.

318 J. O. Stone, *1929 and All That* (Perth, WA: University of Western Australia Department of Economics, 1984).

319 Paul Strangio and Brian J. Costar, *The Victorian Premiers, 1856-2006* (Federation Press, 2006), 367.

320 Thomas Piketty, "Brahmin Left vs Merchant Right: Rising Inequality & the Changing Structure of Political Conflict" (World Inequality Lab, March 2018).

321 This was, albeit, the high water mark of the *Fightback!* election campaign, see McAllister et al., "Australian Election Study."

322 Arguably certain policies, like the Howard era family tax benefits, the aged pension, and regional spending, are targeted pay-offs to Outers' interests in policymaking.

323 McAllister et al., "Australian Election Study."

324 Otto Kirchheimer, "The Transformation of the Western European Party Systems," in *Political Parties and Political Development* (Princeton University Press, 1966), 177–200.

325 Mair, "The Challenge to Party Government."

326 For discussion of the increasing importance of political leadership, see, for example, Glenn Kefford, *All Hail the Leaders: The Australian Labor Party and Political Leadership*, 2015; Kelly, *Triumph and Demise.*

327 Kirchheimer, "The Transformation of the Western European Party Systems," 193.

328   Katz and Mair descrive this as the 'cartel party,' which comes after the catch-all party, see Richard S. Katz and Peter Mair, "Changing Models of Party Organization and Party Democracy: The Emergence of the Cartel Party," *Party Politics* 1, no. 1 (January 1, 1995): 5–28.

329   André Krouwel, "Otto Kirchheimer and the Catch-All Party," *West European Politics* 26, no. 2 (April 1, 2003): 23–40.

330   See Paul Pierson, ed., *The New Politics Of The Welfare State* (Oxford England ; New York: Oxford University Press, U.S.A., 2001); Volker Schneider, Simon Fink, and Marc Tenbücken, "Buying Out the State: A Comparative Perspective on the Privatization of Infrastructures," *Comparative Political Studies* 38, no. 6 (August 1, 2005): 704–27; Alain Noel and Jean-Philippe Therien, "From Domestic to International Justice: The Welfare State and Foreign Aid," *International Organization* 49, no. 3 (1995): 523–53.

331   Louis M. Imbeau, François Pétry, and Moktar Lamari, "Left–right Party Ideology and Government Policies: A Meta–analysis," *European Journal of Political Research* 40, no. 1 (August 1, 2001): 1–29.

332   Russell J. Dalton, *Democratic Challenges, Democratic Choices: The Erosion of Political Support in Advanced Industrial Democracies*, Comparative Politics (London: Oxford University Press, 2004).

333   See Anika Gauja, Narelle Miragliotta, and Smith Smith, eds., *Contemporary Australian Political Party Organisation* (Clayton, Vic: Monash University Publishing, 2015); Rune Karlsen and Jo Saglie, "Party Bureaucrats, Independent Professionals, or Politicians? A Study of Party Employees," *West European Politics* 40, no. 6 (November 2, 2017): 1331–51; Warhurst and Parkin, *The Machine*.

334   The precise figure is contested, however, it is clear that party membership was more common in the mid-20th century, see I. Marsh, "Australia's Political Institutions and the Corruption of Public Opinion," *The Australian Journal of Public Administration* 66, no. 3 (September 2007): 333.

335   The precise number of party members is difficult to ascertain, these numbers are based on published figures, see Troy Bramston, "Labor Officially Going Backwards," April 16, 2018; Jane Norman, "Liberals Deny Tony Abbott's Claim Party Is 'Haemorrhaging Members,'" *ABC News*, July 3, 2017.

336   Rodney Smith, "Disciplined Parties and Australian Parliamentary Politics," in *Contemporary Australian Political Party Organisation*, ed. Anika Gauja, Narelle Miragliotta, and Smith Smith (Clayton, Vic: Monash University Publishing, 2015).

337   Haydon Manning, "Hunting the Swing Voter," in *Contemporary Australian Political Party Organisation*, ed. Anika Gauja, Narelle Miragliotta, and Smith Smith (Clayton, Vic: Monash University Publishing, 2015).

338   Kemp, "Liberalism, Conservatism and the Growth of Government in Australia," 61.

339   For quote, see Kelly, *The End of Certainty*, 1. The system was maintained post-World War II by the Menzies and Fraser governments, who were, arguably, establishment figures in Australian society; nevertheless, the system they maintained was *for* Outer sensibilities as it minimised change and dynamism that is sought by Inners. The Liberal Party did not transform in disposition towards the Australian Settlement until the economically liberal leadership of John Hewson and John Howard.

340   For discussion of how tariffs benefits are condense, and costs disperse, see J. J. Pincus,

"Pressure Groups and the Pattern of Tariffs," *Journal of Political Economy* 83, no. 4 (1975): 757–78.

341 Judith Brett, *The Enigmatic Mr Deakin* (Text Publishing, 2017), 265.

342 Jim Macken and James Joseph Macken, *Australia's Unions: A Death Or a Difficult Birth?* (Federation Press, 1997), 72.

343 W. K. Hancock, *Australia* (London: Ernest Benn, 1930), 72.

344 Francis G Castles, "The Wage Earners' Welfare State Revisited: Refurbishing the Established Model of Australian Social Protection, 1983–93," *Australian Journal of Social Issues* 29, no. 2 (May 1, 1994): 120–45.

345 Frank R. Baumgartner and Bryan D. Jones, *Agendas and Instability in American Politics*, vol. American politics and political economy series (Chicago: University of Chicago Press, 1993); Paul J. DiMaggio and Walter W. Powell, "The Iron Cage Revisited: Institutional Isomorphism and Collective Rationality in Organizational Fields," *American Sociological Review* 48, no. 2 (1983): 147–60.

346 This was the argument made in Wolfgang Kasper et al., *Australia at the Crossroads: Our Choices to the Year 2000* (Sydney, NSW: Harcourt Bruce Jovanovich Group, 1980).

347 See Milton Friedman and Rose Friedman, *Free to Choose: A Personal Statement* (New York, N.Y: Harcourt Bruce Jovanovich, 1980); Andrew Adonis and Tim Hames, eds., *A Conservative Revolution?: The Thatcher-Reagan Decade in Perspective* (Manchester, UK: Manchester University Press, 1994).

348 For further discussion of the rise of the regulatory state see chapter, Ch 7.

349 ALP, "National Platform" (Australian Labor Party, July 2015).

350 Kelly, *The End of Certainty*, 2.

351 Peter Beilharz, *Transforming Labor: Labour Tradition and the Labor Decade in Australia* (Cambridge, UK: Cambridge Univ Press, 1994).

352 For further discussion see Beilharz, 150; Capling and Galligan, *Beyond the Protective State*, 42.

353 Quoted in Beilharz, *Transforming Labor*, 151.

354 John Ahlquist, "Policy by Contract: Social Pacts in Australia and New Zealand," in *Midwest Political Science Association Meeting* (Chicago, 2008).

355 Australian Government, *Proceedings*.

356 For discussion of the trade-offs and negotiations process, see Government of Australia, "Cabinet Submission 168 - Transition to Centralised Wage Fixation - Decisions 580/ EP and 629" (National Archives of Australia, May 1983), 629.

357 This point is made by Peter Hartcher, *The Sweet Spot: How Australia Made Its Own Luck - And Could Now Throw It All Away* (Black Inc., 2014).

358 Gall Gregor, Richard Hurd, and Adrian Wilkinson, *The International Handbook of Labour Unions: Responses to Neo-Liberalism* (Cheltenham, UK: Edward Elgar, 2012).

359 See Liz Ross, Tom O'Lincoln, and Graham Willett, "Labor's Accord: Why It's a Fraud" (Melbourne, VIC: Socialist Action, 1986); Rick Kuhn, "The Limits of Social Democratic Economic Policy in Australia," *Capital & Class* 17, no. 3 (October 1, 1993): 17–52; Herb Thompson, "Australia Reconstructed: Socialism Deconstructed," *Journal of Australian Political Economy, The*, no. 23 (August 1988): 87; Terry Flew, "The Limits to Political Unionism," *Journal of Australian Political Economy, The*, no. 24 (March 1989): 77.

360 Tom Bramble, "Our Unions in Crisis: How Did It Come to This?," *Marxist Left Review* Summer 2018, no. 15 (2018).

361 For discussion of the accords process and impact on unions, including union consolidation, see John Buchanan, Damian Oliver, and Chris Briggs, "Solidarity Reconstructed: The Impact of the Accord on Relations within the Australian Union Movement," *Journal of Industrial Relations* 56, no. 2 (April 1, 2014): 288–307; Peter Ewer, ed., *Politics and the Accord* (Leichhardt, NSW: Pluto Press, 1991); Geoff Dow and George Lafferty, "Decades of Disillusion: Reappraising the ALP-ACTU Accord 1983-1996," *Australian Journal of Politics And History* 53, no. 4 (January 1, 2007): 552–68.

362 Anne Trebilcock, "Australia," in *Towards Social Dialogue: Tripartite Cooperation in National Economic and Social Policy Making* (International Labour Organization, 1994).

363 See Dow Geoff and Lafferty George, "Decades of Disillusion: Reappraising the ALP/ ACTU Accord 1983–1996," *Australian Journal of Politics & History* 53, no. 4 (November 21, 2007); Doug McEachern, *Business Mates: The Power and Politics of the Hawke Era* (New York: Prentice Hall, 1991).

364 See Stephen Bell, "Australian Business Associations: New Opportunities and Challenges," *Australian Journal of Management* 19, no. 2 (December 1, 1994): 147.

365 Many cases of unions acting in their own benefit, and against those of their members, were discussed in the Royal Commission, see Royal Commission into Trade Union Governance and Corruption, "Final Report" (Canberra, ACT: Commonwealth of Australia, December 28, 2015).

366 Ben Schneiders, Royce Millar, and Nick Toscano, "Coles Admits Much of Its Workforce Underpaid after SDA Deals," *The Sydney Morning Herald*, June 9, 2017.

367 Ben Schneiders, Nick Toscano, and Royce Millar, "Sold out: Quarter of a Million Workers Underpaid in Union Deals," *The Sydney Morning Herald*, August 30, 2016.

368 Castles claims the model did not disappear till the Howard era, however, considering the wage freeze and growing public spending of the Hawke-Keating era, the origins were earlier, see Francis G. Castles, "A Farewell to Australia's Welfare State," *International Journal of Health Services* 31, no. 3 (July 1, 2001): 537–44.

369 Also see Peter Saunders, "Selectivity and Targeting in Income Support: The Australian Experience," *Journal of Social Policy* 20, no. 3 (July 1991): 299–326; Alan Fenna and Alan Tapper, "The Australian Welfare State and the Neoliberalism Thesis," *Australian Journal of Political Science* 47, no. 2 (June 1, 2012): 155–72, https://doi.org/10.1080/10 361146.2012.677007; Christopher Deeming, "Social Democracy and Social Policy in Neoliberal Times," *Journal of Sociology* 50, no. 4 (2014): 577–600.

370 Mendes Philip, "Retrenching or Renovating the Australian Welfare State: The Paradox of the Howard Government's Neo-liberalism," *International Journal of Social Welfare* 18, no. 1 (December 5, 2008): 102–10; Andrew Norton, "The Rise of Big Government Conservatism: The Centre-Right's Policy Agenda Killed Hopes of Smaller Government," *Policy: A Journal of Public Policy and Ideas* 22, no. 4 (Summer 2006): 15.

371 Fenna and Tapper, "The Australian Welfare State and the Neoliberalism Thesis."

372 E.A.D.W., "How Australia Broke the Record for Economic Growth," *The Economist*, September 5, 2017.

373 Australian Bureau of Statistics, "5204.0 - Australian System of National Accounts, 2016-17," October 27, 2017, 2016-17.

374 Daniel Wild, "How Regulation And Red Tape Makes Families Poorer" (Melbourne, VIC: Institute of Public Affairs, March 12, 2018).

375 Kemp, "Liberalism, Conservatism and the Growth of Government in Australia," 91.

376 Jonathan Kelley and Joanna Sikora, "Australian Public Opinion on Privatisation, 1986-2002," *Growth*, no. 50 (December 2002): 54; John Braithwaite, "Economic Policy: What the Electorate Thinks," in *Australian Attitudes: Social and Political Analyses from the National Social Science Survey*, ed. Clive Bean and Jonathan Kelley (Sydney: Allen & Unwin, 1988), 26–35.

377 Alex Oliver), "The Lowy Institute Poll 2017" (Sydney, NSW: Lowy Institute, June 21, 2017).

378 Marsh, "Australia's Political Institutions and the Corruption of Public Opinion"; Clint Jasper, Arlie Felton-Taylor, and Anna Vidot, "Vote Compass: Australians Want Closer Eye on Farm Sales to Foreigners," Text, ABC News, May 25, 2016.

379 Bryan Caplan, *The Myth of the Rational Voter: Why Democracies Choose Bad Policies* (Princeton, NJ: Princeton University Press, 2008).

380 Caplan, 32.

381 Melinda Cilento, "Community Pulse 2018: The Economic Disconnect" (Melbourne, VIC: Committee for Economic Development of Australia, June 2018).

382 Hugh Mackay, *Reinventing Australia the Mind and Mood of Australia in the 90s*, Updated ed (Pymble, NSW, Australia Angus & Robertson, 1993), 18.

383 Mackay, 19.

384 Kelly, *The End of Certainty*, vii.

385 Historian Frank Bongiorno describe the recession and coming of Keating the end of the 1980s optimism, see Bongiorno, *The Eighties*.

386 Tom Bramble and Rick Kuhn, "Continuity or Discontinuity in the Recent History of the Australian Labor Party?," *Australian Journal of Political Science* 44, no. 2 (June 1, 2009): 281–94.

387 Terry Nichols Clark, "The Breakdown of Class Politics," *The American Sociologist* 34, no. 1–2 (March 1, 2003): 17–32.

388 L. F. Crisp and Barbara Atkinson, *Australian Labor Party : Federal Personnel 1901-1975* (Canberra, ACT: Dept. of Political Science, Australian National University, 1975), 57.

389 Arthur Augustus Calwell, *Be Just and Fear Not* (Lloyd O'Neil, 1972), 263.

390 Michael Thompson, *Labor Without Class: The Gentrification of the ALP* (Annandale, N.S.W: Pluto Pr Australia, 2001).

391 Mark Latham, *The Latham Diaries* (Melbourne Univ. Publishing, 2005).

392 For the original video of this comment, see *Paul Keating 'This Is the Recession That Australia Had to Have,"* accessed April 18, 2018.

393 Australian Treasury, "Appendix D: Historical Australian Government Data" (Canberra, ACT: Commonwealth of Australia, 2015).

394 Keating, for instance, merged Qantas with Australia Airlines against the advice of Treasury in order to maximise the potential revenue from privitisation, see Australian Government, "Submission - Sales of Qantas and Australian Airlines - Decision 456," June 1, 1992, National Archives of Australia. For general discussion of privatisation motivations in Australia, see Chris Aulich and Janine L. O'Flynn, "From Public to Private: The Australian Experience of Privatisation," SSRN Scholarly Paper (Rochester, NY: Social Science Research Network, September 14, 2011); Ali Farazmand, *Privatization Or Public Enterprise Reform?: International Case Studies with Implications for Public Management* (Greenwood Publishing Group, 2001); Shawn Sherlock, "The Privatisation Debate

and Labor Tradition," *Labour & Community - Sixth National Conference of the Australian Society for the Study of Labour History*, October 3, 1999.

395 Brett, *Australian Liberals and the Moral Middle Class*, 183.

396 Kelly, *The End of Certainty*, xx.

397 Department of the Prime Minister and Cabinet, "Closing the Gap: Prime Minister's Report 2018" (Canberra, ACT: Commonwealth of Australia, 2018).

398 Geoffrey Blainey, "Drawing up a Balance Sheet of Our History," *Quadrant* 37, no. 7–8 (August 1993): 10.

399 Pamela Williams, *The Victory: The Inside Story of the Takeover of Australia* (St. Leonards, NSW: Allen & Unwin, 1997).

400 John Howard, "Election Speeches · John Howard, 1996" (February 18, 1996).

401 Robert Manne, *The Howard Years* (Melbourne, VIC: Black Inc., 2009), 82.

402 This story is told in Latham, *The Latham Diaries*, 52.

403 Brett, *Australian Liberals and the Moral Middle Class*, 185.

404 John Howard, "Address by the Prime Minister" (January 24, 1997).

405 Independent Economics, "The Economic Impact of Migration" (Canberra, ACT: Migration Council Australia, June 2016).

406 Public attitudes to immigration have most strongly been linked to 'sociotropic concerns about its cultural impacts—and to a lesser extent its economic impacts—on the nation,' see Hainmueller and Hopkins, "Public Attitudes Toward Immigration."

407 Putnam Robert D., "E Pluribus Unum: Diversity and Community in the Twenty-first Century The 2006 Johan Skytte Prize Lecture," *Scandinavian Political Studies* 30, no. 2 (June 15, 2007): 137–74.

408 See Geoffrey Blainey, *All for Australia* (Methuen Haynes, 1984).

409 Kelly, *The End of Certainty*, 424.

410 Greg Sheridan, "Howard's Big Regret," *The Weekend Australian*, January 8, 1995.

411 John Howard, "Election Speeches · John Howard, 2001" (October 28, 2001).

412 John Howard, "Australia and Asia: An Enduring Engagement," (May 8, 1997).

413 Betts, "Cosmopolitans and Patriots."

414 Betts.

415 Betts.

416 For a discussion of Howard's style and success, see Howard, *Lazarus Rising: A Personal and Political Autobiography* (Pymble, N.S.W: Harper, 2010).

417 SMH, "Rudd Denies He Is 'John Howard Lite,'" *The Sydney Morning Herald*, August 3, 2007.

418 Australian Labor Party, "Kevin Rudd: Economic Conservative," YouTube, July 26, 2007.

419 Rudd used the GFC to justify the new economic direction, see Kevin Rudd, "The Global Financial Crisis," *The Monthly*, February 1, 2009.

420 This took the form of the 2010 debate contesting a 'big Australia,' as discussed by Rudd, versus a 'sustainable Australia' as discussed by his successor, Julia Gillard, for discussion see Bonny Symons-Brown, "Gillard Rejects Rudd's 'Big Australia,'" *The Sydney Morning Herald*, June 27, 2010; Peter Van Onselen, "Populist Pitch on Population," *The Australian*, July 25, 2010; Fran Kelly, "Bring on the Population Debate," *ABC News*, April 8, 2010.

421 For the best exploration of this period see Kelly, *Triumph and Demise*.

422 Sid Maher, "PM Makes Stand as a Social Conservative," *The Australian*, March 20, 2011.

423 SBS, "Gillard to Spend a Week in Western Sydney," *SBS News*, accessed April 16, 2018.

424 Kelly, *Triumph and Demise.*

425 Niki Savva, *The Road to Ruin: How Tony Abbott and Peta Credlin Destroyed Their Own Government* (Melbourne, Vic: Scribe Publications, 2016); Wayne Errington and Peter Van Onselen, *Battleground: Why the Liberal Party Shirtfronted Tony Abbott* (Carlton, VIC: Melbourne University Publishing, 2015).

Chapter 6

426 Western Sydney University, "Australian Cultural Fields," accessed April 12, 2018.

427 Pierre Bourdieu, *Distinction: A Social Critique of the Judgement of Taste* (Routledge, 2013).

428 A similar argument about tastes creating a class system is made by Paul Fussell, *Class: A Guide Through the American Status System*, Reissue edition (New York: Touchstone, 1992).

429 Ting et al., "Good Taste, Bad Taste? What Your Habits Reveal about Social Class."

430 Brett, *Australian Liberals and the Moral Middle Class*, 145.

431 Vera Hoorens, "Self-Enhancement and Superiority Biases in Social Comparison," *European Review of Social Psychology* 4, no. 1 (January 1, 1993): 113–39; Bram P. Buunk and Nico W. Van Yperen, "Referential Comparisons, Relational Comparisons, and Exchange Orientation: Their Relation to Marital Satisfaction," *Personality and Social Psychology Bulletin* 17, no. 6 (December 1, 1991): 709–17.

432 Cross K. Patricia, "Not Can, but Will College Teaching Be Improved?," *New Directions for Higher Education* 1977, no. 17 (August 18, 2006): 1–15.

433 See Figure 8.

434 The tendency to compare oneself in comparison to known reference groups is example of 'availability heuristic', see Alain de Botton, *Status Anxiety* (Penguin UK, 2005); Leon Festinger, "A Theory of Social Comparison Processes," *Human Relations* 7, no. 2 (May 1, 1954): 117–40; Jonathan Kelley and M. D. R. Evans, "Societal Inequality and Individual Subjective Well-Being: Results from 68 Societies and over 200,000 Individuals, 1981–2008," *Social Science Research* 62 (February 1, 2017): 1–23.

435 The gap between graduates and non-graduates, and The New Elite's party, the Greens, and the rest is substantial, see Table 5.

436 Timna Jacks, "White Flight: Race Segregation in Melbourne State Schools," *The Age*, May 2, 2016.

437 P. J. Henry & Jaime L. Napier, "Education Is Related to Greater Ideological Prejudice," *Public Opinion Quarterly* 81, no. 4 (December 12, 2017): 930-42; Sean Stevens, "Research Summary: Education Is Related to Greater Ideological Prejudice," *Heterodox Academy*, May 5, 2018.

438 Brown, "Green Voters Snobs."

439 Noah Carl, "Who Doesn't Want to Hear the Other Side's View?," *Noah Carl* (blog), April 28, 2017.

440 See Matthew Lesh, "No Room for Differing Views," *The Australian*, May 25, 2018.

441 Mitchell Langbert, Anthony Quain, and Daniel B. Klein, "Faculty Voter Registration in Economics, History, Journalism, Law, and Psychology," *Econ Journal Watch* 13 (October 4, 2016): 422–51; Neil Gross and Solon Simmons, "The Social and Political Views of American Professors," September 24, 2007.

442 Jon Haidt, "New Study Indicates Existence of Eight Conservative Social Psychologists," *Heterodox Academy* (blog), January 7, 2016.

443 Neema Parvini, "The Incentives for Groupthink," *Quillette*, April 22, 2018.

444 Private correspondence.

445 Matthew Blackwell, "The Psychology of Progressive Hostility," *Quillette* (blog), March 10, 2018.

446 Outers do this as well, which helps explain growing polarisation, see R. Kelly Garrett, "Echo Chambers Online?: Politically Motivated Selective Exposure among Internet News Users," *Journal of Computer-Mediated Communication* 14, no. 2 (January 1, 2009): 265–85; Hywel T. P. Williams et al., "Network Analysis Reveals Open Forums and Echo Chambers in Social Media Discussions of Climate Change," *Global Environmental Change* 32 (May 1, 2015): 126–38.

447 Newman, Levy, and Nielsen, "Reuters Institute Digital News Report 2017."

448 Chua, *Political Tribes*.

449 Amy Chozick, "Hillary Clinton Calls Many Trump Backers 'Deplorables,' and G.O.P. Pounces," *The New York Times*, September 10, 2016, sec. Politics.

450 Donald J. Trump, "Wow, Hillary Clinton...," Tweet, *@realDonaldTrump* (blog), September 10, 2016.

451 Marina Fang, "Hillary Clinton: Calling Trump Supporters 'Deplorables' Handed Him 'A Political Gift,'" *Huffington Post*, September 11, 2017, sec. World.

452 Chris Berg et al., "The Case for the Repeal of Section 18C" (Melbourne, VIC: Institute of Public Affairs, December 2016).

453 Inglehart, "The Silent Revolution in Europe".

454 Angelo M. Codevilla, "America's Ruling Class — And the Perils of Revolution," *The American Spectator*, July 16, 2010.

455 Guy Rundle, "The Left Side of Politics as We Know It Is Dead," *Crikey*, November 30, 2016.

456 Nassim Nicholas Taleb, "The Most Intolerant Wins: The Dictatorship of the Small Minority," in *Skin in the Game: Hidden Asymmetries in Daily Life* (New York, NY: Random House, 2018).

457 Wood and Daley, "A Crisis of Trust: The Rise of Protest Politics in Australia."

458 Markus, "Mapping Social Cohesion 2017: The Scanlon Foundation Surveys Report."

459 Robert A. Dahl, "The Concept of Power," *Behavioral Science* 2, no. 3 (January 1, 1957): 201–15.

460 Peter Bachrach and Morton S. Baratz, "Two Faces of Power," *The American Political Science Review* 56, no. 4 (1962): 952.

461 Maxwell E. McCombs and Donald L. Shaw, "The Agenda-Setting Function of Mass Media," *Public Opinion Quarterly* 36, no. 2 (January 1, 1972): 176–87; Maxwell McCombs, *Setting the Agenda: Mass Media and Public Opinion*, 2nd Revised edition (Polity Press, 2014).

462 Alex Chan, "Guiding Public Opinion through Social Agenda-Setting: China's Media Policy since the 1990s," *Journal of Contemporary China* 16, no. 53 (November 1, 2007): 547-59.

463 This is 'bounded rationality,' see Herbert A. Simon, "Rational Decision Making in Business Organizations," *The American Economic Review* 69, no. 4 (1979): 493–513.

464 This is the classic finding by Shaw and McCombs; it is possible that, particularly in the Internet age where users can seek out their own information sources, there are many more issues considered by different people, see Donald Lewis Shaw and Maxwell E. McCombs, *The Emergence of American Political Issues: The Agenda-Setting Function of the Press* (West Pub. Co., 1977).

465 Issues come in and out of attention, see Anthony Downs, "Up and Down with Ecology-the Issue-Attention Cycle," *The Public InterestThe Public Interest*, no. 28 (Summer

1972): 38–50; Baumgartner and Jones, *Agendas and Instability in American Politics.*

466 This is shown by Maxwell McCombs and Jian-Hua Zhu, "Capacity, Diversity, and Volatility of the Public Agenda: Trends From 1954 to 1994," *The Public Opinion Quarterly* 59, no. 4 (1995): 495–525.

467 Pia Akerman, "Easy Being Green at the ABC," *The Australian*, May 20, 2013.

468 Edelman Trust, "Barometer Global Report," 17.

469 Jim Spigelman, "National Press Club Address" (December 12, 2013).

470 Michael Koziol, "ABC Must Spend 'More Time Talking to Ordinary Australians' about Hip Pocket Issues, Internal Review Finds," *The Age*, March 16, 2018.

471 Gordon Tullock, *The Politics of Bureaucracy* (Public Affairs Press, 1965); William A. Niskanen, "The Peculiar Economics of Bureaucracy," *The American Economic Review* 58, no. 2 (1968): 293–305.

472 Mark Higgie, "Eyeballing DFAT," *The Spectator Australia*, February 10, 2018.

473 There are also the few who do speak out, see Janet Albrechtsen, "In Defence of Capitalism," *The Australian*, May 18, 2018.

474 See Australian Marriage Equality, "Corporate Support," accessed April 9, 2018, http://www.australianmarriageequality.org/open-letter-of-support/.

475 Australian Bureau of Statistics, "8165.0 - Counts of Australian Businesses, Including Entries and Exits, Jun 2013 to Jun 2017" (Canberra, ACT, February 20, 2018).

476 Ross Douthat, "Opinion | The Rise of Woke Capital," *The New York Times*, February 28, 2018, sec. Opinion.

477 George Orwell, *Second Thoughts on James Burnham* (Adelaide, SA: eBooks@Adelaide, The University of Adelaide Library, 1946).

478 International Social Survey Programme, "ZA4700: Role of Government IV."

479 Adam Smith, *The Theory of Moral Sentiments and Essays on Philosophical Subjects* (Online Library of Liberty, 1869).

480 James Paterson, "Tim Flannery: Climate Prophet," Institute of Public Affairs Australia, May 15, 2013.

481 Clive Hamilton, "The Great Climate Silence: We Are on the Edge of the Abyss but We Ignore It," *Brisbane Times*, May 9, 2017.

482 Ramona Koval, "Human Rights Commission president Gillian Triggs speaks out," *The Saturday Paper*, April 23, 2016.

483 Michael Koziol, "'I Was Very Frustrated': Gillian Triggs Apologises for Calling Politicians 'Ill-Informed', 'Uneducated,'" *The Sydney Morning Herald*, December 12, 2016.

484 Tom Elliott, "We Need Real Leadership from Our Politicians," *Herald Sun*, February 6, 2015.

485 See Richard Wike et al., "Globally, Broad Support for Representative and Direct Democracy" (Washington, D.C.: Pew Research Center's Global Attitudes Project, October 16, 2017). The fondness for technocracy may help explain the lower level of support for democracy expressed by young Australians, see Oliver, "The Lowy Institute Poll 2017."

486 Ross Gittins, "Rudd's Vision for the Bureaucrats," *The Age*, May 5, 2008.

487 The Public Sector Informant, "Outside Experts Could Reduce Intrusion of Politics in Public Service Work," *Canberra Times*, August 1, 2017.

488 Plato, *Republic*, ed. C. J. Emlyn-Jones and William Preddy (Cambridge, MA: Harvard University Press, 2014); Tom Angier, "Governments Should Resist the 'technocratic Temptation' and Maintain Their Commitment to Democracy.," *EUROPP* (blog), January 3, 2013.

489 Woodrow Wilson and Ronald J. Pestritto, *Woodrow Wilson: The Essential Political Writings* (Lexington Books, 2005), 328.

490 Michael Lind, "Insider Nation V Outsider Nation", *The Smart Set*, April 29, 2016.

491 Yascha Mounk, *The People vs. Democracy: Why Our Freedom Is in Danger and How to Save It* (Cambridge, Massachusetts: Harvard University Press, 2018).

492 This has been called the rise of the 'regulatory state,' see Giandomenico Majone, "The Rise of the Regulatory State in Europe," *West European Politics* 17, no. 3 (July 1, 1994): 77–101.

493 Nassim Nicholas Taleb, "The Intellectual Yet Idiot," in *Skin in the Game: Hidden Asymmetries in Daily Life* (New York, NY: Random House, 2018).

494 This is ultimately an argument for decentralisation – the more local a politician the more they are responsive to their constituents, see Nassim Nicholas Taleb, *Skin in the Game: Hidden Asymmetries in Daily Life* (New York, NY: Random House, 2018).

495 Quoted in Paul Cartledge, *Democracy: A Life* (Oxford University Press, 2016), 308.

496 For discussion of trade-offs in tax policy, see Arthur B. Laffer et al., *An Inquiry into the Nature and Causes of the Wealth of States: How Taxes, Energy, and Worker Freedom Change Everything*, 1 edition (Wiley, 2014).

497 Harold D. Lasswell, "The Political Science of Science: An Inquiry into the Possible Reconciliation of Mastery and Freedom," *The American Political Science Review* 50, no. 4 (1956).

498 Thomas Sowell, *Intellectuals and Society: Revised and Expanded Edition* (New York, NY: Basic Books, 2012).

499 Dan M. Kahan et al., "Motivated Numeracy and Enlightened Self-Government," *Behavioural Public Policy* 1, no. 1 (May 2017): 54–86.

500 Simon, "Rational Decision Making in Business Organizations."

501 Nassim Nicholas Taleb, *The Black Swan: The Impact of the Highly Improbable* (New York: Random House, 2010).

502 F. A. Hayek, "The Use of Knowledge in Society," *The American Economic Review* 35, no. 4 (1945): 519–30.

503 This point is elegantly made by Leonard Read's class pamphlet, *I, Pencil*, see Read Leonard E., *I, Pencil* (Irvington-on-Hudson, NY: The Foundation for Economic Education, Inc., 1999).

504 Philip E. Tetlock, *Expert Political Judgment: How Good Is It? How Can We Know?* (Princeton, N.J.: Princeton University Press, 2006).

505 Policy makers often lack humility, see Sheila Jasanoff, "Technologies of Humility: Citizen Participation in Governing Science," *Minerva* 41, no. 3 (September 1, 2003): 223–44.

506 Bent Flyvbjerg, "What You Should Know About Megaprojects and Why: An Overview," *Project Management Journal* 45 (February 1, 2014).

507 Geraldine Chua, "New Royal Adelaide Hospital Named Third Most Expensive Building in the World," *Architecture And Design*, March 23, 2015; Meredith Booth, "Hospital $640m over Budget Opens," *The Australian*, September 5, 2017.

508 This is the essential insight of the public choice school, see Niskanen, "The Peculiar Economics of Bureaucracy."

509 See David Collingridge and Colin Reeve, *Science Speaks to Power: The Role of Experts in Policy Making* (Pinter, 1986).

510 Daniel P. Carpenter, "Groups, the Media, Agency Waiting Costs, and FDA Drug Approval," *American Journal of Political Science* 46, no. 3 (2002): 490–505.

511 See, for example, A. E. J. M. Cavelaars et al., "Educational Differences in Smoking: International Comparison," *BMJ* 320, no. 7242 (April 22, 2000): 1102–7.

512 Berg discusses the push by councils, non-profits, health networks, and university public

health departments pushing paternalistic policy, see Chris Berg, "Healthy Living... in a Nanny State," *ABC News*, November 3, 2010.

513 Chris Berg, *Liberty, Equality & Democracy* (Ballarat, VIC: Connor Court, 2015).

514 Olivier Allais, Patrice Bertail, and Véronique Nichèle, "The Effects of a Fat Tax on French Households' Purchases: A Nutritional Approach," *American Journal of Agricultural Economics* 92, no. 1 (January 1, 2010): 228–45.

515 Richard H. Thaler & Cass R. Sunstein, *Nudge* (New York: Penguin Group USA, 2009).

516 C. Berg and S. Davidson, "Nudging, Calculation, and Utopia," *Journal of Behavioral Economics for Policy* 1, no. Special Issue (2017): 49–52.

517 Michael David Thomas, "Reapplying Behavioral Symmetry: Public Choice and Choice Architecture," *Public Choice*, March 21, 2018, 1–15.

518 Fraser Nelson, "Michael Gove Was (Accidentally) Right about Experts," *The Spectator*, January 14, 2017.

519 Chris York, "Professor Brian Cox Says Michael Gove's 'Anti-Expert' Stance Is The 'Road Back To The Cave,'" *HuffPost UK*, July 2, 2016.

520 Patrick Minford, "The Treasury's Economic Modelling of Brexit Has Been Proven Wrong," *BrexitCentral*, November 15, 2016.

521 Fraser Nelson, "The U.K. Is Doing Just Fine, Thanks," *Wall Street Journal*, March 23, 2018, sec. Life.

522 Justin Kruger and David Dunning, "Unskilled and Unaware of It: How Difficulties in Recognizing One's Own Incompetence Lead to Inflated Self-Assessments," *Journal of Personality and Social Psychology* 77, no. 6 (December 1999): 1121–34.

Chapter 7

523 Institute of Public Affairs, *The Human Cost of Red Tape*, 2016.

524 David Goodwin, "Let Truckies Drive Own Bargain," April 14, 2016.

525 PricewaterhouseCoopers Australia, *Road Safety Remuneration System: Regulatory Impact Statement* (Canberra, ACT: Department of Education, Employment and Workplace Relations, 2011), 53.

526 Bill Shorten, "National Road Safety Tribunal to Improve Safety for Australian Road Users," Bill Shorten, accessed March 29, 2018.

527 For discussion of the public interest justification for regulation, see Arthur C. Pigou, *The Economics of Welfare* (London, UK: Macmillan and Co., 1932).

528 Rex Deighton-Smith, "Review of the Road Safety Remuneration System" (Jaguar Consulting Pty Ltd, April 16, 2014); PricewaterhouseCoopers, "Review of the Road Safety Remuneration System," January 2016.

529 James Massola, "Former TWU Official Blasts Safe Rates Created to 'Destroy' Owner-Drivers," *The Sydney Morning Herald*, April 10, 2016.

530 Anna Vidot, "Farmers, Rural Truckers Welcome Abolition of Road Safety Tribunal," *ABC Rural*, April 19, 2016.

531 Gordon Tullock, Gordon Brady, and Arthur Seldon, *Government Failure* (Washington, D.C.: Cato Institute, 2010), https://store.cato.org/book/government-failure.

532 McAllister et al., "Australian Election Study."

533 For further discussion of this metaphor, see Adam Smith and Bruce Yandle, *Bootleggers and Baptists: How Economic Forces and Moral Persuasion Interact to Shape Regulatory Politics* (Washington, D.C.: Cato Institute, 2014).

534 On the day I wrote this chapter Cirkey political editor Bernard Keane asserted that "The role of government in the economy has been curtailed" over the past 30 years,

see Bernard Keane, "Company Tax Robbery Is Everything That Is Wrong with Our Governance," *Crikey*, March 26, 2018.

535 See Bernhard Kittel and Herbert Obinger, "Political Parties, Institutions, and the Dynamics of Social Expenditure in Times of Austerity," *Journal of European Public Policy* 10, no. 1 (January 1, 2003): 20–45.

536 Paul Pierson, "The New Politics of the Welfare State," *World Politics* 48, no. 2 (1996): 158; John Hills, "Thatcherism, New Labour and the Welfare State," CASEpaper (London, UK: Centre for Analysis of Social Exclusion, London School of Economics, August 1998).

537 Office of Management and Budget, "Historical Tables," The White House, accessed April 16, 2018.

538 Norton, "The Rise of Big Government Conservatism."

539 See Schneider, Fink, and Tenbücken, "Buying Out the State"; Chris Aulich and Janine O'Flynn, "From Public to Private: The Australian Experience of Privatisation," *Asia Pacific Journal of Public Administration* 29, no. 2 (December 1, 2007): 153–71; Privatization Barometer, "Database," Privatization Barometer, 2013.

540 For this argument, see Steven Kent Vogel, *Freer Markets, More Rules: Regulatory Reform in Advanced Industrial Countries* (Cornell University Press, 1996).

541 Majone, "The Rise of the Regulatory State in Europe."

542 Michael Moran, *The British Regulatory State: High Modernism and Hyper-Innovation* (Oxford: Oxford University Press, 2007), 6.

543 James Q. Wilson argues that bureaucrats are 'turf' maximises, that is, they want the power to do the most interesting and lowest tasks, see James Q. Wilson, *Bureaucracy: What Government Agencies Do and Why They Do It* (New York: Basic Books, 2000).

544 Harold Seidman and Robert Scott Gilmour, *Politics, Position, and Power: From the Positive to the Regulatory State* (Oxford University Press, 1986), 128.

545 This was argued by Sam Peltzman, "Toward a More General Theory of Regulation," *The Journal of Law and Economics* 19, no. 2 (August 1, 1976): 211–40.

546 See discussion of this phenomena the Israeli, British and Swedish cases, Hanan Haber, "Regulating for Welfare: A Comparative Study of 'Regulatory Welfare Regimes' in the Israeli, British, and Swedish Electricity Sectors," *Law & Policy* 33, no. 1 (October 22, 2010): 116–48.

547 For further discussion on 'regulatory capture' see Gary S. Becker, "A Theory of Competition Among Pressure Groups for Political Influence," *The Quarterly Journal of Economics* 98, no. 3 (1983): 371–400; George J. Stigler, "The Theory of Economic Regulation," *The Bell Journal of Economics and Management Science* 2, no. 1 (1971): 3–21; Marver H. Bernstein, *Regulating Business by Independent Commission* (Princeton, N.J: Princeton University Press, 1955).

548 McAllister et al., "Australian Election Study 2016."

549 McAllister et al.

550 Dustin Chambers, Courtney A. Collins, and Alan Krause, "How Do Federal Regulations Affect Consumer Prices? An Analysis of the Regressive Effects of Regulation," *Public Choice*, October 9, 2017, 1–34.

551 United Voice, "United Voice Submission to Producitvity Commissions' Education and Training Workforce: Early Childhood Development" (Canberra, ACT: Productivity Commission, December 2011), 15.

552 There are a range of reasons for increased price, including various demand and supply factors, see Wild, "How Regulation And Red Tape Makes Families Poorer."

553 Gideon Rozner, "Your Licence to Work," *IPA Review*, May 2018.

554 Gideon Rozner, "Childcare Costs? Thank Unions and Government," *The Spectator Australia* (blog), March 29, 2018.

555 The Early Learning and Care Council of Australia, the association of "large providers of early learning" supports the qualification requirements, see Early Learning and Care Council of Australia Inc., "Submission DR897" (Melbourne, VIC: Productivity Commission, March 10, 2014).

556 Mark Sperling, "Submission DR170" (Melbourne, VIC: Productivity Commission, March 10, 2014).

557 David Coen and Mark Thatcher, "The New Governance of Markets and Non-Majoritarian Regulators," *Governance* 18, no. 3 (June 13, 2005): 329–46; John Braithwaite and Peter Drahos, *Global Business Regulation* (Cambridge University Press, 2000).

558 Chris Berg, *The Growth Of Australia's Regulatory State: Ideology, Accountability And The Mega-Regulators* (Melbourne, VIC: Institute of Public Affairs, 2008).

559 Berg, *Liberty, Equality & Democracy*, 90.

560 Australian Government, "List of Departments and Agencies," accessed March 29, 2018.

561 Stephen Wilks and Ian Bartle, "The Unanticipated Consequences of Creating Independent Competition Agencies," *West European Politics* 25, no. 1 (January 1, 2002): 148–72.

562 For discussion of Australia's 'gold plated' system see Phillip Lasker, "We Have a Gold-Plated Electricity Grid Consumers Can't Afford," Text, ABC News, July 18, 2017.

563 For this, and other examples of red tape pushing up energy costs, see Wild, "How Regulation And Red Tape Makes Families Poorer."

564 Malcolm Turnbull, "Environment & Energy," Prime Minister of Australia, accessed March 27, 2018.

565 For further discussion of 'path dependence' in policymaking see Paul Pierson, "Increasing Returns, Path Dependence, and the Study of Politics," *The American Political Science Review* 94, no. 2 (2000): 251–67.

566 I have argued that this helps explain Australia's regulatory culture, see Lesh, "A Regulatory Culture?"

567 Gordon Tullock, *The Rent-Seeking Society*, vol. 5, The Selected Works of Gordon Tullock (Carmel, IN: Liberty Fund Inc, 2005).

568 See, for example, James B. Bailey, Diana W. Thomas, and Joseph R. Anderson, "Regressive Effects of Regulation on Wages," *Public Choice*, February 26, 2018, 1–13.

569 Novak, "The $176 Billion Tax on Our Prosperity."

570 Kenneth A. Shepsle, "Bureaucratic Drift, Coalitional Drift, and Time Consistency: A Comment on Macey," *Journal of Law, Economics, & Organization* 8, no. 1 (1992): 111–18.

571 Mancur OLSON, *The Logic of Collective Action: Public Goods and the Theory of Groups, Second Printing with New Preface and Appendix* (Harvard University Press, 1965).

572 Stigler, "The Theory of Economic Regulation"; Peltzman, "Toward a More General Theory of Regulation."

573 For further discussion of Australia's banking regulation, see Chris Berg, "Safety and Soundness: An Economic History of Prudential Bank Regulation in Australia, 1893-2008" (RMIT University, 2016).

574 Michael Maloney and Robert McCormick, "A Positive Theory of Environmental Quality Regulation," *Journal of Law and Economics* 25, no. 1 (1982): 99–123.

575 Matthew Lesh, "The Decline of Small Business: How Red Tape Is Undermining

Opportunity, Prosperity, and Community" (Melbourne, VIC: Institute of Public Affairs, July 2018).

576 Mark J. Perry, "Fortune 500 Firms in 1955 v. 2015; Only 12% Remain, Thanks to the Creative Destruction That Fuels Economic Prosperity," American Enterprise Institute, *AEIdeas* (blog), October 12, 2015; John McDuling, "Corporate Australia's Real Problem: Ancient Companies," *The Sydney Morning Herald*, November 26, 2015.

577 Vincenzo Quadrini, "Entrepreneurship, Saving and Social Mobility," *Review of Economic Dynamics* 3, no. 1 (2000): 1–40; Jock Collins, *A Shop Full of Dreams: Ethnic Small Business in Australia* (Leichhardt, NSW: Pluto Press Australia, 1995).

578 Chad Syverson, "What Determines Productivity?," Working Paper (National Bureau of Economic Research, January 2010).

579 Joseph A Schumpeter, *Capitalism, Socialism, and Democracy* (London: Harper & Brothers, 1942).

580 See discussion in Majone Giandomenico, "From Regulatory State to a Democratic Default," *JCMS: Journal of Common Market Studies* 52, no. 6 (August 5, 2014): 1216–23.

581 See Cornelius M. Kerwin and Scott R. Furlong, *Rulemaking: How Government Agencies Write Law and Make Policy* (Washington, D.C: CQ Press, 2010).

582 For further discussion of central banking independence and democracy see Robert Elgie, "The Politics of the European Central Bank: Principal-Agent Theory and the Democratic Deficit," *Journal of European Public Policy* 9, no. 2 (January 1, 2002): 186–200.

583 Kaare Strøm, "Delegation and Accountability in Parliamentary Democracies," *European Journal of Political Research* 37, no. 3 (September 26, 2003): 267.

584 Smith, "Disciplined Parties and Australian Parliamentary Politics."

585 For example, since 1990, just 28 pieces of legislation have attracted more than 20 hours of debate in the Senate, and less than 40 per cent of time is spent debating legislation, most legislation is 'non-controversial' and attracts minimal debate, see Parliament of Australia, "Senate StatsNet."

586 See, for example, Joshua B. Kennedy, "'Do This! Do That!' And Nothing Will Happen': Executive Orders and Bureaucratic Responsiveness," *American Politics Research* 43, no. 1 (January 1, 2015): 59–82.

587 This is the classic principal-agent problem. Many ministers have said that *Yes Minister* is less fiction and more documentary of the reality of being a minister.

588 Michael Lipsky, *Street-Level Bureaucracy: The Dilemmas of the Individual in Public Service* (Russell Sage Foundation, 1983); Edward C. Page, "The Civil Servant as Legislator: Law Making in British Administration," *Public Administration* 81, no. 4 (December 1, 2003): 651–79; Bernardo Zacka, *When the State Meets the Street: Public Service and Moral Agency* (Harvard University Press, 2017).

589 Giandomenico Majone, ed., *Regulating Europe* (London: Routledge, 1996), 284.

590 James Madison, "The Federalist Papers No. 10," 10.

591 See Mark Thatcher and Alec Stone Sweet, "Theory and Practice of Delegation to Non-Majoritarian Institutions," *West European Politics* 25, no. 1 (January 1, 2002): 1–22.

592 George W. Hilton, "The Basic Behavior of Regulatory Commissions," *The American Economic Review* 62, no. 1/2 (1972): 47–54.

593 Christopher Adolph, *Bankers, Bureaucrats, and Central Bank Politics: The Myth of Neutrality* (Cambridge University Press, 2013).

594 Berg, *The Growth Of Australia's Regulatory State*, 3.

595 Matt Chambers, "Tighten Power Rules: ACCC," *The Australian*, September 20, 2017.

596 Tim Soutphommasane, "Speeches," accessed March 29, 2018.

597 Majone makes this point about who makes up the agencies, see Majone, *Regulating Europe*, 22.

598 Michael Roddan, "Disclose Climate Risks, Firms Told," June 18, 2018.

599 Braithwaite and Drahos, *Global Business Regulation*, 3–4.

600 John O. McGinnis and Ilya Somin, "Should International Law Be Part of Our Law?," *Stanford Law Review* 59, no. 5 (September 11, 2006): 1175–1247.

601 Posner links this point to the populist backlash, see Eric A. Posner, "Liberal Internationalism and the Populist Backlash," SSRN Scholarly Paper (Rochester, NY: Social Science Research Network, January 11, 2017).

Chapter 8

602 Posner links this point to the populist backlash, see Posner.

603 "The Anti-Dray and Land-Tax League," *South Australian Register*, June 28, 1850, 3.

604 "The South Australian Anti-Dray and Land Tax League," *South Australian Register*, May 17, 1850.

605 "The Anti-Dray and Land-Tax League," *South Australian Register*, September 28, 1850.

606 Jim Moss, *Sound of Trumpets: History of the Labour Movement in South Australia* (Wakefield Press, 1985), 65.

607 "A constitution," *Adelaide Observer*, June 29, 1850, 1.

608 For a broad discussion of the rise of authoritarian populism, see Dalibor Rohac, Liz Kennedy, and Vikram Singh, "Drivers of Authoritarian Populism in the United States" (Washington, D.C.: Center for American Progress & American Enterprise Institute, May 2018).

609 Authoritarian populists tend to claim that certain groups, such as immigrants, Muslims, and blacks, are being championed by an elite against the people's will, see John B. Judis, "Us v Them: The Birth of Populism | John B Judis | The Long Read," *The Guardian*, October 13, 2016.

610 For discussion on how One Nation voters are fuelled by Greens style completionism, see Ch 4.

611 Haidt, "When and Why Nationalism Beats Globalism."

612 Bagehot, "Some Thoughts on the Crisis of Liberalism—and How to Fix It," *The Economist*, June 12, 2018.

613 Note: Liberal Populism is different to authoritarian populism in three core elements. Firstly, Liberal Populism is built on pluralist individualist foundations and the idea that *all* voices are worthy, not an in-group and out-group rivalry that diminishes minority voices. Secondly, Liberal Populism is sceptical of leaders who claim represent 'the people', and believes the most effective way to ensure people are represented is through decentralisation to more accountable local jurisdictions. Finally, Liberal Populism understands the social world is complex and cannot be fixed with simplistic policy solutions. The similarity between liberal and authoritarian populism is the joint realisation that people are frustrated with the operation of the political system, and change is necessary to better represent the unheard voices in our national debate.

614 This issue is apparent in the field of education, in which the traditional social mores of Outers are being replaced by the social mores of Inners in sexual education as in the

case of the controversial 'Safe Schools' program.

615   This is the basic individualist notion, for discussion, see Berg, *Liberty, Equality & Democracy*; Stephen Macedo, *Liberal Virtues: Citizenship, Virtue, and Community in Liberal Constitutionalism* (Clarendon Press, 1990).

616   Populism often becomes illiberal because 'the people' are defined in a narrow sense.

617   Pauline Maier, *American Scripture: Making the Declaration of Independence*, 1st ed (New York: Knopf : Distributed by Random House, Inc, 1997).

618   For discussion of the spread of this idea, see Daniel Hannan, *Inventing Freedom: How the English-Speaking Peoples Made the Modern World*, New edition (New York: Broadside Books, 2013).

619   For recent discussion on how to define populism, see Harry C. Boyte, "Introduction:: Reclaiming Populism as a Different Kind of Politics," *The Good Society* 21, no. 2 (2012): 173–76; Daniele Albertazzi and Duncan McDonnell, "Introduction: The Sceptre and the Spectre," in *Twenty-First Century Populism* (Palgrave Macmillan, London, 2008), 1–11.

620   See Alexander Hamilton, James Madison, and John Jay, *The Federalist Papers*, The Avalon Project (Yalw Law School), accessed November 13, 2017.

621   James Burnham classically made this point, albeit in defence, in James Burnham, *The Machiavellians, Defenders of Freedom* (John Day, 1943).

622   Bagehot, "Some Thoughts on the Crisis of Liberalism—and How to Fix It."

623   Daron Acemoglu and James Robinson, *Why Nations Fail: The Origins of Power, Prosperity, and Poverty* (New York, NY: Currency, 2013).

624   See Brian Galligan, "Federalism," in *The Oxford Companion to Australian Politics*, ed. Brian Galligan and Winsome Roberts (South Melbourne, VIC: Oxford University Press, 2007); Brian Galligan, ed., *Australian Federalism* (Melbourne: Longman Cheshire, 1989).

625   Charles M. Tiebout, "A Pure Theory of Local Expenditures," *Journal of Political Economy* 64, no. 5 (1956): 416–24.

626   This is the 'correspondence principle' as outlined by Wallace E. Oates, *Fiscal Federalism*, Harbrace Series in Business and Economics (New York: Harcourt Brace Jovanovich, 1972).

627   The physical movement of people tends to be limited in practice, however, even if people don't actively move they can still be better represented in smaller groups.

628   Dan Stegarescu, "Public Sector Decentralisation: Measurement Concepts and Recent International Trends*," *Fiscal Studies* 26, no. 3 (September 1, 2005): 301–33; Jean-Paul Faguet, "Decentralization and Governance," *World Development*, Decentralization and Governance, 53 (January 2014): 2–13; Nick Devas and Simon Delay, "Local Democracy and the Challenges of Decentralising the State: An International Perspective," *Local Government Studies* 32, no. 5 (November 1, 2006): 677–95.

629   For example, see the recent devolution efforts in the United Kingdom, Mark Sandford, "Devolution to Local Government in England" (House of Commons Library, November 24, 2017).

630   Wallace E. Oates, "An Essay on Fiscal Federalism," *Journal of Economic Literature* 37, no. 3 (1999): 1120–49; Anwar Shah and Jeff Huther, *Applying a Simple Measure of Good Governance to the Debate on Fiscal Decentralization*, Policy Research Working Papers (The World Bank, 1999); Axel Dreher, "Power to the People? The Impact of Decentralization on Governance," SSRN Scholarly Paper (Rochester, NY: Social Science Research Network, January 1, 2006).

631   Hansjörg Blöchliger, "Decentralisation and Economic Growth - Part 1: How Fiscal Federalism Affects Long-Term Development," OECD Working Papers on Fiscal

Federalism (Paris: Organisation for Economic Co-operation and Development, June 3, 2013); Nobuo Akai and Masayo Sakata, "Fiscal Decentralization Contributes to Economic Growth: Evidence from State-Level Cross-Section Data for the United States," *Journal of Urban Economics* 52, no. 1 (July 1, 2002): 93–108; Iwan Barankay and Ben Lockwood, "Decentralization and the Productive Efficiency of Government: Evidence from Swiss Cantons," *Journal of Public Economics* 91, no. 5–6 (June 2007): 1197–1218; David Cantarero Prieto and Marta Pascual Saez, "Decentralisation and Health Care Outcomes: An Empirical Analysis within the European Union," *ResearchGate*, accessed November 15, 2016; Antonis Adam, Manthos D. Delis, and Pantelis Kammas, "Fiscal Decentralization and Public Sector Efficiency: Evidence from OECD Countries," *Economics of Governance* 15, no. 1 (February 1, 2014): 17–49.

632 Geoffrey Brennan and James M. Buchanan, *The Power to Tax: Analytical Foundations of a Fiscal Constitution: 9* (Cambridge: Cambridge University Press, 1980).

633 Ben Lockwood, "The Political Economy of Decentralization," in *Handbook of Fiscal Federalism*, ed. Ehtisham Ahmad and Giorgio Brosio (Cheltenham, UK: Edward Elgar, 2006); Ehtisham Ahmad and Giorgio Brosio, *Handbook of Fiscal Federalism* (Cheltenham: Edward Elgar Publishing Limited, 2006), 5–7; Raymond Fisman and Roberta Gatti, "Decentralization and Corruption: Evidence across Countries," *Journal of Public Economics* 83, no. 3 (March 2002): 325–45.

634 Senator James Paterson has suggested multiple competing private curricula, which schools can choose, see James Paterson, "Maiden Speech" (Canberra, ACT, March 16, 2016).

635 See Swiss Government, "Regular Naturalisation in Switzerland," accessed April 17, 2018.

636 Christopher Snowdon, "The Wages of Sin Taxes" (London, UK: Adam Smith Institute, May 15, 2012), 51–54.

637 This argument is made by Hayek, *The Road to Serfdom*.

638 John Stuart Mill, *On Liberty* (Project Gutenberg, 2011).

639 Chris Doucouliagos and Mehmet Ali Ulubasoglu, "Economic Freedom and Economic Growth: Does Specification Make a Difference?," *European Journal of Political Economy* 22, no. 1 (2006): 60–81.

640 Max Roser and Esteban Ortiz-Ospina, "Global Extreme Poverty," Our World in Data, accessed June 12, 2018.

641 Lesh, "A Regulatory Culture?"

642 See Yuval Noah Harari, *Sapiens: A Brief History of Humankind*, 1st edition (New York: Harper, 2015).

643 Pierson, "Increasing Returns, Path Dependence, and the Study of Politics."

644 Albert Jay Nock, *Jefferson* (Ludwig von Mises Institute, 1940), 110.

645 Alexis de Tocqueville, *Democracy in America*, trans. Henry Reeve (The Project Gutenberg EBook, 1835).

646 Michael Polanyi, *The Tacit Dimension* (University of Chicago Press, 2009); Elinor Ostrom, *Governing the Commons* (Cambridge University Press, 2015).

647 Robert D. Putnam, *Bowling Alone: The Collapse and Revival of American Community* (New York: Simon & Schuster, 2000).

648 In just the past decade numbers have trended downwards further, for instance, involvement in social groups has declined from 63% in 2006 to 51% in 2014, see Australian Bureau of Statistics, "4159.0 - General Social Survey."

649 Kemp, "Liberalism, Conservatism and the Growth of Government in Australia," 48.

650 Brink Lindsey and Steven Teles, *The Captured Economy: How the Powerful Enrich Themselves,*

Slow Down Growth, and Increase Inequality (New York, NY: Oxford University Press, n.d.).

651 Arthur C. Brooks, "The Dignity Deficit," *Foreign Affairs*, February 13, 2017.

652 Department of Jobs and Small Business, "Skill Shortage List Australia" (Australian Government, March 2018).

653 Department of Jobs and Small Business, "Labour Market Research - Construction Trades" (Australian Government, March 2018).

654 Jo Hargreaves and Michelle Circelli, "Choosing VET: Aspirations, Intentions and Choice" (National Centre for Vocational Education Research, October 23, 2017).

655 Gore et al., "Choosing VET: Investigating the VET Aspirations of School Students."

656 Australian Bureau of Statistics, "6227.0 - Education and Work, Australia, May 2017."

657 See, for example, SEEK, "Electrician Jobs in All Australia," accessed April 18, 2018.

658 Pilcher and Torii, "Expenditure on Education and Training in Australia 2017."

659 For example, see Yarrow Dunham, Andrew Scott Baron, and Susan Carey, "Consequences of 'Minimal' Group Affiliations in Children," *Child Development* 82, no. 3 (June 2011): 793–811.

660 Marilynn B Brewer, "When Contact Is Not Enough: Social Identity and Intergroup Cooperation," *International Journal of Intercultural Relations*, Prejudice, Discrimination and Conflict, 20, no. 3 (June 1, 1996): 291–303.

661 Matthew J. Hornsey and Jolanda Jetten, "The Individual within the Group: Balancing the Need to Belong with the Need to Be Different," *Personality and Social Psychology Review: An Official Journal of the Society for Personality and Social Psychology, Inc* 8, no. 3 (2004): 248–64.

662 The idea that attacking a group makes them more defensive and insular is established in psychology literature, see Jolanda Jetten et al., "Rebels with a Cause: Group Identification as a Response to Perceived Discrimination from the Mainstream," *Personality and Social Psychology Bulletin* 27, no. 9 (September 1, 2001): 1204–13; Paul M. Sniderman, Louk Hagendoorn, and Markus Prior, "Predisposing Factors and Situational Triggers: Exclusionary Reactions to Immigrant Minorities," *The American Political Science Review* 98, no. 1 (2004): 35–49.

663 Lincoln Quillian, "Prejudice as a Response to Perceived Group Threat: Population Composition and Anti-Immigrant and Racial Prejudice in Europe," *American Sociological Review* 60, no. 4 (1995): 586–611.

664 Australian Consortium for Social & Political Research Inc., "Australian Survey of Social Attitudes 2013."

665 Australian Consortium for Social & Political Research Inc.

666 World Values Survey

667 Australian Consortium for Social & Political Research Inc., "Australian Survey of Social Attitudes 2013."

668 OECD Data, "Migration - Foreign-Born Population," The OECD, accessed April 27, 2018.

669 Stokes, "What It Takes to Truly Be 'One of Us.'"

670 For discussion of the concept of the expanding moral sympathy circle, see Peter Singer, *The Expanding Circle: Ethics, Evolution, and Moral Progress* (Princeton University Press, 2011).

671 The 'imagined community' concept is a critique of nationalism, see Benedict Anderson, *Imagined Communities: Reflections on the Origin and Spread of Nationalism* (Verso, 2006).

672 Yael Tamir, *Liberal Nationalism* (Princeton, N.J.: Princeton University Press, 1995); Michael

Lind, "In Defense of Liberal Nationalism," *Foreign Affairs* 73, no. 3 (1994): 87–99.

673 Roger Scruton, "The Truth in Nationalism," in *How to Be a Conservative* (A&C Black, 2014).

674 Frank Furedi, "Why the People Must Be Sovereign," *Spiked!*, March 2018.

675 This point is made by Yascha Mounk, see Yascha Mounk, "How Liberals Can Reclaim Nationalism," *The New York Times*, March 3, 2018, sec. Opinion.

676 Furedi, "Why the People Must Be Sovereign."

Conclusion

677 This is the point made by Stenner, *The Authoritarian Dynamic.*

678 Douglas Murray, *The Strange Death of Europe: Immigration, Identity, Islam* (Bloomsbury Publishing, 2017), 169.

679 See Chris Berg, ed., *The National Curriculum: A Critique*, Foundations of Western Civilisation Program (Melbourne, Victoria: Institute of Public Affairs, 2010); Matthew Lesh and Bella d'Abrera, "Learning When to Catch Blackfish," *The Spectator Australia*, July 30, 2016; d'Abrera, "The Rise Of Identity Politics History In Australian Universities."

680 See Matthew Lesh, "Growing Freedom," *IPA Review*, April 23, 2017.

681 Amy Chua describes this as a 'super-group,' in her case America, which includes sub-groups such as Irish Americans and Japanese Americans, that are nevertheless united, see Chua, *Political Tribes.*

682 Pew found it to be 26% and ANU Poll found it to be 28%, see Travis Mitchell, "Spring 2015 Survey Data," Pew Research Center's Global Attitudes Project, May 27, 2015;a

Bibliography

"A CONSTITUTION FOR SOUTH AUSTRALIA." *Adelaide Observer*. June 29, 1850.

A. H., Maslow. "A Theory of Human Motivation." *Psychological Review* 50, no. 4 (1943).

AAP. "Joe Hockey Commits to First-Year Surplus." *News.com.au*, March 7, 2012. https://www.news.com.au/finance/business/joe-hockey-commits-to-first-year-surplus/news-story/53cdd6f7ed44030aa9a1b0fed09b102a.

Abdel-Magied, Yassmin. "I Tried to Fight Racism by Being a 'Model Minority' — and Then It Backfired." *Teen Vogue*, September 28, 2017. https://www.teenvogue.com/story/fight-racism-model-minority-yassmin-abdel-magied.

Abramson, Paul R., and Ronald Inglehart. "Education, Security, and Postmaterialism: A Comment on Duch and Taylor's 'Postmaterialism and the Economic Condition.'" *American Journal of Political Science* 38, no. 3 (1994): 797–814. https://doi.org/10.2307/2111607.

Abrera, Bella d.' "The Rise Of Identity Politics History In Australian Universities." Melbourne, VIC: Institute of Public Affairs, October 17, 2017. http://ipa.org.au/publications-ipa/media-releases/rise-identity-politics-audit-history-teaching-australian-universities-2017.

ABS. "6333.0 - Characteristics of Employment, Australia, August 2016," May 2, 2017. http://www.abs.gov.au/AUSSTATS/abs@.nsf/allprimarymainfeatures/79BF DF96A3DCCB70CA25823D0018FAF7?opendocument.

Acemoglu, Daron, and James Robinson. *Why Nations Fail: The Origins of Power, Prosperity, and Poverty*. New York, NY: Currency, 2013.

Adam, Antonis, Manthos D. Delis, and Pantelis Kammas. "Fiscal Decentralization and Public Sector Efficiency: Evidence from OECD Countries." *Economics of Governance* 15, no. 1 (February 1, 2014): 17–49. https://doi.org/10.1007/s10101-013-0131-4.

Adolph, Christopher. *Bankers, Bureaucrats, and Central Bank Politics: The Myth of Neutrality*. Cambridge University Press, 2013.

Adonis, Andrew, and Tim Hames, eds. *A Conservative Revolution?: The Thatcher-Reagan Decade in Perspective*. Manchester, UK: Manchester University Press, 1994.

Ahlquist, John. "Policy by Contract: Social Pacts in Australia and New Zealand." In *Midwest Political Science Association Meeting*. Chicago, 2008.

Ahmad, Ehtisham, and Giorgio Brosio. *Handbook of Fiscal Federalism*. Cheltenham: Edward Elgar Publishing Limited, 2006.

Aitkin, Don. *Stability and Change in Australian Politics*. Canberra, ACT: Australian National University Press, 1977.

Akai, Nobuo, and Masayo Sakata. "Fiscal Decentralization Contributes to Economic Growth: Evidence from State-Level Cross-Section Data for the United

States." *Journal of Urban Economics* 52, no. 1 (July 1, 2002): 93–108. https://doi.org/10.1016/S0094-1190(02)00018-9.

Akerman, Pia. "Easy Being Green at the ABC." *The Australian*. May 20, 2013. https://www.theaustralian.com.au/national-affairs/its-easy-being-green-at-the-abc-survey-finds/story-fn59niix-1226647246897?sv=ada2b3719a7659bc9eabfc7bf18bbb09.

Albertazzi, Daniele, and Duncan McDonnell. "Introduction: The Sceptre and the Spectre." In *Twenty-First Century Populism*, 1–11. Palgrave Macmillan, London, 2008. https://doi.org/10.1057/9780230592100_1.

Albrechtsen, Janet. "In Defence of Capitalism." *The Australian*. May 18, 2018. https://www.theaustralian.com.au/news/inquirer/chris-corrigan-issues-a-defence-of-capitalism-during-brief-return/news-story/4f9845c29927115567de341af5d237cf.

Alford, Robert R. *Party and Society: The Anglo-American Democracies*. Westport, Conn.: Greenwood Press, 1963.

Alison, Genevieve. "Youth Crime, Gang Violence a 'failure' of Andrews: PM." *Herald Sun*. January 1, 2018. http://www.heraldsun.com.au/news/victoria/prime-minister-malcolm-turnbull-says-youth-crime-gang-violence-failure-of-andrews-government/news-story/8dd7060fc77b2fd780d80f5e08a3a03a.

Allais, Olivier, Patrice Bertail, and Véronique Nichèle. "The Effects of a Fat Tax on French Households' Purchases: A Nutritional Approach." *American Journal of Agricultural Economics* 92, no. 1 (January 1, 2010): 228–45. https://doi.org/10.1093/ajae/aap004.

ALP. "National Platform." Australian Labor Party, July 2015. https://cdn.australianlabor.com.au/documents/ALP_National_Platform.pdf.

Anderson, Benedict. *Imagined Communities: Reflections on the Origin and Spread of Nationalism*. Verso, 2006.

Angier, Tom. "Governments Should Resist the 'technocratic Temptation' and Maintain Their Commitment to Democracy." *EUROPP* (blog), January 3, 2013. http://blogs.lse.ac.uk/europpblog/2013/01/03/the-technocratic-temptation-tom-angier/.

"ANTI-DRAY TAX LEAGUE." *South Australian Register*. June 28, 1850.

Arntz, Melanie, Terry Gregory, and Ulrich Zierahn. "The Risk of Automation for Jobs in OECD Countries," May 14, 2016. https://doi.org/10.1787/5jlz9h56dvq7-en.

Ashenden, Dean. "The Australian Skills Agenda: Productivity versus Credentialism?" *Educational and Training Technology International* 29, no. 3 (August 1, 1992): 240–48. https://doi.org/10.1080/0954730920290307.

Aslanidis, Paris. "Avoiding Bias in the Study of Populism." *Chinese Political Science Review* 2, no. 3 (September 1, 2017): 266–87. https://doi.org/10.1007/s41111-017-0064-0.

Aulich, Chris, and Janine O'Flynn. "From Public to Private: The Australian Experience of Privatisation." *Asia Pacific Journal of Public Administration* 29, no. 2 (December 1, 2007): 153–71. https://doi.org/10.1080/23276665.2007.1077 9332.

Aulich, Chris, and Janine L. O'Flynn. "From Public to Private: The Australian Experience of Privatisation." SSRN Scholarly Paper. Rochester, NY: Social Science Research Network, September 14, 2011. https://papers.ssrn.com/abstract=1927674.

Australian Bureau of Statistics. "1800.0 - Australian Marriage Law Postal Survey," November 15, 2017. http://www.abs.gov.au/ausstats/abs@.nsf/mf/1800.0.

———. "4159.0 - General Social Survey," June 29, 2015. http://www.abs.gov.au/ausstats/abs@.nsf/mf/4159.0.

———. "5204.0 - Australian System of National Accounts, 2016-17," October 27, 2017. http://www.abs.gov.au/ausstats/abs@.nsf/mf/5204.0.

———. "6227.0 - Education and Work, Australia, May 2017," November 6, 2017. http://www.abs.gov.au/AUSSTATS/abs@.nsf/Lookup/6227.0Main+Features1May%202017?OpenDocument.

———. "6523.0 - Household Income and Wealth, Australia," September 13, 2017. http://www.abs.gov.au/ausstats/abs@.nsf/mf/6523.0.

———. "8155.0 - Australian Industry, 2015-16," May 26, 2017. http://www.abs.gov.au/ausstats/abs@.nsf/mf/8155.0.

———. "8165.0 - Counts of Australian Businesses, Including Entries and Exits, Jun 2013 to Jun 2017." Canberra, ACT, February 20, 2018. http://www.abs.gov.au/ausstats/abs@.nsf/mf/8165.0.

Australian Consortium for Social & Political Research Inc. "Australian Survey of Social Attitudes 2013," 2013. https://www.acspri.org.au/aussa/2013.

Australian Data Archive. "ANU Poll: Changing Views of Governance," 2014. http://www.ada.edu.au/ada/01284.

Australian Electoral Commission. "2016 Federal Election." Australian Electoral Commission, 2016. https://results.aec.gov.au/20499/Website/HouseDefault-20499.htm.

———. "Tally Room." Canberra, ACT: Australian Electoral Commission, 2016.

Australian Government. "List of Departments and Agencies." Accessed March 29, 2018. https://www.australia.gov.au/about-government/departments-and-agencies/list-of-departments-and-agencies.

———. *Proceedings: National Economic Summit Conference April 1983, Canberra.* Canberra, ACT: Australian Government Publishing Service, 1983.

———. "Submission - Sales of Qantas and Australian Airlines - Decision 456," June 1, 1992. National Archives of Australia. http://www.naa.gov.au/go.aspx?i=32176790.

"Australian Greens." Australian Greens. Accessed April 9, 2018. https://greens.org.au/.

Australian Greens. "Change the Date." Australian Greens, January 25, 2017. https://greens.org.au/change-the-date.

———. "Reject Trump." Australian Greens, December 21, 2016. https://greens.org.au/reject-trump.

Australian Labor Party. "Kevin Rudd: Economic Conservative." YouTube, July 26, 2007. https://www.youtube.com/watch?v=lQN_btzkg0U.

Australian Marriage Equality. "Corporate Support." Accessed April 9, 2018. http://www.australianmarriageequality.org/open-letter-of-support/.

Australian Treasury. "Appendix D: Historical Australian Government Data." Canberra, ACT: Commonwealth of Australia, 2015. http://www.budget.gov.au/2015-16/content/myefo/html/16_appendix_d.htm.

Bachrach, Peter, and Morton S. Baratz. "Two Faces of Power." *The American Political Science Review* 56, no. 4 (1962): 947–52.

Bacon, Wendy. "Sceptical Climate Part 2: CLIMATE SCIENCE IN AUSTRALIAN NEWSPAPERS." Australian Centre for Independent Journalism, 2013.

Bagehot. "Some Thoughts on the Crisis of Liberalism—and How to Fix It." *The Economist*, June 12, 2018. https://www.economist.com/bagehots-notebook/2018/06/12/some-thoughts-on-the-crisis-of-liberalism-and-how-to-fix-it.

Bailey, James B., Diana W. Thomas, and Joseph R. Anderson. "Regressive Effects of Regulation on Wages." *Public Choice*, February 26, 2018, 1–13. https://doi.org/10.1007/s11127-018-0517-5.

Ballas, Dimitris, Danny Dorling, and Benjamin Hennig. "Analysing the Regional Geography of Poverty, Austerity and Inequality in Europe: A Human Cartographic Perspective." *Regional Studies* 51, no. 1 (January 2, 2017): 174–85. https://doi.org/10.1080/00343404.2016.1262019.

Barankay, Iwan, and Ben Lockwood. "Decentralization and the Productive Efficiency of Government: Evidence from Swiss Cantons." *Journal of Public Economics* 91, no. 5–6 (June 2007): 1197–1218. https://doi.org/10.1016/j.jpubeco.2006.11.006.

Baumgartner, Frank R., and Bryan D. Jones. *Agendas and Instability in American Politics.* Vol. American politics and political economy series. Chicago: University of Chicago Press, 1993.

Bean, Clive, and Ian McAllister. "Documenting the Inevitable: Voting Behaviour at the 2013 Australian Election." In *Abbott's Gambit*, edited by Carol Johnson, Hsu-Ann Lee, and John Wanna. ANU Press. Accessed April 16, 2018. https://doi.org/10.22459/AG.01.2015.

Becker, Gary S. "A Theory of Competition Among Pressure Groups for Political Influence." *The Quarterly Journal of Economics* 98, no. 3 (1983): 371–400. https://doi.org/10.2307/1886017.

Beilharz, Peter. *Transforming Labor: Labour Tradition and the Labor Decade in Australia.* Cambridge, UK: Cambridge Univ Press, 1994.

Bell, Stephen. "Australian Business Associations: New Opportunities and Challenges." *Australian Journal of Management* 19, no. 2 (December 1, 1994): 137–58. https://doi.org/10.1177/031289629401900202.

Benson, Simon. "Two-Thirds Reject Push for Australia Day Switch: Newspoll." *The Australian*. February 6, 2018. https://www.theaustralian.com.au/national-affairs/newspoll/twothirds-reject-push-for-australia-day-switch/news-story/36bae5347f0d70f8e97c7e181c6c9860.

Benson, Simon, and Ben Packham. "Labor Warns Shorten over Adani." *The Australian*. February 6, 2018. https://www.theaustralian.com.au/national-affairs/labor-warnings-for-bill-shorten-on-opposing-adani/news-story/110faeced8162de304964496052b7c5c.

Berg, C., and S. Davidson. "Nudging, Calculation, and Utopia." *Journal of Behavioral Economics for Policy* 1, no. SpecialIssue (2017): 49–52.

Berg, Chris. "Healthy Living… in a Nanny State." *ABC News*, November 3, 2010. http://www.abc.net.au/news/2010-11-03/health_help/40690.

———. *Liberty, Equality & Democracy*. Ballarat, VIC: Connor Court Publishing, 2015.

———. "Safety and Soundness: An Economic History of Prudential Bank Regulation in Australia, 1893-2008." RMIT University, 2016. https://researchbank.rmit.edu.au/view/rmit:161883.

———. *The Growth Of Australia's Regulatory State: Ideology, Accountability And The Mega-Regulators*. Melbourne, VIC: Institute of Public Affairs, 2008. http://ipa.org.au/publications-ipa/books/growth-australias-regulatory-state-ideology-accountability-mega-regulators.

———, ed. *The National Curriculum: A Critique*. Foundations of Western Civilisation Program. Melbourne, Victoria: Institute of Public Affairs, 2010.

Berg, Chris, Simon Breheny, Morgan Begg, Andrew Bushnell, and Sebastian Reinehr. "The Case for the Repeal of Section 18C." Melbourne, VIC: Institute of Public Affairs, December 2016.

Bernstein, Marver H. *Regulating Business by Independent Commission*. Princeton, N.J: Princeton University Press, 1955.

Betts, Katharine. "Cosmopolitans and Patriots: Australia's Cultural Divide and Attitudes to Immigration." *People and Place* 13, no. 2 (2005): 29.

———. *The Great Divide: Immigration Politics in Australia*. Sydney, NSW: Duffy and Snellgrove, 1999.

Betts, Katharine, and Bob Birrell. "Australian Voters' Views on Immigration Policy." Middle Camberwell, VIC: The Australian Population Research Institute, October 2017. http://tapri.org.au/wp-content/uploads/2016/04/TAPRI-survey-19-Oct-2017-final-3.pdf.

Blackwell, Matthew. "The Psychology of Progressive Hostility." *Quillette* (blog), March 10, 2018. http://quillette.com/2018/03/10/psychology-progressive-hostility/.

Blainey, Geoffrey. *All for Australia*. Methuen Haynes, 1984.

———. "Drawing up a Balance Sheet of Our History." *Quadrant* 37, no. 7–8 (August 1993): 10.

Blöchliger, Hansjörg. "Decentralisation and Economic Growth - Part 1: How Fiscal Federalism Affects Long-Term Development." OECD Working Papers on Fiscal Federalism. Paris: Organisation for Economic Co-operation and Development, June 3, 2013. http://www.oecd-ilibrary.org/content/workingpaper/5k4559gx1q8r-en.

Blyberg, Andrew. "Old Parties Fail to Protect Australian Athletes: Greens." Australian Greens, July 23, 2013. https://greens.org.au/old-parties-fail-protect-australian-athletes-greens.

Bobo, Lawrence, and Frederick C. Licari. "EDUCATION AND POLITICAL TOLERANCETESTING THE EFFECTS OF COGNITIVE SOPHISTICATION AND TARGET GROUP AFFECT." *Public Opinion Quarterly* 53, no. 3 (January 1, 1989): 285–308. https://doi.org/10.1086/269154.

Bongiorno, Frank. *The Eighties: The Decade That Transformed Australia.* Black Inc., 2015.

Booth, Meredith. "Hospital $640m over Budget Opens." *The Australian*, September 5, 2017. https://www.theaustralian.com.au/national-affairs/health/640m-over-budget-royal-adelaide-hospital-opens-at-last/news-story/466a739d36e0c19 0f948c26caa7f44e2.

Borland, Jeff, and Michael Coelli. "Are Robots Taking Our Jobs?" *Australian Economic Review* 50, no. 4 (December 1, 2017): 377–97. https://doi.org/10.1111/1467-8462.12245.

Bornschier, Simon. *Cleavage Politics and the Populist Right: The New Cultural Conflict in Western Europe.* Temple University Press, 2010.

Botton, Alain de. *Status Anxiety.* Penguin UK, 2005.

Bourdieu, Pierre. *Distinction: A Social Critique of the Judgement of Taste.* Routledge, 2013.

Boyte, Harry C. "Introduction:: Reclaiming Populism as a Different Kind of Politics." *The Good Society* 21, no. 2 (2012): 173–76. https://doi.org/10.5325/goodsociety.21.2.0173.

Braithwaite, John. "Economic Policy: What the Electorate Thinks." In *Australian Attitudes: Social and Political Analyses from the National Social Science Survey,* edited by Clive Bean and Jonathan Kelley, 26–35. Sydney: Allen & Unwin, 1988.

Braithwaite, John, and Peter Drahos. *Global Business Regulation.* Cambridge University Press, 2000.

Bramble, Tom. "Our Unions in Crisis: How Did It Come to This?" *Marxist Left Review* Summer 2018, no. 15 (2018). http://marxistleftreview.org/index.php/no-15-summer-2018/154-our-unions-in-crisis-how-did-it-come-to-this.

Bramble, Tom, and Rick Kuhn. "Continuity or Discontinuity in the Recent History of the Australian Labor Party?" *Australian Journal of Political Science* 44, no. 2

(June 1, 2009): 281–94. https://doi.org/10.1080/10361140902862792.

Bramston, Troy. "Labor Officially Going Backwards," April 16, 2018. https://www.theaustralian.com.au/national-affairs/members-flee-labor-despite-shortens-target/news-story/b1da2d450780aa14eac5ecbff2dd7360.

Brennan, Geoffrey, and James M. Buchanan. *The Power to Tax: Analytical Foundations of a Fiscal Constitution: 9*. Cambridge: Cambridge University Press, 1980.

Brennan, John, Jenny Chanfreau, Jerome Finnegan, Julia Griggs, Zsolt Kiss, and Alison Park. "The Effect of Higher Education on Graduates' Attitudes: Secondary Analysis of the British Social Attitudes Survey." BIS RESEARCH PAPER NO. 200. London, UK: Department of Business innovation and Skills, November 2015.

Brett, Judith. *Australian Liberals and the Moral Middle Class: From Alfred Deakin to John Howard*. Cambridge University Press, 2003.

———. "Class, Religion and the Foundation of the Australian Party System: A Revisionist Interpretation." *Australian Journal of Political Science* 37, no. 1 (March 1, 2002): 39–56. https://doi.org/10.1080/13603100220119010.

———. *The Enigmatic Mr Deakin*. Text Publishing, 2017.

Brewer, Mrilynn B. "When Contact Is Not Enough: Social Identity and Intergroup Cooperation." *International Journal of Intercultural Relations*, Prejudice, Discrimination and Conflict, 20, no. 3 (June 1, 1996): 291–303.

Brinsden, Colin. "Budget on Course for Surplus in 2012-13: Treasurer Wayne Swan," May 10, 2011. https://www.theaustralian.com.au/business/latest/budget-on-course-for-surplus-in-2012-13-treasurer-wayne-swan/story-e6frg90f-1226053510856?sv=7307f57e99746f397b0357297f2a9258.

Broinowski, Anna. *Please Explain: The Rise, Fall and Rise Again of Pauline Hanson*. Penguin Books Limited, 2017.

Brooks, Arthur C. *The Conservative Heart: How to Build a Fairer, Happier, and More Prosperous America*. HarperCollins, 2017.

———. "The Dignity Deficit." *Foreign Affairs*, February 13, 2017.

Brown, Greg. "Green Voters Snobs: Research." *The Australian*. November 20, 2017. https://www.theaustralian.com.au/national-affairs/green-voters-are-snobs-says-labor-survey/news-story/9966be6beaf5020c3a82616d7d923a96.

Bucci, Nino, and Anthony Colangelo. "'It Felt like a War Zone': Party-Goers at Werribee Airbnb House Pelt Police with Rocks." *The Age*. December 20, 2017. https://www.theage.com.au/national/victoria/werribee-partygoers-pelt-police-with-rocks-20171220-h07m6q.html.

Buchanan, John, Damian Oliver, and Chris Briggs. "Solidarity Reconstructed: The Impact of the Accord on Relations within the Australian Union Movement." *Journal of Industrial Relations* 56, no. 2 (April 1, 2014): 288–307. https://doi.org/10.1177/0022185613514976.

Burgess, Katie, and Clare Sibthorpe. "Australians' Trust in Politicians Hits Two-

Decade Low." *Sydney Morning Herald.* June 28, 2016. https://www.smh. com.au/politics/federal/australians-trust-in-politicians-hits-twodecade-low-20160624-gpqq9r.html.

Burke, Edmund. *Reflections on the Revolution in France.* Adelaide, SA: eBooks@Adelaide, The University of Adelaide Library, 1790.

Burnham, James. *The Machiavellians, Defenders of Freedom.* John Day, 1943.

Buunk, Bram P., and Nico W. Van Yperen. "Referential Comparisons, Relational Comparisons, and Exchange Orientation: Their Relation to Marital Satisfaction." *Personality and Social Psychology Bulletin* 17, no. 6 (December 1, 1991): 709–17. https://doi.org/10.1177/0146167291176015.

Calwell, Arthur Augustus. *Be Just and Fear Not.* Lloyd O'Neil, 1972.

Caplan, Bryan. *The Myth of the Rational Voter: Why Democracies Choose Bad Policies.* Princeton, NJ: Princeton University Press, 2008.

Capling, Ann, and Brian Galligan. *Beyond the Protective State.* CUP Archive, 1992.

Carl, Noah. "Who Doesn't Want to Hear the Other Side's View?" *Noah Carl* (blog), April 28, 2017. https://medium.com/@NoahCarl/who-doesnt-want-to-hear-the-other-side-s-view-9a7cdf3ad702.

Carnes, Nicholas, and Noam Lupu. "It's Time to Bust the Myth: Most Trump Voters Were Not Working Class." *Washington Post,* June 5, 2017, sec. Monkey Cage Analysis   Analysis Interpretation of the news based on evidence, including data, as well as anticipating how events might unfold based on past events. https://www.washingtonpost.com/news/monkey-cage/wp/2017/06/05/its-time-to-bust-the-myth-most-trump-voters-were-not-working-class/.

Carpenter, Daniel P. "Groups, the Media, Agency Waiting Costs, and FDA Drug Approval." *American Journal of Political Science* 46, no. 3 (2002): 490–505. https://doi.org/10.2307/3088394.

Cartledge, Paul. *Democracy: A Life.* Oxford University Press, 2016.

Castles, Francis G. "A Farewell to Australia's Welfare State." *International Journal of Health Services* 31, no. 3 (July 1, 2001): 537–44. https://doi.org/10.2190/E6W8-3HYY-EHJ5-7VFK.

Castles, Francis G. "The Wage Earners' Welfare State Revisited: Refurbishing the Established Model of Australian Social Protection, 1983–93." *Australian Journal of Social Issues* 29, no. 2 (May 1, 1994): 120–45. https://doi.org/10.1002/j.1839-4655.1994.tb00939.x.

Cater, Nick. *The Lucky Culture.* HarperCollins Australia, 2013.

Cato Institute. "Human Progress," 2017. http://humanprogress.org/.

Cavelaars, A. E. J. M., A. E. Kunst, J. J. M. Geurts, R. Crialesi, L. Grötvedt, U. Helmert, E. Lahelma, et al. "Educational Differences in Smoking: International Comparison." *BMJ* 320, no. 7242 (April 22, 2000): 1102–7. https://doi.org/10.1136/bmj.320.7242.1102.

Chambers, Dustin, Courtney A. Collins, and Alan Krause. "How Do Federal

Regulations Affect Consumer Prices? An Analysis of the Regressive Effects of Regulation." *Public Choice*, October 9, 2017, 1–34. https://doi.org/10.1007/s11127-017-0479-z.

Chambers, Matt. "Tighten Power Rules: ACCC." *The Australian*. September 20, 2017. https://www.theaustralian.com.au/business/tighten-power-rules-to-cut-costs-accc/news-story/77ebb3e54f4fa65d822d95db0f7644e3.

Chan, Alex. "Guiding Public Opinion through Social Agenda-Setting: China's Media Policy since the 1990s." *Journal of Contemporary China* 16, no. 53 (November 1, 2007): 547–59. https://doi.org/10.1080/10670560701562267.

Chan, Tak Wing, and John H. Goldthorpe. "Social Status and Newspaper Readership." *American Journal of Sociology* 112, no. 4 (January 1, 2007): 1095–1134. https://doi.org/10.1086/508792.

Cherastidtham, Ittima, and Andrew Norton. "University Attrition: What Helps and What Hinders University Completion?" Grattan Institute, April 29, 2018.

Chozick, Amy. "Hillary Clinton Calls Many Trump Backers 'Deplorables,' and G.O.P. Pounces." *The New York Times*, September 10, 2016, sec. Politics. https://www.nytimes.com/2016/09/11/us/politics/hillary-clinton-basket-of-deplorables.html.

Chua, Amy. *Political Tribes: Group Instinct and the Fate of Nations*. New York: Penguin Press, 2018.

Chua, Geraldine. "New Royal Adelaide Hospital Named Third Most Expensive Building in the World." *Architecture And Design*, March 23, 2015. http://www.architectureanddesign.com.au/news/new-royal-adelaide-hospital-named-third-most-expen.

Cilento, Melinda. "Community Pulse 2018: The Economic Disconnect." Melbourne, VIC: Committee for Economic Development of Australia, June 2018.

Clark, Terry Nichols. "The Breakdown of Class Politics." *The American Sociologist* 34, no. 1–2 (March 1, 2003): 17–32. https://doi.org/10.1007/s12108-003-1003-0.

Clark, Terry Nichols, and Vincent Hoffmann-martinot, eds. *The New Political Culture*. Boulder, Colo.: Routledge, 1998.

Clark, Terry Nichols, and Seymour Martin Lipset. *The Breakdown of Class Politics: A Debate on Post-Industrial Stratification*. Woodrow Wilson Center Press, 2001.

Clark, Terry Nichols, Seymour Martin Lipset, and Michael Rempel. "THE DECLINING POLITICAL SIGNIFICANCE OF SOCIAL CLASS." *International Sociology* 8, no. 3 (September 1, 1993): 293–316. https://doi.org/10.1177/026858093008003003.

Codevilla, Angelo M. "America's Ruling Class — And the Perils of Revolution." *The American Spectator*, July 16, 2010. https://spectator.org/39326_americas-ruling-class-and-perils-revolution/.

Coen, David, and Mark Thatcher. "The New Governance of Markets and Non-Majoritarian Regulators." *Governance* 18, no. 3 (June 13, 2005): 329–46.

https://doi.org/10.1111/j.1468-0491.2005.00279.x.

Collingridge, David, and Colin Reeve. *Science Speaks to Power: The Role of Experts in Policy Making*. Pinter, 1986.

Collins, Hugh. "Political Ideology in Australia: The Distinctiveness of a Benthamite Society." *Daedalus* 114, no. 1 (January 1, 1985): 147–69.

Collins, Jock. *A Shop Full of Dreams: Ethnic Small Business in Australia*. Leichhardt, NSW: Pluto Press Australia, 1995.

Connolly, Ellis, and Christine Lewis. "Structural Change in the Australian Economy." Sydney, NSW: Reserve Bank of Australia, September 2010. https://www.rba. gov.au/publications/bulletin/2010/sep/pdf/bu-0910-1.pdf.

Cowan, Tyler. *Average Is Over: Powering America Beyond the Age of the Great Stagnation*. First Edition edition. New York, New York: Dutton, 2013.

Creighton, Adam. "Labor's Elitist Obsessions." *The Australian*. April 29, 2018. https:// www.theaustralian.com.au/opinion/columnists/labors-identity-politics-the-lefts-blight-on-the-hill/news-story/f2d7121f2222262f00c71f1cbb113cec.

Crisp, L. F., and Barbara Atkinson. *Australian Labor Party : Federal Personnel 1901-1975*. Canberra, ACT: Dept. of Political Science, Australian National University, 1975.

Cross K. Patricia. "Not Can, but Will College Teaching Be Improved?" *New Directions for Higher Education* 1977, no. 17 (August 18, 2006): 1–15. https://doi. org/10.1002/he.36919771703.

Croucher, Gwilym, Simon Marginson, Julie Wells, and Andrew Norton. *The Dawkins Revolution: 25 Years on*. Melbourne, VIC: Melbourne University Press, 2014.

Crowe, David. "Major Parties Warned on Need to Win Back Angry Voters." *The Sydney Morning Herald*, May 14, 2018. https://www.smh.com.au/politics/federal/ major-parties-warned-on-need-to-win-back-angry-voters-20180514-p4zf99.html.

Crowe, David, and Paige Taylor. "Newspoll Finds Overwhelming Support to Leave Statues Alone." *The Australian*. September 4, 2017. https://www.theaustralian. com.au/news/nation/newspoll-finds-overwhelming-support-to-leave-statues-alone/news-story/41ccc61bffaccca0614ae48c497f2cbb.

Curry, Philip, and Michael F. O'connell. "Post-Materialist Values and Political Preference: Some Unlikely Findings from Northern Ireland." *European Journal of Political Research* 37, no. 1 (January 1, 2000): 19–30. https://doi. org/10.1111/1475-6765.00502.

Dahl, Robert A. "The Concept of Power." *Behavioral Science* 2, no. 3 (January 1, 1957): 201–15. https://doi.org/10.1002/bs.3830020303.

Dalton, Professor Russell J., and Steven A. Weldon. "Public Images of Political Parties: A Necessary Evil?" *West European Politics* 28, no. 5 (November 1, 2005): 931–51. https://doi.org/10.1080/01402380500310527.

Dalton, Russell J. "Cognitive Mobilization and Partisan Dealignment in Advanced

Industrial Democracies." *The Journal of Politics* 46, no. 1 (1984): 264–84. https://doi.org/10.2307/2130444.

————. *Democratic Challenges, Democratic Choices: The Erosion of Political Support in Advanced Industrial Democracies*. Comparative Politics. London: Oxford University Press, 2004.

————. "Economics, Environmentalism and Party Alignments: A Note on Partisan Change in Advanced Industrial Democracies." *European Journal of Political Research* 48, no. 2 (March 1, 2009): 161–75. https://doi.org/10.1111/j.1475-6765.2008.00831.x.

Darwin, Charles. *The Voyage of the Beagle*. Murray, 1876.

Deeming, Christopher. "Social Democracy and Social Policy in Neoliberal Times." *Journal of Sociology* 50, no. 4 (2014): 577–600. https://doi.org/10.1177/1440783313492240.

Deighton-Smith, Rex. "Review of the Road Safety Remuneration System." Jaguar Consulting Pty Ltd, April 16, 2014. https://docs.jobs.gov.au/system/files/doc/other/2014_review_of_the_rsrs.pdf.

Deneen, Patrick J. *Why Liberalism Failed*. New Haven, CT: Yale University Press, 2018.

Department of Education. "Higher Education Statistics," 2018. http://highereducationstatistics.education.gov.au/.

Department of Infrastructure and Regional Development. "State of Australian Cities 2014–2015." Canberra, ACT: Commonwealth of Australia, 2015. https://infrastructure.gov.au/infrastructure/pab/soac/.

Department of Jobs and Small Business. "Labour Market Research - Construction Trades." Australian Government, March 2018. https://docs.jobs.gov.au/system/files/doc/other/ausconstructiontrades_3.pdf.

————. "Skill Shortage List Australia." Australian Government, March 2018. https://docs.jobs.gov.au/system/files/doc/other/skillshortagelistaus_8.pdf.

Department of the Prime Minister and Cabinet. "Closing the Gap: Prime Minister's Report 2018." Canberra, ACT: Commonwealth of Australia, 2018. https://closingthegap.pmc.gov.au/sites/default/files/ctg-report-2018.pdf.

Deutrom, Rhian, and Sarah Elks. "Shorten 'vowed to Kill Adani.'" *The Australian*. February 27, 2018. https://www.theaustralian.com.au/news/nation/geoff-cousins-says-labor-leader-bill-shorten-vowed-to-revoke-adani-mine-licence-if-labor-win-election/news-story/697cbdae70fd9ae492aabf5cbb3eabbd.

Devas, Nick, and Simon Delay. "Local Democracy and the Challenges of Decentralising the State: An International Perspective." *Local Government Studies* 32, no. 5 (November 1, 2006): 677–95. https://doi.org/10.1080/03003930600896293.

Di Natale, Richard. "2016 Federal Policy Initiatives: National Anti-Corruption Commission." The Greens, 2016. https://greens.org.au/sites/default/files/2018-06/20160628_National%20Anti-Corruption%20Commission_0.pdf.

———. "The Trickle Down Hoax & the Need for Government to Step In." presented at the National Press Club, Canberra, ACT, April 4, 2018. https://greens.org. au/sites/greens.org.au/files/National%20Press%20Club%20040418.pdf.

DiMaggio, Paul J., and Walter W. Powell. "The Iron Cage Revisited: Institutional Isomorphism and Collective Rationality in Organizational Fields." *American Sociological Review* 48, no. 2 (1983): 147–60. https://doi.org/10.2307/2095101.

Donoughue, Paul. "Hottest 100 Will No Longer Be Held on Australia Day." *ABC News*, November 27, 2017. http://www.abc.net.au/news/2017-11-27/hottest-100-wont-be-held-on-australia-day-triple-j-says/9197014.

Doucouliagos, Chris, and Mehmet Ali Ulubasoglu. "Economic Freedom and Economic Growth: Does Specification Make a Difference?" *European Journal of Political Economy* 22, no. 1 (2006): 60–81.

Douthat, Ross. "Opinion | The Rise of Woke Capital." *The New York Times*, February 28, 2018, sec. Opinion. https://www.nytimes.com/2018/02/28/opinion/ corporate-america-activism.html.

Dow, Geoff, and George Lafferty. "Decades of Disillusion: Reappraising the ALP-ACTU Accord 1983-1996." *Australian Journal of Politics And History* 53, no. 4 (January 1, 2007): 552–68. https://doi.org/10.1111/j.1467-8497.2007.00474.x.

Dow Geoff, and Lafferty George. "Decades of Disillusion: Reappraising the ALP-ACTU Accord 1983–1996." *Australian Journal of Politics & History* 53, no. 4 (November 21, 2007): 552–68. https://doi.org/10.1111/j.1467-8497.2007.00474.x.

Downs, Anthony. "An Economic Theory of Political Action in a Democracy." *Journal of Political Economy* 65, no. 2 (1957): 135–50.

———. "Up and Down with Ecology-the Issue-Attention Cycle." *The Public InterestThe Public Interest*, no. 28 (Summer 1972): 38–50.

Dreher, Axel. "Power to the People? The Impact of Decentralization on Governance." SSRN Scholarly Paper. Rochester, NY: Social Science Research Network, January 1, 2006. https://papers.ssrn.com/abstract=881542.

Duch, Raymond M., and Michaell A. Taylor. "Postmaterialism and the Economic Condition." *American Journal of Political Science* 37, no. 3 (1993): 747–79. https://doi.org/10.2307/2111573.

Dunham, Yarrow, Andrew Scott Baron, and Susan Carey. "Consequences Of 'minimal' group Affiliations in Children." *Child Development* 82, no. 3 (June 2011): 793–811.

E.A.D.W. "How Australia Broke the Record for Economic Growth." *The Economist*, September 5, 2017. https://www.economist.com/blogs/economist-explains/2017/09/economist-explains-3.

Early Learning and Care Council of Australia Inc. "Submission DR897." Melbourne, VIC: Productivity Commission, March 10, 2014. https://www.pc.gov.au/ inquiries/completed/childcare/submissions/post-draft/submission-counter/

subdr897-childcare.pdf.

Economou, Nick. "From the Inner Cities to the Outer Suburbs: Voting, Parties, Politics and A Post-Industrial Australia." *Journal of Australian Studies* 29 (2016): 50–61. https://doi.org/10.20764/asaj.29.0_50.

Edelman Trust. "Barometer Global Report." Edelman Trust, 2018. https://cms.edelman.com/sites/default/files/2018-01/2018%20Edelman%20Trust%20Barometer%20Global%20Report.pdf.

Elgie, Robert. "The Politics of the European Central Bank: Principal-Agent Theory and the Democratic Deficit." *Journal of European Public Policy* 9, no. 2 (January 1, 2002): 186–200. https://doi.org/10.1080/13501760110120219.

Elliott, Tom. "We Need Real Leadership from Our Politicians." *Herald Sun*. February 6, 2015. http://www.heraldsun.com.au/news/opinion/we-need-real-leadership-and-real-democracy-from-our-politicians/news-story/f37a3a3951aa78df868 92c71166fdbb5.

Encel, Solomon. *Equality and Authority : A Study of Class Status and Power in Australia*. Melbourne, VIC: Cheshire, 1970.

Errington, Wayne, and Peter Van Onselen. *Battleground: Why the Liberal Party Shirtfronted Tony Abbott*. Carlton, VIC: Melbourne University Publishing, 2015.

Essential Polling. "Energy Policy." The Essential Report, December 11, 2017. http://www.essentialvision.com.au/energy-policy-2.

Essential Research. "Satisfaction with Democracy in Australia." The Essential Report, November 20, 2017. http://www.essentialvision.com.au/satisfaction-democracy-australia.

Evans, Mark, Max Halupka, and Gerry Stoker. "How Australians Imagine Their Democracy: The 'Power of Us.'" Canberra, ACT: Governance Institute, 2017. http://www.governanceinstitute.edu.au/magma/media/upload/publication/408_Democracy100-report-IGPA.pdf.

Ewer, Peter, ed. *Politics and the Accord*. Leichhardt, NSW: Pluto Press, 1991.

Faguet, Jean-Paul. "Decentralization and Governance." *World Development*, Decentralization and Governance, 53 (January 2014): 2–13. https://doi.org/10.1016/j.worlddev.2013.01.002.

Fairfax Media. "How the Political Persona Project Works." *The Sydney Morning Herald*, February 6, 2017. https://www.smh.com.au/national/how-the-political-persona-project-works-20170206-gu66c0.html.

Fang, Marina. "Hillary Clinton: Calling Trump Supporters 'Deplorables' Handed Him 'A Political Gift.'" *Huffington Post*, September 11, 2017, sec. World. https://www.huffingtonpost.com.au/2017/09/10/hillary-clinton-calling-trump-supporters-deplorables-handed-him-a-political-gift_a_23203564/.

Farazmand, Ali. *Privatization Or Public Enterprise Reform?: International Case Studies with Implications for Public Management*. Greenwood Publishing Group, 2001.

Fenna, Alan, and Alan Tapper. "The Australian Welfare State and the Neoliberalism Thesis." *Australian Journal of Political Science* 47, no. 2 (June 1, 2012): 155–72. https://doi.org/10.1080/10361146.2012.677007.

Ferguson, John, and Simon Benson. "Labor in Fast Retreat over Adani." *The Australian.* February 2, 2018. https://www.theaustralian.com.au/national-affairs/bill-shorten-in-fast-retreat-over-adani-mine/news-story/19a624d7749f93418e6 04afc0d5ee7d4.

Ferguson, Richard. "'No Ethnic Gang Link to Crime.'" *The Australian.* December 27, 2017. https://www.theaustralian.com.au/national-affairs/state-politics/no-ethnic-gang-link-to-crime-say-victoria-police/news-story/16f2a3b734e423 b7bd453d1555a36879.

Festinger, Leon. "A Theory of Social Comparison Processes." *Human Relations* 7, no. 2 (May 1, 1954): 117–40. https://doi.org/10.1177/001872675400700202.

Fisman, Raymond, and Roberta Gatti. "Decentralization and Corruption: Evidence across Countries." *Journal of Public Economics* 83, no. 3 (March 2002): 325–45.

FLANAGAN, SCOTT C. "Changing Values in Advanced Industrial Societies: Inglehart's Silent Revolution from the Perspective of Japanese Findings." *Comparative Political Studies* 14, no. 4 (January 1, 1982): 403–44. https://doi. org/10.1177/0010414082014004001.

Flew, Terry. "The Limits to Political Unionism." *Journal of Australian Political Economy, The,* no. 24 (March 1989): 77.

Flight, Ingrid, Phillip Leppard, and David N Cox. "Food Neophobia and Associations with Cultural Diversity and Socio-Economic Status amongst Rural and Urban Australian Adolescents." *Appetite* 41, no. 1 (August 1, 2003): 51–59. https://doi.org/10.1016/S0195-6663(03)00039-4.

Flyvbjerg, Bent. "What You Should Know About Megaprojects and Why: An Overview." *Project Management Journal* 45 (February 1, 2014). https://doi. org/10.1002/pmj.21409.

Frank, Thomas. *What's the Matter with Kansas?: How Conservatives Won the Heart of America.* New York: Holt Paperbacks, 2005.

Franklin, Mark N. *The Decline of Class Voting in Britain: Changes in the Basis of Electoral Choice, 1964-1983.* Oxford : New York: Oxford University Press, 1985.

Franklin, Mark N, Thomas T Mackie, and Henry Valen. *Electoral Change: Responses to Evolving Social and Attitudinal Structures in Western Countries.* New York, NY: Cambridge University Press, 1992.

Fredman, Nick. "Watermelons or Tomatoes? Social Democracy, Class and the Australian Greens." *Capitalism Nature Socialism* 24, no. 4 (December 1, 2013): 86–104. https://doi.org/10.1080/10455752.2013.845585.

Friedman, Milton, and Rose Friedman. *Free to Choose: A Personal Statement.* New York, N.Y: Harcourt Bruce Jovanovich, 1980.

Furedi, Frank. "Why the People Must Be Sovereign." *Spiked!* March 2018. http://www.

spiked-online.com/spiked-review/article/why-the-people-ought-to-be-sovereign/21171.

Fussell, Paul. *Class: A Guide Through the American Status System*. Reissue edition. New York: Touchstone, 1992.

Galligan, Brian, ed. *Australian Federalism*. Melbourne: Longman Cheshire, 1989.

———. "Federalism." In *The Oxford Companion to Australian Politics*, edited by Brian Galligan and Winsome Roberts. South Melbourne, VIC: Oxford University Press, 2007.

Garrett, R. Kelly. "Echo Chambers Online?: Politically Motivated Selective Exposure among Internet News Users." *Journal of Computer-Mediated Communication* 14, no. 2 (January 1, 2009): 265–85. https://doi.org/10.1111/j.1083-6101.2009.01440.x.

Gauja, Anika, and Stewart Jackson. "Australian Greens Party Members and Supporters: Their Profiles and Activities." *Environmental Politics* 25, no. 2 (March 3, 2016): 359–79. https://doi.org/10.1080/09644016.2015.1104803.

Gauja, Anika, Narelle Miragliotta, and Smith Smith, eds. *Contemporary Australian Political Party Organisation*. Clayton, Vic: Monash University Publishing, 2015.

Gittins, Ross. "Rudd's Vision for the Bureaucrats." *The Age*. May 5, 2008. http://www.theage.com.au/business/rudds-vision-for-the-bureaucrats-20080504-2au6.html.

Global Scan. "Global Citizenship A Growing Sentiment Among Citizens Of Emerging Economies." BBC World Service, April 27, 2016. https://globescan.com/wp-content/uploads/2016/04/BBC_GlobeScan_Identity_Season_Press_Release_April%2026.pdf.

Golebiowska, Ewa A. "Individual Value Priorities, Education, and Political Tolerance." *Political Behavior* 17, no. 1 (1995): 23–48.

Goodhart, David. "Last Hope for the Left." *Prospect Magazine*. March 19, 2012. https://www.prospectmagazine.co.uk/magazine/haidt-weird-liberals-righteous-mind-america.

———. *The Road to Somewhere: The Populist Revolt and the Future of Politics*. London: C Hurst & Co Publishers Ltd, 2017.

Goodwin, David. "Let Truckies Drive Own Bargain," April 14, 2016. https://www.theaustralian.com.au/opinion/let-truckies-drive-their-own-bargain-not-regulators/news-story/5493b451df418ffe3fafce1d18a7201f.

Goot, Murray, and Ian Watson. "Explaining Howard's Success: Social Structure, Issue Agendas and Party Support, 1993–2004." *Australian Journal of Political Science* 42, no. 2 (June 1, 2007): 253–76. https://doi.org/10.1080/10361140701320018.

———. "One Nation's Electoral Support: Where Does It Come From, What Makes It Different and How Does It Fit?" *Australian Journal of Politics & History* 47, no. 2 (June 1, 2001): 159–91. https://doi.org/10.1111/1467-8497.00226.

Gore, Jennifer, Hywel Ellis, Leanne Fray, Maxwell Smith, Adam Lloyd, Carly Berrigan, Andrew Lyell, Natasha Weaver, and Kathryn Holmes. "Choosing VET: Investigating the VET Aspirations of School Students." National Centre for Vocational Education Research, October 23, 2017. https://www.ncver.edu. au/publications/publications/all-publications/from-school-to-vet-choices,-experiences-and-outcomes.

Government of Australia. "Cabinet Submission 168 - Transition to Centralised Wage Fixation - Decisions 580/EP and 629." National Archives of Australia, May 1983.

Grant, Stan. *IQ2 Racism Debate: Stan Grant.* The Ethics Centre, 2016. https://www. youtube.com/watch?v=uEOssW1rw0I.

Gray, Freddy. "Corbyn Copy: Why Jeremy and Trump Are (Almost) the Same." *The Spectator.* June 17, 2017. https://www.spectator.co.uk/2017/06/corbyn-copy-why-jeremy-and-trump-are-almost-the-same/.

Gregor, Gall, Richard Hurd, and Adrian Wilkinson. *The International Handbook of Labour Unions: Responses to Neo-Liberalism.* Cheltenham, UK: Edward Elgar Pub, 2012.

Gross, Neil, and Solon Simmons. "The Social and Political Views of American Professors," September 24, 2007. https://www.conservativecriminology.com/uploads/5/6/1/7/56173731/lounsbery_9-25.pdf.

Grubel, James, and Jill Sheppard. "Voter Interest Hits Record Low in 2016 - ANU Election Study." ANU, December 20, 2016. http://www.anu.edu.au/news/all-news/voter-interest-hits-record-low-in-2016-anu-election-study.

Gruen, F. H. "Australia's Long-Term Economic Strategy." *Economic Papers: A Journal of Applied Economics and Policy* 3, no. 2 (June 1, 1984): 40–50. https://doi. org/10.1111/j.1759-3441.1984.tb00454.x.

Haber, Hanan. "Regulating-for-Welfare: A Comparative Study of 'Regulatory Welfare Regimes' in the Israeli, British, and Swedish Electricity Sectors." *Law & Policy* 33, no. 1 (October 22, 2010): 116–48. https://doi.org/10.1111/j.1467-9930.2010.00332.x.

Haidt, Jon. "New Study Indicates Existence of Eight Conservative Social Psychologists." *Heterodox Academy* (blog), January 7, 2016. https://heterodoxacademy.org/new-study-finds-conservative-social-psychologists/.

Haidt, Jonathan. *The Righteous Mind: Why Good People Are Divided by Politics and Religion.* New York: Vintage, 2013.

———. "When and Why Nationalism Beats Globalism." *The American Interest* (blog), July 10, 2016. https://www.the-american-interest.com/2016/07/10/when-and-why-nationalism-beats-globalism/.

———. "Why Working-Class People Vote Conservative." *The Guardian,* June 5, 2012. http://www.theguardian.com/society/2012/jun/05/why-working-class-people-vote-conservative.

Hainmueller, Jens, and Daniel J. Hopkins. "Public Attitudes Toward Immigration."

Annual Review of Political Science 17, no. 1 (2014): 225–49. https://doi. org/10.1146/annurev-polisci-102512-194818.

Hair, Jonathan. "Victorian Liberals May Not Run in Inner-City Seats, State Director Says." *ABC News.* November 19, 2017. http://www.abc.net.au/news/2017-11-19/victorian-liberals-may-not-run-in-inner-city-seats-director-says/9165698.

Hamid, Shadi. "The Rise of Anti-Liberalism." *The Atlantic,* February 20, 2018. https://www.theatlantic.com/international/archive/2018/02/liberalism-trump/553754/.

Hamilton, Alexander, James Madison, and John Jay. *The Federalist Papers.* The Avalon Project. Yalw Law School. Accessed November 13, 2017. http://avalon.law. yale.edu/subject_menus/fed.asp.

Hamilton, Clive. "The Great Climate Silence: We Are on the Edge of the Abyss but We Ignore It." *Brisbane Times.* May 9, 2017. https://www.brisbanetimes.com.au/opinion/the-great-climate-silence-we-are-on-the-edge-of-the-abyss-but-we-ignore-it-20170509-gw0ro2.html.

Hammond, Holly. "Power to the People." *Greens Magazine,* February 23, 2014. https://greens.org.au/magazine/power-people.

Hancock, W. K. *Australia.* London: Ernest Benn, 1930.

Hannan, Daniel. *Inventing Freedom: How the English–Speaking Peoples Made the Modern World.* New edition. New York: Broadside Books, 2013.

Hanson, Pauline. "Pauline Hanson's Please Explain." Facebook, January 14, 2018. https://www.facebook.com/PaulineHansonAu/posts/australia-day-2018-under-attack/715171752020473/.

Harari, Yuval Noah. *Sapiens: A Brief History of Humankind.* 1st edition. New York: Harper, 2015.

Hargreaves, Jo, and Michelle Circelli. "Choosing VET: Aspirations, Intentions and Choice." National Centre for Vocational Education Research, October 23, 2017. https://www.ncver.edu.au/publications/publications/all-publications/from-school-to-vet-choices,-experiences-and-outcomes.

Hartcher, Peter. "Fairfax-Ipsos Poll: Voters Feel the Seven-Month Itch." *The Sydney Morning Herald,* March 13, 2016.

———. *The Sweet Spot: How Australia Made Its Own Luck - And Could Now Throw It All Away.* Black Inc., 2014.

Hawke, Robert. "Address by the Prime Minister." presented at the National Economic Summit Conference, House of Represenatives, Canberra, April 11, 1983. https://pmtranscripts.pmc.gov.au/release/transcript-6083.

Hayek, F. A. *The Road to Serfdom.* Routledge, 1976.

———. "The Use of Knowledge in Society." *The American Economic Review* 35, no. 4 (1945): 519–30.

Henrich, Joseph, Steven J. Heine, and Ara Norenzayan. "The Weirdest People in the

World?" *Behavioral and Brain Sciences* 33, no. 2–3 (June 2010): 61–83. https://doi.org/10.1017/S0140525X0999152X.

Henry, P. J., and Jaime L. Napier. "Education Is Related to Greater Ideological Prejudice." *Public Opinion Quarterly* 81, no. 4 (December 12, 2017): 930–42. https://doi.org/10.1093/poq/nfx038.

Higgie, Mark. "Eyeballing DFAT." *The Spectator Australia*, February 10, 2018. https://www.spectator.co.uk/2018/02/eyeballing-dfat/.

Hills, John. "Thatcherism, New Labour and the Welfare State." CASEpaper. London, UK: Centre for Analysis of Social Exclusion, London School of Economics, August 1998. https://core.ac.uk/download/pdf/93746.pdf.

Hilton, George W. "The Basic Behavior of Regulatory Commissions." *The American Economic Review* 62, no. 1/2 (1972): 47–54.

Holt, Norman, and C. E. Tygart. "Political Tolerance and Higher Education." *The Pacific Sociological Review* 12, no. 1 (1969): 27–33. https://doi.org/10.2307/1388211.

Hoorens, Vera. "Self-Enhancement and Superiority Biases in Social Comparison." *European Review of Social Psychology* 4, no. 1 (January 1, 1993): 113–39. https://doi.org/10.1080/14792779343000040.

Horne, Donald. *The Lucky Country: Australia in the Sixties.* 2nd ed. Melbourne: Penguin, 1964.

Hornsey, Matthew J., and Jolanda Jetten. "The Individual within the Group: Balancing the Need to Belong with the Need to Be Different." *Personality and Social Psychology Review: An Official Journal of the Society for Personality and Social Psychology, Inc* 8, no. 3 (2004): 248–64. https://doi.org/10.1207/s15327957pspr0803_2.

Hout, Michael, Clem Brooks, and Jeff Manza. "The Democratic Class Struggle in the United States, 1948-1992." *American Sociological Review* 60, no. 6 (1995): 805–28. https://doi.org/10.2307/2096428.

Howard. *Lazarus Rising: A Personal and Political Autobiography.* Pymble, N.S.W: Harper, 2010.

Howard, John. "Address by the Prime Minister." presented at the Australia Day Council's Australia Day Luncheon, Darling Harbour, Sydney, January 24, 1997. https://pmtranscripts.pmc.gov.au/sites/default/files/original/00010217.pdf.

———. "Australia and Asia: An Enduring Engagement." presented at the Australia-Asia Society, May 8, 1997. http://pmtranscripts.pmc.gov.au/sites/default/files/original/00010336.pdf.

———. "Election Speeches · John Howard, 1996." Sydney, NSW, February 18, 1996. https://electionspeeches.moadoph.gov.au/speeches/1996-john-howard.

———. "Election Speeches · John Howard, 2001." Sydney, NSW, October 28, 2001. https://electionspeeches.moadoph.gov.au/speeches/2001-john-howard.

Hutchens, Gareth. "Australian Wages Growing More Slowly than Cost of Living." *The Guardian*, May 17, 2017, sec. Business. http://www.theguardian.com/

business/2017/may/17/australian-wages-growing-more-slowly-than-cost-of-living.

Imbeau, Louis M., François Pétry, and Moktar Lamari. "Left–right Party Ideology and Government Policies: A Meta–analysis." *European Journal of Political Research* 40, no. 1 (August 1, 2001): 1–29. https://doi.org/10.1111/1475-6765.00587.

Independent Economics. "The Economic Impact of Migration." Canberra, ACT: Migration Council Australia, June 2016. http://migrationcouncil.org.au/wp-content/uploads/2016/06/2015_EIOM.pdf.

Inglehart, Ronald. "The Silent Revolution in Europe: Intergenerational Change in Post-Industrial Societies." *The American Political Science Review* 65, no. 4 (1971): 991–1017. https://doi.org/10.2307/1953494.

Inglehart, Ronald F. "Changing Values among Western Publics from 1970 to 2006." *West European Politics* 31, no. 1–2 (January 1, 2008): 130–46. https://doi.org/10.1080/01402380701834747.

Inglehart, Ronald, and Pippa Norris. "Trump, Brexit, and the Rise of Populism: Economic Have-Nots and Cultural Backlash." SSRN Scholarly Paper. Rochester, NY: Social Science Research Network, July 29, 2016. https://papers.ssrn.com/abstract=2818659.

Institute of Public Affairs. "Dignity of Work." IPA - The Voice For Freedom, n.d. https://ipa.org.au/research-areas/dignity-of-work.

———. *The Human Cost of Red Tape*, 2016. https://www.youtube.com/watch?v=EGBiI2OvSZw.

International Social Survey Programme. "ZA4700: Role of Government IV," 2015.

———. "ZA5900: Family and Changing Gender Roles IV," 2012.

———. "ZA6670: Citizenship II," 2014.

———. "ZA6770: Work Orientations IV," 2015.

Ipsos Global Trends. "Government Prioritising Concerns," 2016. https://www.ipsosglobaltrends.com/government-prioritising-concerns/.

Jackman, Simon. "Political Parties and Electoral Behavior." In *The Cambridge Handbook of Cocial Sciences in Australia*, edited by Riaz Hassan, Ian McAllister, and Steve Dowrick. Cambridge., England: Cambridge University Press, 2003.

Jacks, Timna. "White Flight: Race Segregation in Melbourne State Schools." *The Age*, May 2, 2016. https://www.theage.com.au/national/victoria/white-flight-race-segregation-in-melbourne-state-schools-20160501-goj516.html.

Jacoby, William G. "The Sources of Liberal-Conservative Thinking: Education and Conceptualization." *Political Behavior* 10, no. 4 (December 1, 1988): 316–32. https://doi.org/10.1007/BF00990806.

Jaensch, Dean. *The Hawke–Keating Hijack : The ALP in Transition*. Sydney, NSW: Allen & Unwin, 1989.

James Madison. "The Federalist Papers No. 10," November 23, 1787. http://avalon.law.yale.edu/18th_century/fed10.asp.

Jansen, Giedo, Geoffrey Evans, and Nan De Graaf. "Class Voting and Left-Right Party Positions: A Comparative Study of 15 Western Democracies, 1960-2005." *Social Science Research* 42 (March 1, 2013): 376–400. https://doi.org/10.1016/j.ssresearch.2012.09.007.

Jasanoff, Sheila. "Technologies of Humility: Citizen Participation in Governing Science." *Minerva* 41, no. 3 (September 1, 2003): 223–44. https://doi.org/10.1023/A:1025557512320.

Jasper, Clint, Arlie Felton-Taylor, and Anna Vidot. "Vote Compass: Australians Want Closer Eye on Farm Sales to Foreigners." Text. ABC News, May 25, 2016. http://www.abc.net.au/news/2016-05-25/vote-compass-foreign-investment/7432598.

Jeansch, Dean. *The Australian Party System.* Sydney, NSW: George Allen & Unwin, 1983.

Jennings Will, and Stoker Gerry. "The Bifurcation of Politics: Two Englands." *The Political Quarterly* 87, no. 3 (September 9, 2016): 372–82. https://doi.org/10.1111/1467-923X.12228.

Jetten, Jolanda, Nyla R. Branscombe, Michael T. Schmitt, and Russell Spears. "Rebels with a Cause: Group Identification as a Response to Perceived Discrimination from the Mainstream." *Personality and Social Psychology Bulletin* 27, no. 9 (September 1, 2001): 1204–13. https://doi.org/10.1177/0146167201279012.

Johnson, Matt. "Victorians Give Andrews a Whack." *Herald Sun.* November 20, 2016. http://www.heraldsun.com.au/news/victoria/victorians-think-officials-are-losing-apex-battle/news-story/4a876303352bbdfba00456e18d81d956.

Jones, Barry. "The need for a new political party." *The Saturday Paper,* February 11, 2017.

Judis, John B. "Us v Them: The Birth of Populism | John B Judis | The Long Read." *The Guardian,* October 13, 2016, sec. Politics. http://www.theguardian.com/politics/2016/oct/13/birth-of-populism-donald-trump.

Kahan, Dan M., Ellen Peters, Erica Cantrell Dawson, and Paul Slovic. "Motivated Numeracy and Enlightened Self-Government." *Behavioural Public Policy* 1, no. 1 (May 2017): 54–86. https://doi.org/10.1017/bpp.2016.2.

Karlsen, Rune, and Jo Saglie. "Party Bureaucrats, Independent Professionals, or Politicians? A Study of Party Employees." *West European Politics* 40, no. 6 (November 2, 2017): 1331–51. https://doi.org/10.1080/01402382.2017.1290403.

Karp, Paul. "Australia Day's Date Will Not Change While I'm Prime Minister, Turnbull Says." *The Guardian,* January 29, 2018, sec. Australia news. http://www.theguardian.com/australia-news/2018/jan/29/australia-days-date-will-not-change-while-im-prime-minister-turnbull-says.

———. "Too Many Graduates: Universities Chief Warns against Degrees for All." *The Guardian,* August 1, 2016. http://www.theguardian.com/australia-news/2016/aug/01/too-many-graduates-universities-chief-warns-against-degrees-for-all.

Kasper, Wolfgang, Richard Blandy, John Freebarin, Douglas Hocking, and Robert O'Niell. *Australia at the Crossroads: Our Choices to the Year 2000*. Sydney, NSW: Harcourt Bruce Jovanovich Group, 1980.

Katz, Richard S., and Peter Mair. "Changing Models of Party Organization and Party Democracy: The Emergence of the Cartel Party." *Party Politics* 1, no. 1 (January 1, 1995): 5–28. https://doi.org/10.1177/1354068895001001001.

Kaufmann, Eric. "Trump and Brexit: Why It's Again NOT the Economy, Stupid." *British Politics and Policy at LSE* (blog), November 9, 2016. http://blogs.lse. ac.uk/politicsandpolicy/trump-and-brexit-why-its-again-not-the-economy-stupid/.

Keane, Bernard. "Company Tax Robbery Is Everything That Is Wrong with Our Governance." *Crikey*. March 26, 2018. https://www.crikey.com. au/2018/03/26/company-tax-robbery-is-everything-that-is-wrong-with-our-governance/.

Kefford, Glenn. *All Hail the Leaders: The Australian Labor Party and Political Leadership*, 2015.

Kelley, Jonathan, and M. D. R. Evans. "Societal Inequality and Individual Subjective Well-Being: Results from 68 Societies and over 200,000 Individuals, 1981–2008." *Social Science Research* 62 (February 1, 2017): 1–23. https://doi. org/10.1016/j.ssresearch.2016.04.020.

Kelley, Jonathan, and Joanna Sikora. "Australian Public Opinion on Privatisation, 1986-2002." *Growth*, no. 50 (December 2002): 54.

Kelly, Fran. "Bring on the Population Debate." *ABC News*, April 8, 2010. http://www. abc.net.au/news/2010-04-08/bring-on-the-population-debate/2577832.

Kelly, Paul. *The End of Certainty: Power, Politics & Business in Australia*. St. Leonards, NSW: Allen & Unwin, 1994.

———. *Triumph and Demise: The Broken Promise of a Labor Generation*. Carlton, Vic: Melbourne University Publishing, 2014.

Kemp, D. A. *Society and Electoral Behaviour in Australia: A Study of Three Decades*. St. Lucia, Qld: University of Queensland Press, 1978.

Kemp D. A. "The National Economic Summit: Authority, Persuasion and Exchange*." *Economic Record* 59, no. 3 (October 22, 2007): 209–19. https://doi. org/10.1111/j.1475-4932.1983.tb00810.x.

Kemp, David. "Liberalism, Conservatism and the Growth of Government in Australia." In *Liberalism and Conservatism*, edited by Greg Melleuish. Ballarat: Connor Court Publishing, 2015.

Kennedy, Joshua B. ""Do This! Do That!" and Nothing Will Happen': Executive Orders and Bureaucratic Responsiveness." *American Politics Research* 43, no. 1 (January 1, 2015): 59–82. https://doi.org/10.1177/1532673X14534062.

Kerwin, Cornelius M., and Scott R. Furlong. *Rulemaking: How Government Agencies Write Law and Make Policy*. Washington, D.C: CQ Press, 2010.

Kingston, Margo. *Off the Rails: The Pauline Hanson Trip*. Allen & Unwin, 2001.

Kirchheimer, Otto. "The Transformation of the Western European Party Systems." In *Political Parties and Political Development*, 177–200. Princeton University Press, 1966.

Kittel, Bernhard, and Herbert Obinger. "Political Parties, Institutions, and the Dynamics of Social Expenditure in Times of Austerity." *Journal of European Public Policy* 10, no. 1 (January 1, 2003): 20–45. https://doi.org/10.1080/1350176032000 046912.

Koval, Ramona. "Human Rights Commission president Gillian Triggs speaks out." *The Saturday Paper*, April 23, 2016. https://www.thesaturdaypaper.com.au/news/politics/2016/04/23/human-rights-commission-president-gillian-triggs-speaks-out/14613336003160.

Koziol, Michael. "ABC Must Spend 'More Time Talking to Ordinary Australians' about Hip Pocket Issues, Internal Review Finds." *The Age*. March 16, 2018. https://www.smh.com.au/politics/federal/abc-must-spend-more-time-talking-to-ordinary-australians-about-hip-pocket-issues-internal-review-finds-20180316-p4z4r1.html.

———. "How Malcolm Turnbull's Innovation Agenda Failed to Take Flight." *The Sydney Morning Herald*, July 18, 2016. http://www.smh.com.au/federal-politics/political-news/how-malcolm-turnbulls-innovation-agenda-failed-to-take-flight-20160714-gq5dwu.html.

———. "'I Was Very Frustrated': Gillian Triggs Apologises for Calling Politicians 'Ill-Informed', 'Uneducated.'" *The Sydney Morning Herald*, December 12, 2016. https://www.smh.com.au/politics/federal/i-was-very-frustrated-gillian-triggs-apologises-for-calling-politicians-illinformed-uneducated-20161212-gt8xwb.html.

Krouwel, André. "Otto Kirchheimer and the Catch-All Party." *West European Politics* 26, no. 2 (April 1, 2003): 23–40. https://doi.org/10.1080/01402380512331 341091.

Kruger, Justin, and David Dunning. "Unskilled and Unaware of It: How Difficulties in Recognizing One's Own Incompetence Lead to Inflated Self-Assessments." *Journal of Personality and Social Psychology* 77, no. 6 (December 1999): 1121–34.

Kuhn, Rick. "The Limits of Social Democratic Economic Policy in Australia." *Capital & Class* 17, no. 3 (October 1, 1993): 17–52. https://doi.org/10.1177/030981689305100102.

———. "Xenophobic Racism and Class During the Howard Years." *Marxist Interventions*, no. 1 (2009): 53–82.

Laffer, Arthur B., Stephen Moore, Rex A. Sinquefield, and Travis H. Brown. *An Inquiry into the Nature and Causes of the Wealth of States: How Taxes, Energy, and Worker Freedom Change Everything*. 1 edition. Wiley, 2014.

Langbert, Mitchell, Anthony Quain, and Daniel B. Klein. "Faculty Voter Registration in Economics, History, Journalism, Law, and Psychology." *Econ Journal Watch* 13 (October 4, 2016): 422–51.

Lasker, Phillip. "We Have a Gold-Plated Electricity Grid Consumers Can't Afford." Text. ABC News, July 18, 2017. http://www.abc.net.au/news/2017-07-18/australian-gold-plated-power-grid/8721566.

Lasswell, Harold D. "The Political Science of Science: An Inquiry into the Possible Reconciliation of Mastery and Freedom." *The American Political Science Review* 50, no. 4 (1956): 961–79. https://doi.org/10.2307/1951330.

Latham, Mark. "Insiders and Outsiders." presented at the The 2002 Menzies Lecture, Menzies Centre for Australian Studies, King's College London, September 17, 2002. http://www.outsiders.org.au/insiders-and-outsiders.html.

———. *The Latham Diaries*. Melbourne Univ. Publishing, 2005.

Le Grand, Chip, and Samantha Hutchinson. "Invasion Rally Exposes Left's Split." *The Australian*. January 26, 2018. https://www.theaustralian.com.au/national-affairs/indigenous/australia-day-hardline-group-not-interested-in-changing-date/news-story/e6a807841a1e2ea3f7613c9cf7577a97.

Leigh, Andrew. "Economic Voting and Electoral Behavior: How Do Individual, Local, and National Factors Affect the Partisan Choice?" *Economics & Politics* 17, no. 2 (July 1, 2005): 265–96. https://doi.org/10.1111/j.1468-0343.2005.00154.x.

———. "How Do Unionists Vote? Estimating the Causal Impact of Union Membership on Voting Behaviour from 1966 to 2004." *Australian Journal of Political Science* 41, no. 4 (December 1, 2006): 537–52. https://doi.org/10.1080/10361140600959767.

Leonard E., Read. *I, Pencil*. Irvington-on-Hudson, NY: The Foundation for Economic Education, Inc., 1999. https://fee.org/resources/i-pencil/.

Lesh, Matthew. "A Regulatory Culture?" In *Australia's Red Tape Crisis: The Costs and Consequences of Over-Regulation*, edited by Darcy WE Allen and Chris Berg. Australia: Conor Court Publishers, Fourthcoming.

———. "A Universal Basic Income Would Create a Permanent Underclass." *The Sydney Morning Herald*. April 4, 2018. https://www.smh.com.au/national/a-universal-basic-income-would-create-a-permanent-underclass-20180404-p4z7se.html.

———. "Growing Freedom." *IPA Review*, April 23, 2017. http://ipa.org.au/publications-ipa/ipa-review-articles/growing-freedom.

———. "No Room for Differing Views." *The Australian*. May 25, 2018. https://www.theaustralian.com.au/news/inquirer/no-room-for-differing-views/news-story/70c3e73570eccb414eb26fb22c31e6f9.

———. "Reigniting Australia's Entrepreneurial Flame: Finding The Missing 275,000 Businesses." Melbourne, VIC: Institute of Public Affairs, November 5, 2017. http://ipa.org.au/publications-ipa/research-papers/reigniting-australias-entrepreneurial-flame-finding-missing-275000-businesses.

Lesh, Matthew, and Bella d'Abrera. "Learning When to Catch Blackfish." *The Spectator Australia*, July 30, 2016. https://www.spectator.co.uk/2016/07/learning-catch-blackfish/.

Levitsky, Steven, and Daniel Ziblatt. *How Democracies Die*. New York: Crown, 2018.

Lilla, Mark. "Opinion | The End of Identity Liberalism." *The New York Times*, November 18, 2016, sec. Opinion. https://www.nytimes.com/2016/11/20/opinion/sunday/the-end-of-identity-liberalism.html.

Lind, Michael. "In Defense of Liberal Nationalism." *Foreign Affairs* 73, no. 3 (1994): 87–99. https://doi.org/10.2307/20046660.

Lindsey, Brink, and Steven Teles. *The Captured Economy: How the Powerful Enrich Themselves, Slow Down Growth, and Increase Inequality*. New York, NY: Oxford University Press, n.d.

Linton, Ralph. *The Study of Man: An Introduction*. D. Appleton-Century Company, 1936.

Lipset, Seymour Martin. *Political Man: The Social Bases of Politics*. Baltimore: Johns Hopkins University Press, 1960.

Lipsky, Michael. *Street-Level Bureaucracy: The Dilemmas of the Individual in Public Service*. Russell Sage Foundation, 1983.

Llewellyn, David Geoffrey Matthew. "Australia Felix: Jeremy Bentham and Australian Colonial Democracy." University of Melbourne, 2016. http://minerva-access.unimelb.edu.au/handle/11343/108748.

Lockwood, Ben. "The Political Economy of Decentralization." In *Handbook of Fiscal Federalism*, edited by Ehtisham Ahmad and Giorgio Brosio. Cheltenham, UK: Edward Elgar, 2006.

Lucas, Clay. "Poll Shows African Youth Crime a Key Issue, and Andrews Better to Deal with It." *The Age*, January 7, 2018. http://www.theage.com.au/national/victoria/poll-shows-african-youth-crime-a-key-issue-and-andrews-better-to-deal-with-it-20180107-h0enyq.html.

Macedo, Stephen. *Liberal Virtues: Citizenship, Virtue, and Community in Liberal Constitutionalism*. Clarendon Press, 1990.

Mackay, Hugh. *Reinventing Australia the Mind and Mood of Australia in the 90s*. Updated ed. Pymble, NSW, Australia Angus & Robertson, 1993. https://trove.nla.gov.au/version/208173172.

Macken, Jim, and James Joseph Macken. *Australia's Unions: A Death Or a Difficult Birth?* Federation Press, 1997.

Maher, Sid. "PM Makes Stand as a Social Conservative." *The Australian*. March 20, 2011. https://www.theaustralian.com.au/national-affairs/julia-gillard-makes-stand-as-a-social-conservative/story-fn59niix-1226025066869?sv=9 01c3045cd965e136f9cb44c30718279.

Maier, Pauline. *American Scripture: Making the Declaration of Independence*. 1st ed. New York: Knopf : Distributed by Random House, Inc, 1997.

Mair, Peter. "The Challenge to Party Government." *West European Politics* 31, no. 1–2 (January 1, 2008): 211–34. https://doi.org/10.1080/01402380701835033.

Majone Giandomenico. "From Regulatory State to a Democratic Default." *JCMS: Journal of Common Market Studies* 52, no. 6 (August 5, 2014): 1216–23. https://doi.org/10.1111/jcms.12190.

Majone, Giandomenico, ed. *Regulating Europe*. London: Routledge, 1996.

———. "The Rise of the Regulatory State in Europe." *West European Politics* 17, no. 3 (July 1, 1994): 77–101. https://doi.org/10.1080/01402389408425031.

Maloney, Michael, and Robert McCormick. "A Positive Theory of Environmental Quality Regulation." *Journal of Law and Economics* 25, no. 1 (1982): 99–123.

Manne, Robert. *The Howard Years*. Melbourne, VIC: Black Inc., 2009. https://www.blackincbooks.com.au/books/howard-years.

Manning, Haydon. "Hunting the Swing Voter." In *Contemporary Australian Political Party Organisation*, edited by Anika Gauja, Narelle Miragliotta, and Smith Smith. Clayton, Vic: Monash University Publishing, 2015.

Mansillo, Luke, and Nick Evershed. "Australian Politics Becoming More Polarised." the Guardian, August 7, 2014. http://www.theguardian.com/news/datablog/2014/aug/07/australian-politics-becoming-more-polarised.

Marks, Gary N., and Clive S. Bean. "Sources of Electoral Support for Minor Parties: The Case of the Australian Democrats." *Electoral Studies* 11, no. 4 (December 1, 1992): 311–33. https://doi.org/10.1016/0261-3794(92)90004-P.

Markus, Andrew. "Mapping Social Cohesion 2017: The Scanlon Foundation Surveys Report." Melbourne, VIC: Scanlon Foundation, 2017. https://www.monash.edu/mapping-population/public-opinion/social-cohesion-report.

Marr, David. *The White Queen: One Nation and the Politics of Race*. Quarterly Essay, 2017.

Marsh, I. "Australia's Political Institutions and the Corruption of Public Opinion." *The Australian Journal of Public Administration* 66, no. 3 (September 2007): 329–41.

Massola, James. "Former TWU Official Blasts Safe Rates Created to 'Destroy' Owner-Drivers." *The Sydney Morning Herald*, April 10, 2016. https://www.smh.com.au/politics/federal/former-twu-official-blasts-safe-rates-created-to-destroy-ownerdrivers-20160410-go2w96.html.

Matthewson, Paula. "The Crashing Disappointment That Is Malcolm Turnbull." *The New Daily*, September 15, 2017. https://thenewdaily.com.au/news/national/2017/09/15/malcolm-turnbull-two-years-leadership-disappointment/.

———. "Turnbull Looks More Dodgy than Decisive These Days." *ABC News*, March 14, 2016. http://www.abc.net.au/news/2016-03-14/matthewson-turnbull-looks-more-dodgy-than-decisive-these-days/7243804.

Mayer, Alexander K. "Does Education Increase Political Participation?" *The Journal of Politics* 73, no. 3 (2011): 633–45. https://doi.org/10.1017/s002238161100034x.

McAllister, Ian. *Political Behaviour: Citizens, Parties and Elites in Australia*. Melbourne, VIC: Longman Cheshire, 1992.

———. "The Australian Democrats: Protest Vote or Portent of Realignment?" *Politics* 17, no. 1 (May 1, 1982): 68–73. https://doi.org/10.1080/00323268208401832.

———. *The Australian Voter: 50 Years of Change*. University of New South Wales Press, 2011.

McAllister, Ian, Clive Bean, Rachel Gibson, and Toni Makkai. "Australian Election Study," 2016. http://australianelectionstudy.org/.

McCombs, Maxwell. *Setting the Agenda: Mass Media and Public Opinion*. 2nd Revised edition edition. Polity Press, 2014.

McCombs, Maxwell E., and Donald L. Shaw. "THE AGENDA-SETTING FUNCTION OF MASS MEDIA." *Public Opinion Quarterly* 36, no. 2 (January 1, 1972): 176–87. https://doi.org/10.1086/267990.

McCombs, Maxwell, and Jian-Hua Zhu. "Capacity, Diversity, and Volatility of the Public Agenda: Trends From 1954 to 1994." *The Public Opinion Quarterly* 59, no. 4 (1995): 495–525.

McDuling, John. "Corporate Australia's Real Problem: Ancient Companies." *The Sydney Morning Herald*, November 26, 2015. http://www.smh.com.au/business/the-economy/corporate-australias-real-problem-ancient-companies-20151125-gl7wu2.html.

McEachern, Doug. *Business Mates: The Power and Politics of the Hawke Era*. New York: Prentice Hall, 1991.

McGinnis, John O., and Ilya Somin. "Should International Law Be Part of Our Law?" *Stanford Law Review* 59, no. 5 (September 11, 2006): 1175–1247.

McGlade, Hannah. "Australia Is Still Fighting Racism and It's Time We Faced up to It." *ABC News*, November 27, 2017. http://www.abc.net.au/news/2017-11-27/australias-race-relations-will-be-examined-by-un-in-geneva/9198272.

McIlroy, Tom. "Election Slogans: Voters Disagree 'There's Never Been a More Exciting Time to Be an Australian.'" *The Sydney Morning Herald*, June 26, 2016. http://www.smh.com.au/federal-politics/federal-election-2016/election-slogans-voters-disagree-theres-never-been-a-more-exciting-time-to-be-an-australian-20160623-gpq359.html.

McMillan, Julie, Adrian Beavis, and Frank L. Jones. "The AUSEI06: A New Socioeconomic Index for Australia." *Journal of Sociology* 45, no. 2 (June 1, 2009): 123–49.

Mendes Philip. "Retrenching or Renovating the Australian Welfare State: The Paradox of the Howard Government's Neo-liberalism." *International Journal of Social Welfare* 18, no. 1 (December 5, 2008): 102–10. https://doi.org/10.1111/j.1468-2397.2008.00569.x.

Mill, John Stuart. *On Liberty*. Project Gutenberg, 2011. http://www.gutenberg.org/ebooks/34901.

Minford, Patrick. "The Treasury's Economic Modelling of Brexit Has Been Proven Wrong." *BrexitCentral*, November 15, 2016. http://brexitcentral.com/patrick-minford-treasurys-economic-modelling-brexit-proven-wrong-yet-failed-abandon-unjustified-pessimism/.

Mission Australia. "Youth Survey Report 2015." Sydney, Australia: Mission Australia, June 29, 2016. https://www.missionaustralia.com.au/what-we-do/research-evaluation/youth-survey.

Mitchell, Travis. "Spring 2015 Survey Data." Pew Research Center's Global Attitudes Project, May 27, 2015. http://www.pewglobal.org/2015/05/27/spring-2015-survey-data/.

Mols, Frank, and Jolanda Jetten. "One Nation's Support: Why 'Income' Is a Poor Predictor." *Australasian Parliamentary Review* 32, no. 1 (Autumn/Winter 2017): 92.

Moran, Michael. *The British Regulatory State: High Modernism and Hyper-Innovation.* Oxford: Oxford University Press, 2007.

Morin, Rich. "New Academic Study Links Rising Income Inequality to 'assortative Mating.'" *Pew Research Center* (blog), January 29, 2014. http://www.pewresearch.org/fact-tank/2014/01/29/new-academic-study-links-rising-income-inequality-to-assortive-mating/.

Moss, Jim. *Sound of Trumpets: History of the Labour Movement in South Australia.* Wakefield Press, 1985.

Mounk, Yascha. "How Liberals Can Reclaim Nationalism." *The New York Times*, March 3, 2018, sec. Opinion. https://www.nytimes.com/2018/03/03/opinion/sunday/liberals-reclaim-nationalism.html.

———. *The People vs. Democracy: Why Our Freedom Is in Danger and How to Save It.* Cambridge, Massachusetts: Harvard University Press, 2018.

Muller, Jerry Z. *The Tyranny of Metrics.* Princeton: Princeton University Press, 2018.

Murphy, Katharine. "Bill Shorten Says There's a 'Role for Coal' and Adani Mine Just 'Another Project.'" *The Guardian*, February 19, 2018. http://www.theguardian.com/business/2018/feb/19/bill-shorten-says-theres-a-role-for-coal-and-adani-mine-just-another-project.

Murray, Charles. *Coming Apart: The State of White America, 1960-2010.* New York, N.Y: Crown Forum, 2013.

Murray, Douglas. *The Strange Death of Europe: Immigration, Identity, Islam.* Bloomsbury Publishing, 2017.

Mutz, Diana C. "Status Threat, Not Economic Hardship, Explains the 2016 Presidential Vote." *Proceedings of the National Academy of Sciences of the United States of America* 115, no. 19 (May 8, 2018): E4330–39. https://doi.org/10.1073/pnas.1718155115.

NCVER. "Apprentices and Trainees." National Centre for Vocational Education Research, 2016.

Nelson, Fraser. "Michael Gove Was (Accidentally) Right about Experts." *The Spectator*, January 14, 2017. https://www.spectator.co.uk/2017/01/michael-gove-was-accidentally-right-about-experts/.

———. "The U.K. Is Doing Just Fine, Thanks." *Wall Street Journal*, March 23, 2018, sec. Life. https://www.wsj.com/articles/the-u-k-is-doingjust-fine-thanks-1521819089.

Newman, Nic, David A. L. Levy, and Rasmus Kleis Nielsen. "Reuters Institute Digital News Report 2017." Oxford, UK: Reuters Institute, University of Oxford, 2017.

News.com.au. "Yarra Council Cancels Australia Day out of Respect to Aboriginal Australians," August 16, 2017. http://www.news.com.au/finance/work/leaders/yarra-council-scraps-australia-day-celebrations-wont-hold-citizenship-ceremonies/news-story/de3f0b228d3d9f30476ef1e7f3de3780.

Niall, Jake. "Labor Fiddled with Factions While the Land of Tofu Burned." *The Age*. March 10, 2018. https://www.theage.com.au/national/victoria/labor-fiddled-with-factions-while-the-land-of-tofu-burned-20180309-p4z3o0.html.

Niskanen, William A. "The Peculiar Economics of Bureaucracy." *The American Economic Review* 58, no. 2 (1968): 293–305.

Nock, Albert Jay. *Jefferson*. Ludwig von Mises Institute, 1940.

Noel, Alain, and Jean-Philippe Therien. "From Domestic to International Justice: The Welfare State and Foreign Aid." *International Organization* 49, no. 3 (1995): 523–53.

Norberg, Johan. *Progress: Ten Reasons to Look Forward to the Future*. Oneworld Publications, 2016.

Norman, Jane. "Liberals Deny Tony Abbott's Claim Party Is 'Haemorrhaging Members.'" *ABC News*, July 3, 2017. http://www.abc.net.au/news/2017-07-03/liberals-deny-abbotts-accusation-of-haemorrhaging-members/8674756.

Norris, Pippa. "Authoritarian Populist Vote and GINI." Tweet. @PippaN15, April 25, 2018. https://twitter.com/PippaN15/status/988812376320479233.

Norton, Andrew. "Mapping Australian Higher Education 2016." Melbourne, VIC: Grattan Institute, August 7, 2016. https://grattan.edu.au/report/mapping-australian-higher-education-2016/.

———. "The Rise of Big Government Conservatism: The Centre-Right's Policy Agenda Killed Hopes of Smaller Government." *Policy: A Journal of Public Policy and Ideas* 22, no. 4 (Summer 2006): 15.

———. "To Avoid Uni Drop Outs, Vocational Ed Needs a Boost." *The Sydney Morning Herald*, May 11, 2018.

———. "Universities and the Evolving Graduate Labour Market." Melbourne, VIC: Grattan Institute, February 28, 2017.

———. "Was Higher Education Ever Likely to Reduce Inequality?" *Andrew Norton* (blog), February 21, 2018. http://andrewnorton.net.au/2018/02/21/was-higher-education-ever-likely-to-reduce-inequality/.

Novak, Mikayla. "The $176 Billion Tax on Our Prosperity." Melbourne, VIC: Institute of Public Affairs, May 2016. http://ipacutredtape.org.au/wp-content/uploads/2016/05/The-176-Billion-Tax-On-Our-Prosperity.pdf.

Oates, Wallace E. "An Essay on Fiscal Federalism." *Journal of Economic Literature* 37, no. 3 (1999): 1120–49.

———. *Fiscal Federalism.* Harbrace Series in Business and Economics. New York: Harcourt Brace Jovanovich, 1972.

OECD Data. "Migration - Foreign-Born Population." The OECD. Accessed April 27, 2018. http://data.oecd.org/migration/foreign-born-population.htm.

Office of Management and Budget. "Historical Tables." The White House. Accessed April 16, 2018. https://www.whitehouse.gov/omb/historical-tables/.

Oliver, Alex. "The Lowy Institute Poll 2017." Sydney, NSW: Lowy Institute, June 21, 2017. https://www.lowyinstitute.org/publications/2017-lowy-institute-poll.

OLSON, Mancur. *The Logic of Collective Action: Public Goods and the Theory of Groups, Second Printing with New Preface and Appendix.* Harvard University Press, 1965.

Onselen, Peter Van. "Populist Pitch on Population." *The Australian.* July 25, 2010. https://www.theaustralian.com.au/national-affairs/populist-pitch-on-population/news-story/d472f050f255710e721c08b381aaf187.

Orwell, George. *Second Thoughts on James Burnham.* Adelaide, SA: eBooks@Adelaide, The University of Adelaide Library, 1946. https://ebooks.adelaide.edu.au/o/orwell/george/james_burnham/.

Ostrom, Elinor. *Governing the Commons.* Cambridge University Press, 2015.

O'Sullivan, John. "Hungary Embraces National Conservatism." *National Review,* April 9, 2018. https://www.nationalreview.com/2018/04/hungary-embraces-national-conservatism/.

Page, Edward C. "The Civil Servant as Legislator: Law Making in British Administration." *Public Administration* 81, no. 4 (December 1, 2003): 651–79. https://doi.org/10.1111/j.0033-3298.2003.00366.x.

Parliament of Australia. "Senate StatsNet." Text, 2018. https://www.aph.gov.au/Parliamentary_Business/Statistics/Senate_StatsNet.

Parliamentary Library of Australia. "Part 5 - Referendums and Plebiscites." In *Parliamentary Handbook of the 44th Parliament.* Canberra, ACT: Parliament of Australia, 2014.

Parvini, Neema. "The Incentives for Groupthink." *Quillette,* April 22, 2018. https://quillette.com/2018/04/22/the-incentives-for-groupthink/.

Paterson, James. "Maiden Speech." Canberra, ACT, March 16, 2016. https://senatorpaterson.com.au/maiden-speech/.

———. "Tim Flannery: Climate Prophet." Institute of Public Affairs Australia, May 15, 2013. https://web.archive.org/web/20130515165635/https://ipa.org.au/

publications/1888/tim-flannery-climate-prophet.

Paul Keating "This Is the Recession That Australia Had to Have." Accessed April 18, 2018. https://www.youtube.com/watch?v=J9MWckEsc2A.

Peltzman, Sam. "Toward a More General Theory of Regulation." *The Journal of Law and Economics* 19, no. 2 (August 1, 1976): 211–40. https://doi.org/10.1086/466865.

Perry, Mark J. "Fortune 500 Firms in 1955 v. 2015; Only 12% Remain, Thanks to the Creative Destruction That Fuels Economic Prosperity." American Enterprise Institute. *AEIdeas* (blog), October 12, 2015. http://www.aei.org/publication/fortune-500-firms-in-1955-vs-2015-only-12-remain-thanks-to-the-creative-destruction-that-fuels-economic-growth/.

Pesutto, John. "Weaker Laws Unleashed Gangs." *The Australian.* January 7, 2018. https://www.theaustralian.com.au/opinion/victoria-shows-how-gangs-flourish-when-justice-system-hobbled/news-story/4b7f290110a0bd792dbef a1059720a5d.

Pierson, Paul. "Increasing Returns, Path Dependence, and the Study of Politics." *The American Political Science Review* 94, no. 2 (2000): 251–67. https://doi.org/10.2307/2586011.

———. "The New Politics of the Welfare State." *World Politics* 48, no. 2 (1996): 143–79.

———, ed. *The New Politics Of The Welfare State.* Oxford England ; New York: Oxford University Press, U.S.A., 2001.

Pigou, Arthur C. *The Economics of Welfare.* London, UK: Macmillan and Co., 1932.

Piketty, Thomas. "Brahmin Left vs Merchant Right: Rising Inequality & the Changing Structure of Political Conflict." World Inequality Lab, March 2018. http://piketty.pse.ens.fr/files/Piketty2018.pdf.

Pilcher, Sarah, and Kate Torii. "Expenditure on Education and Training in Australia 2017." Melbourne, VIC: Mitchell Institute, December 13, 2017.

Pincus, J. J. "Pressure Groups and the Pattern of Tariffs." *Journal of Political Economy* 83, no. 4 (1975): 757–78.

Pinker, Steven. *Enlightenment Now: The Case for Reason, Science, Humanism, and Progress.* Viking, 2018.

Plato. *Republic.* Edited by C. J. Emlyn-Jones and William Preddy. Cambridge, MA: Harvard University Press, 2014.

Polanyi, Michael. *The Tacit Dimension.* University of Chicago Press, 2009.

Posner, Eric A. "Liberal Internationalism and the Populist Backlash." SSRN Scholarly Paper. Rochester, NY: Social Science Research Network, January 11, 2017. https://papers.ssrn.com/abstract=2898357.

Poushter, Jacob. "As Elections Near, Most Australians Trust Turnbull's Handling of World Affairs." *Pew Research Center's Global Attitudes Project* (blog), June 20, 2016. http://www.pewglobal.org/2016/06/20/as-elections-near-most-australians-trust-turnbulls-handling-of-world-affairs/.

PricewaterhouseCoopers. "Review of the Road Safety Remuneration System," January

2016. https://docs.jobs.gov.au/system/files/doc/other/2016_review_of_the_ rsrs.pdf.

PricewaterhouseCoopers Australia. *Road Safety Remuneration System: Regulatory Impact Statement*. Canberra, ACT: Department of Education, Employment and Workplace Relations, 2011. http://ris.pmc.gov.au/sites/default/files/ posts/2011/11/03-Safe-Rates-RIS1.pdf.

Prieto, David Cantarero, and Marta Pascual Saez. "Decentralisation and Health Care Outcomes: An Empirical Analysis within the European Union." *ResearchGate*. Accessed November 15, 2016. https://www.researchgate.net/ publication/5022809_Decentralisation_and_health_care_outcomes_An_ empirical_analysis_within_the_European_Union.

Privatization Barometer. "Database." Privatization Barometer, 2013. http://www. privatizationbarometer.com/database.php.

Putnam, Robert D. *Bowling Alone: The Collapse and Revival of American Community*. New York: Simon & Schuster, 2000.

Putnam Robert D. "E Pluribus Unum: Diversity and Community in the Twenty-first Century The 2006 Johan Skytte Prize Lecture." *Scandinavian Political Studies* 30, no. 2 (June 15, 2007): 137–74. https://doi.org/10.1111/j.1467-9477.2007.00176.x.

Quadrini, Vincenzo. "Entrepreneurship, Saving and Social Mobility." *Review of Economic Dynamics* 3, no. 1 (2000): 1–40.

Quillian, Lincoln. "Prejudice as a Response to Perceived Group Threat: Population Composition and Anti-Immigrant and Racial Prejudice in Europe." *American Sociological Review* 60, no. 4 (1995): 586–611. https://doi. org/10.2307/2096296.

Ratcliff, Shaun. "Do Economic Cleavagesstill Matterin Australian Politics?" presented at the Australian Society of Quantitative Political Science conference, Melbourne, VIC, 2015. https://shaunratcliffdotcom.files.wordpress. com/2015/12/ratcliff-asqps-presentation-do-economic-cleavages-still-matter-in-australian-politics.pdf.

Ridley, Matt. *The Rational Optimist: How Prosperity Evolves*. New York: Harper, 2010.

Roddan, Michael. "Disclose Climate Risks, Firms Told," June 18, 2018. https://www. theaustralian.com.au/business/companies/asic-puts-directors-on-notice-over-disclosure-on-climate-change-risks/news-story/9b189d5b433a78f5430 4065b788cd8a2.

Rodrik, Dani. "Populism and the Economics of Globalization." *Journal of International Business Policy*, February 22, 2018, 1–22. https://doi.org/10.1057/s42214-018-0001-4.

Rohac, Dalibor, Liz Kennedy, and Vikram Singh. "Drivers of Authoritarian Populism in the United States." Washington, D.C.: Center for American Progress & American Enterprise Institute, May 2018. https://www.americanprogress. org/issues/democracy/reports/2018/05/10/450552/drivers-authoritarian-populism-united-states/.

Rohac, Dalibor, Sahana Kumar, and Andreas Johansson Heinö. "The Wisdom of Demagogues: Institutions, Corruption and Support for Authoritarian Populists." *Economic Affairs* 37, no. 3 (October 1, 2017): 382–96. https://doi.org/10.1111/ecaf.12264.

Romios, Yiani Petroulias. "Opinion: Why Can't the Greens Gain Mass Appeal?" *Farrago*, March 17, 2018. http://farragomagazine.com/2018/03/17/op-ed-why-cant-the-greens-gain-mass-appeal/.

Roser, Max, and Esteban Ortiz-Ospina. "Global Extreme Poverty." Our World in Data. Accessed June 12, 2018. https://ourworldindata.org/extreme-poverty.

Ross, Liz, Tom O'Lincoln, and Graham Willett. "Labor's Accord: Why It's a Fraud." Melbourne, VIC: Socialist Action, 1986. http://www.reasoninrevolt.net.au/bib/PR0001136.htm.

Roy Morgan. "Employment at Record High but over 2.5 Million Australians Looking for 'More' Work," April 9, 2018. http://www.roymorgan.com/findings/7553-roy-morgan-australian-unemployment-march-2018-201804060704.

Royal Commission into Trade Union Governance and Corruption. "Final Report." Canberra, ACT: Commonwealth of Australia, December 28, 2015. https://www.tradeunionroyalcommission.gov.au/reports/Pages/Volume-1.aspx.

Rozner, Gideon. "Australia's Silent Crisis In Male Employment." Melbourne, VIC: Institute of Public Affairs, August 19, 2017. https://ipa.org.au/publications-ipa/media-releases/australias-silent-crisis-male-employment.

———. "Childcare Costs? Thank Unions and Government." *The Spectator Australia* (blog), March 29, 2018. https://www.spectator.com.au/2018/03/childcare-costs-thank-unions-and-government/.

———. "Your Licence to Work." *IPA Review*, May 2018.

Rudd, Kevin. "The Global Financial Crisis." *The Monthly*, February 1, 2009. https://www.themonthly.com.au/issue/2009/february/1319602475/kevin-rudd/global-financial-crisis.

Rundle, Guy. *Quarterly Essay 3 The Opportunist: John Howard and the Triumph of Reaction*. Black Inc., 2001.

———. "Rundle: Trump Is the End of the Left as We Know It." *Cirkey*. November 30, 2016. https://www.crikey.com.au/2016/11/30/rundle-trump-changed-everything-the-death-of-the-left/.

———. "The Left Side of Politics as We Know It Is Dead." *Crikey*, November 30, 2016. https://www.crikey.com.au/2016/11/30/rundle-trump-changed-everything-the-death-of-the-left/.

Salt, Bernard. "Australia's Great Tribal Retreat." *The Australian*. April 20, 2018. https://www.theaustralian.com.au/news/inquirer/our-segregated-cities-keep-rich-and-poor-as-far-apart-as-possible/news-story/c5a98e968cd82c7f44079cbfbeac9839.

———. "Evils of the Hipster Cafe." *The Weekend Australian Magazine*, October 16, 2016.

Sandford, Mark. "Devolution to Local Government in England." House of Commons Library, November 24, 2017. http://researchbriefings.parliament.uk/ResearchBriefing/Summary/SN07029.

Saunders, Peter. "Selectivity and Targeting in Income Support: The Australian Experience<a href='#fn01'>*</A>." *Journal of Social Policy* 20, no. 3 (July 1991): 299–326. https://doi.org/10.1017/S0047279400018900.

Savva, Niki. *The Road to Ruin: How Tony Abbott and Peta Credlin Destroyed Their Own Government*. Melbourne, Vic: Scribe Publications, 2016.

Sawer, Marian, and David Laycock. "Down with Elites and Up with Inequality: Market Populism in Australia and Canada." *Commonwealth & Comparative Politics* 47, no. 2 (April 1, 2009): 133–50. https://doi.org/10.1080/14662040902842836.

SBS. "Face Up 2 Racism." Accessed April 27, 2018. https://www.sbs.com.au/programs/fu2racism.

———. "Gillard to Spend a Week in Western Sydney." *SBS News*. Accessed April 16, 2018. https://www.sbs.com.au/news/gillard-to-spend-a-week-in-western-sydney.

Schneider, Volker, Simon Fink, and Marc Tenbücken. "Buying Out the State: A Comparative Perspective on the Privatization of Infrastructures." *Comparative Political Studies* 38, no. 6 (August 1, 2005): 704–27. https://doi.org/10.1177/0010414005274847.

Schneiders, Ben, Royce Millar, and Nick Toscano. "Coles Admits Much of Its Workforce Underpaid after SDA Deals." *The Sydney Morning Herald*. June 9, 2017. https://www.smh.com.au/business/companies/coles-admits-much-of-its-workforce-underpaid-after-sda-deals-20170608-gwnfl4.html.

Schneiders, Ben, Nick Toscano, and Royce Millar. "Sold out: Quarter of a Million Workers Underpaid in Union Deals." *The Sydney Morning Herald*. August 30, 2016. https://www.smh.com.au/business/careers/sold-out-quarter-of-a-million-workers-underpaid-in-union-deals-20160830-gr4f68.html.

Schulz, Jonathan, Duman Barahmi-Rad, Jonathan Beauchamp, and Joseph Henrich. "The Origins of WEIRD Psychology." *PsyArXiv*, June 22, 2018. https://doi.org/10.17605/OSF.IO/D6QHU.

Schumpeter, Joseph A. *Capitalism, Socialism, and Democracy*. London: Harper & Brothers, 1942.

Schwartz, Christine R., and Robert D. Mare. "Trends in Educational Assortative Marriage from 1940 to 2003." *Demography* 42, no. 4 (November 1, 2005): 621–46. https://doi.org/10.1353/dem.2005.0036.

Scruton, Roger. "The Truth in Nationalism." In *How to Be a Conservative*. A&C Black, 2014.

SEEK. "Electrician Jobs in All Australia." Accessed April 18, 2018. https://www.seek.com.au/electrician-jobs.

Seidman, Harold, and Robert Scott Gilmour. *Politics, Position, and Power: From the Positive to the Regulatory State.* Oxford University Press, 1986.

Shah, Anwar, and Jeff Huther. *Applying a Simple Measure of Good Governance to the Debate on Fiscal Decentralization.* Policy Research Working Papers. The World Bank, 1999. http://elibrary.worldbank.org/doi/abs/10.1596/1813-9450-1894.

Shaw, Donald Lewis, and Maxwell E. McCombs. *The Emergence of American Political Issues: The Agenda-Setting Function of the Press.* West Pub. Co., 1977.

Sheppard, Jill. "ANUPoll: Attitudes to National Security." Australian National University, October 2016. http://politicsir.cass.anu.edu.au/sites/default/files/docs/ANUpoll-22-Security_0.pdf.

Sheppard, Jill, and Nicholas Biddle. "Class, Capital, and Identity in Australian Society." *Australian Journal of Political Science*, August 14, 2017. http://www.tandfonline.com/doi/abs/10.1080/10361146.2017.1364342.

Shepsle, Kenneth A. "Bureaucratic Drift, Coalitional Drift, and Time Consistency: A Comment on Macey." *Journal of Law, Economics, & Organization* 8, no. 1 (1992): 111–18.

Sheridan, Greg. "Howard's Big Regret." *The Weekend Australian.* January 8, 1995.

Sherlock, Shawn. "The Privatisation Debate and Labor Tradition." *Labour & Community - Sixth National Conference of the Australian Society for the Study of Labour History*, October 3, 1999. http://ro.uow.edu.au/labour1999/proceedings/refereed/27.

Shields, Bevan. "Government to Launch $28 Million Taxpayer-Funded Ad Campaign to Sell Innovation Policies." *The Sydney Morning Herald*, January 6, 2016. http://www.smh.com.au/federal-politics/political-news/government-to-launch-28-million-taxpayerfunded-ad-campaign-to-sell-innovation-policies-20160105-glznzg.html.

Shorten, Bill. "National Road Safety Tribunal to Improve Safety for Australian Road Users." Bill Shorten. Accessed March 29, 2018. http://www.billshorten.com.au/national_road_safety_tribunal_to_improve_safety_for_australian_roadusers.

Simms, Robert. "The Australian Greens and the Moral Middle Class." Perth, WA: Australian Political Studies Association, 2013. https://www.auspsa.org.au/sites/default/files/the_australian_greens_and_the_moral_middle_class_robert_simms.pdf.

Simon, Herbert A. "Rational Decision Making in Business Organizations." *The American Economic Review* 69, no. 4 (1979): 493–513.

Singer, Peter. *The Expanding Circle: Ethics, Evolution, and Moral Progress.* Princeton University Press, 2011.

Singh, Matt. "Two Years On, Many Still Don't Understand Why the UK Voted for Brexit." *CapX.* June 21, 2018. https://capx.co/two-years-after-the-brexit-vote-too-many-still-dont-get-why-the-uk-voted-leave/.

Smethurst, Annika. "Labor Declares Batman Victory, Greens Stunned." *Herald Sun*. March 17, 2018. http://www.heraldsun.com.au/news/victoria/labor-set-to-lose-melbourne-seat-of-batman-to-greens-alex-bhathal/news-story/ba3dba 5fb630b4c5b9985c9520ef7da1.

SMH. "Rudd Denies He Is 'John Howard Lite.'" *The Sydney Morning Herald*, August 3, 2007. https://www.smh.com.au/national/rudd-denies-he-is-john-howard-lite-20070803-rbe.html.

Smith, Adam. *The Theory of Moral Sentiments and Essays on Philosophical Subjects*. Online Library of Liberty, 1869. http://oll.libertyfund.org/titles/theory-of-moral-sentiments-and-essays-on-philosophical-subjects.

Smith, Adam, and Bruce Yandle. *Bootleggers and Baptists: How Economic Forces and Moral Persuasion Interact to Shape Regulatory Politics*. Washington, D.C: Cato Institute, 2014.

Smith, Rodney. "Disciplined Parties and Australian Parliamentary Politics." In *Contemporary Australian Political Party Organisation*, edited by Anika Gauja, Narelle Miragliotta, and Smith Smith. Clayton, Vic: Monash University Publishing, 2015.

Sniderman, Paul M., Louk Hagendoorn, and Markus Prior. "Predisposing Factors and Situational Triggers: Exclusionary Reactions to Immigrant Minorities." *The American Political Science Review* 98, no. 1 (2004): 35–49.

Snowdon, Christopher. "The Wages of Sin Taxes." London, UK: Adam Smith Institute, May 15, 2012. https://www.adamsmith.org/blog/tax-spending/the-wages-of-sin-taxes-the-true-cost-of-taxing-alcohol-tobacco-and-other-vices.

Socialist Alternative. "Red Flag Newspaper," n.d. http://redflag.org.au/.

Soutphommasane, Tim. "Speeches." Accessed March 29, 2018. https://www.humanrights.gov.au/news/speeches.

Sowell, Thomas. *Intellectuals and Society: Revised and Expanded Edition*. New York, NY: Basic Books, 2012.

Sperling, Mark. "Submission DR170." Melbourne, VIC: Productivity Commission, March 10, 2014. https://www.pc.gov.au/inquiries/completed/childcare/submissions/initial/submission-counter/sub170-childcare.pdf.

Spigelman, Jim. "James Spigelman's National Press Club Address." presented at the National Press Club, Canberra, ACT, December 12, 2013. https://www.smh.com.au/opinion/james-spigelmans-national-press-club-address-20131212-2z6wi.html.

Stegarescu, Dan. "Public Sector Decentralisation: Measurement Concepts and Recent International Trends*." *Fiscal Studies* 26, no. 3 (September 1, 2005): 301–33. https://doi.org/10.1111/j.1475-5890.2005.00014.x.

Stenner, Karen. *The Authoritarian Dynamic*. New York: Cambridge University Press, 2005.

Stevens, Sean. "Research Summary: Education Is Related to Greater Ideological

Prejudice." *Heterodox Academy,* May 5, 2018. https://heterodoxacademy.org/research-summary-education-ideological-prejudice/.

Stewart, Matthew. "The 9.9 Percent Is the New American Aristocracy." *The Atlantic,* June 2018.

Stigler, George J. "The Theory of Economic Regulation." *The Bell Journal of Economics and Management Science* 2, no. 1 (1971): 3–21. https://doi.org/10.2307/3003160.

Stimson, Robert J., and Tung-Kai Shyy. "A Socio-Spatial Analysis of Voting for Political Parties at the 2007 Federal Election." *People and Place* 17, no. 1 (2009).

Stokes, Bruce. "What It Takes to Truly Be 'One of Us.'" *Pew Research Center's Global Attitudes Project* (blog), February 1, 2017. http://www.pewglobal.org/2017/02/01/what-it-takes-to-truly-be-one-of-us/.

Stone, J. O. *1929 and All That.* Perth, WA: University of Western Australia Department of Economics, 1984.

Strangio, Paul, and Brian J. Costar. *The Victorian Premiers, 1856-2006.* Federation Press, 2006.

Strøm, Kaare. "Delegation and Accountability in Parliamentary Democracies." *European Journal of Political Research* 37, no. 3 (September 26, 2003): 261–89. https://doi.org/10.1111/1475-6765.00513.

Swiss Government. "Regular Naturalisation in Switzerland." Accessed April 17, 2018. https://www.ch.ch/en/regular-naturalisation/.

Symons-Brown, Bonny. "Gillard Rejects Rudd's 'Big Australia.'" *The Sydney Morning Herald.* June 27, 2010. https://www.smh.com.au/national/gillard-rejects-rudds-big-australia-20100627-zbov.html.

Syverson, Chad. "What Determines Productivity?" Working Paper. National Bureau of Economic Research, January 2010. http://www.nber.org/papers/w15712.

Taleb, Nassim Nicholas. *Skin in the Game: Hidden Asymmetries in Daily Life.* New York, NY: Random House, 2018.

———. *The Black Swan: The Impact of the Highly Improbable.* New York: Random House, 2010.

———. "The Intellectual Yet Idiot." In *Skin in the Game: Hidden Asymmetries in Daily Life.* New York, NY: Random House, 2018.

———. "The Most Intolerant Wins: The Dictatorship of the Small Minority." In *Skin in the Game: Hidden Asymmetries in Daily Life.* New York, NY: Random House, 2018.

Tamir, Yael. *Liberal Nationalism.* Princeton, N.J.: Princeton University Press, 1995.

Temin, Peter. *The Vanishing Middle Class: Prejudice and Power in a Dual Economy.* Cambridge, Massachusetts: The MIT Press, 2017.

Tetlock, Philip E. *Expert Political Judgment: How Good Is It? How Can We Know?* Princeton, N.J.: Princeton University Press, 2006.

Thaler, Richard H., and Cass R. Sunstein. *Nudge.* New York: Penguin Group USA, 2009.

Thatcher, Mark, and Alec Stone Sweet. "Theory and Practice of Delegation to Non-Majoritarian Institutions." *West European Politics* 25, no. 1 (January 1, 2002): 1–22. https://doi.org/10.1080/713601583.

"THE ANTI-DRAY AND LAND-TAX LEAGUE." *South Australian Register.* September 28, 1850.

The Australian. "Newspoll," n.d. https://www.theaustralian.com.au/national-affairs/newspoll.

———. "Top Unis Tell Students That Vocational Education Is Fine." *The Australian.* June 4, 2018. https://www.theaustralian.com.au/higher-education/higher-ed-daily-brief/top-unis-tell-students-that-vocational-education-is-fine/news-story/0c425035e548544eca55f46b7d63cc9d.

The Public Sector Informant. "Outside Experts Could Reduce Intrusion of Politics in Public Service Work." *Canberra Times.* August 1, 2017. http://www.canberratimes.com.au/national/public-service/outside-experts-could-reduce-intrusion-of-politics-in-public-service-work-20170726-gxixot.html.

"The South Australian Anti-Dray and Land Tax League." *South Australian Register.* May 17, 1850.

The Treasury. "2015 Intergenerational Report: Australia in 2055." Canberra, ACT: Australian Government, March 5, 2015. treasury.gov.au/publication/2015-intergenerational-report/.

Thomas, Michael David. "Reapplying Behavioral Symmetry: Public Choice and Choice Architecture." *Public Choice,* March 21, 2018, 1–15. https://doi.org/10.1007/s11127-018-0537-1.

Thompson, Greg, and Allen G. Harbaugh. "A Preliminary Analysis of Teacher Perceptions of the Effects of NAPLAN on Pedagogy and Curriculum." *The Australian Educational Researcher* 40, no. 3 (August 1, 2013): 299–314. https://doi.org/10.1007/s13384-013-0093-0.

Thompson, Herb. "Australia Reconstructed: Socialism Deconstructed." *Journal of Australian Political Economy, The,* no. 23 (August 1988): 87.

Thompson, Michael. *Labor Without Class: The Gentrification of the ALP.* Annandale, N.S.W: Pluto Pr Australia, 2001.

Tiebout, Charles M. "A Pure Theory of Local Expenditures." *Journal of Political Economy* 64, no. 5 (1956): 416–24.

Ting, Inga. "Melbourne's Political Geography Revealed in Seven Maps." *The Age,* February 19, 2017. https://www.theage.com.au/national/victoria/melbournes-political-geography-revealed-in-seven-maps-20170217-gufqtq.html.

———. "Sydney's Political Geography Revealed in Seven Maps." *The Sydney Morning Herald.* February 18, 2017. https://www.smh.com.au/national/nsw/sydneys-political-geography-revealed-in-seven-maps-20170217-gufncj.html.

Ting, Inga, Ri Liu, Nathanael Scott, and Alex Palmer. "Good Taste, Bad Taste? What

Your Habits Reveal about Social Class." *ABC News*, April 13, 2018. http://amp.abc.net.au/article/9610658.

Tocqueville, Alexis de. *Democracy in America*. Translated by Henry Reeve. The Project Gutenberg EBook, 1835. http://www.gutenberg.org/files/815/815-h/815-h.htm.

Tranter, Bruce. "The Impact of Political Context on the Measurement of Postmaterial Values." *SAGE Open* 5, no. 2 (June 19, 2015): 2158244015591826. https://doi.org/10.1177/2158244015591826.

Trebilcock, Anne. "Australia." In *Towards Social Dialogue: Tripartite Cooperation in National Economic and Social Policy Making*. International Labour Organization, 1994.

Trump, Donald J. "Wow, Hillary Clinton..." Tweet. *@realDonaldTrump* (blog), September 10, 2016. https://twitter.com/realDonaldTrump/status/774590070355529728.

Tullock, Gordon. *The Politics of Bureaucracy*. Public Affairs Press, 1965.

———. *The Rent-Seeking Society*. Vol. 5. The Selected Works of Gordon Tullock. Carmel, IN: Liberty Fund Inc, 2005.

Tullock, Gordon, Gordon Brady, and Arthur Seldon. *Government Failure*. Washington, D.C.: Cato Institute, 2010. https://store.cato.org/book/government-failure.

Turnbull, Malcolm. "Environment & Energy." Prime Minister of Australia. Accessed March 27, 2018. https://www.pm.gov.au/priorities/environment-energy.

———. "This Has Been a Very Important Day in the Life of the Nation...," September 15, 2015. https://www.facebook.com/malcolmturnbull/posts/10153698142356579.

United Voice. "United Voice Submission to Producitvity Commissions' Education and Training Workforce: Early Childhood Development." Canberra, ACT: Productivity Commission, December 2011. https://www.pc.gov.au/inquiries/completed/education-workforce-early-childhood/submissions/subdr166-attachment.pdf.

Urban, Rebecca. "Plea to PM: Smash the Gangs." *The Australian*. Accessed April 27, 2018. https://www.theaustralian.com.au/news/nation/plea-to-turnbull-smash-the-gangs/news-story/d28d380c4e23c723b4903539874b727b.

Vidot, Anna. "Farmers, Rural Truckers Welcome Abolition of Road Safety Tribunal." *ABC Rural*, April 19, 2016. http://www.abc.net.au/news/rural/2016-04-19/farmers-rural-truckers-welcome-rsrt-abolished/7338814.

Vlandas, Tim, and Daphne Halikiopoulou. "Does Unemployment Matter? Economic Insecurity, Labour Market Policies and the Far Right Vote in Europe." *European Political Science*, January 8, 2018.

Vogel, Steven Kent. *Freer Markets, More Rules: Regulatory Reform in Advanced Industrial Countries*. Cornell University Press, 1996.

Wahlquist, Calla. "Is Melbourne in the Grip of African Crime Gangs? The Facts behind the Lurid Headlines." *The Guardian*, January 2, 2018, sec. Australia news. http://www.theguardian.com/australia-news/2018/jan/03/is-melbourne-in-the-grip-of-african-gangs-the-facts-behind-the-lurid-headlines.

Warhurst, John, and Andrew Parkin, eds. *The Machine: Labor Confronts the Future*. St Leonards, NSW: Allen & Unwin, 2000.

Watkins, Emily. "More than 200,000 Words Published about Yassmin Abdel-Magied since Last Anzac Day." *Crikey*. April 26, 2018. https://www.crikey.com. au/2018/04/26/more-than-200000-words-published-about-yassmin-abdel-magied-since-last-anzac-day/.

Watkins, Jerry, Sora Park, R. Warwick Blood, Megan Deas, Michelle Dunne Breen, Caroline Fisher, Glen Fuller, Jee Young Lee, Franco Papandrea, and Matthew Ricketson. "Digital News Report Australia 2016." University of Canberra: News & Media Research Centre, 2017.

Welzel, Christian. *Freedom Rising: Human Empowerment and the Quest for Emancipation*. Cambridge University Press, 2013.

West, Geoffrey. *Scale: The Universal Laws of Life and Death in Organisms, Cities and Companies*. London, UK: Hachette, 2017.

Western, Mark, and Bruce Tranter. "Postmaterialist and Economic Voting in Australia, 1990-98." *Australian Journal of Political Science* 36, no. 3 (November 1, 2001): 439–58. https://doi.org/10.1080/10361140120100659.

Western Sydney University. "Australian Cultural Fields." Accessed April 12, 2018. https://www.westernsydney.edu.au/ACF.

Wiarda, Howard J. *Corporatism and Comparative Politics: The Other Great "Ism."* Routledge, 2016.

Wike, Richard, Katie Simmons, Bruce Stokes, and Janell Fetterolf. "Globally, Broad Support for Representative and Direct Democracy." Washington, D.C.: Pew Research Center's Global Attitudes Project, October 16, 2017. http://www. pewglobal.org/2017/10/16/globally-broad-support-for-representative-and-direct-democracy/.

Wild, Daniel. "Business Investment In Australia Now Lower Than Under Whitlam." Parliamentary Research Brief. Melbourne, VIC: Institute of Public Affairs, March 8, 2017. https://ipa.org.au/publications-ipa/research-papers/business-investment-australia-now-lower-whitlam.

———. "How Regulation And Red Tape Makes Families Poorer." Melbourne, VIC: Institute of Public Affairs, March 12, 2018. https://ipa.org.au/wp-content/ uploads/2018/03/IPA-Report-How-Regulation-and-Red-Tape-Makes-Families-Poorer-1.pdf.

Wilks, Stephen, and Ian Bartle. "The Unanticipated Consequences of Creating Independent Competition Agencies." *West European Politics* 25, no. 1 (January 1, 2002): 148–72. https://doi.org/10.1080/713601589.

Williams, Hywel T. P., James R. McMurray, Tim Kurz, and F. Hugo Lambert. "Network Analysis Reveals Open Forums and Echo Chambers in Social Media

Discussions of Climate Change." *Global Environmental Change* 32 (May 1, 2015): 126–38. https://doi.org/10.1016/j.gloenvcha.2015.03.006.

Williams, Pamela. *The Victory: The Inside Story of the Takeover of Australia*. St. Leonards, NSW: Allen & Unwin, 1997.

Wilson, James Q. *Bureaucracy: What Government Agencies Do and Why They Do It*. New York: Basic Books, 2000.

Wilson, Woodrow, and Ronald J. Pestritto. *Woodrow Wilson: The Essential Political Writings*. Lexington Books, 2005.

Wood, Danielle, and John Daley. "A Crisis of Trust: The Rise of Protest Politics in Australia." Melbourne, VIC: Grattan Institute, March 12, 2018. https://grattan.edu.au/report/a-crisis-of-trust/.

World Economic Forum. "The Global Competitiveness Index 2017-2018 Edition: Australia." Cologny, Switzerland: World Economic Forum, September 27, 2017. http://reports.weforum.org/pdf/gci-2017-2018/WEF_GCI_2017_2018_Profile_AUS.pdf.

"World Values Survey." World Values Survey Association, 2012. worldvaluessurvey.org.

York, Chris. "Professor Brian Cox Says Michael Gove's 'Anti-Expert' Stance Is The 'Road Back To The Cave.'" *HuffPost UK*, July 2, 2016. https://www.huffingtonpost.co.uk/entry/professor-brian-cox-michael-gove-experts_uk_5777dceee4b073366f0f20b5.

Young, Michael. "Comment: Down with Meritocracy." *The Guardian*, June 29, 2001. http://www.theguardian.com/politics/2001/jun/29/comment.

Young, Toby. "The Fall of the Meritocracy." *Quadrant*, September 7, 2015. https://quadrant.org.au/magazine/2015/09/fall-meritocracy/.

———. "The Rise and Fall of the Meritocracy." presented at the BBC Radio 4, London, UK, April 12, 2017. http://www.bbc.co.uk/programmes/b08lgq9n.

Zacka, Bernardo. *When the State Meets the Street: Public Service and Moral Agency*. Harvard University Press, 2017.

Zajda, Joseph. "Globalisation, Credentialism and Human Capital." Text, 2012. https://doi.org/info:doi/10.7459/ept/34.2.04.

Zaller, John. "Floating Voters in US Presidential Elections, 1948-2000." *Studies in Public Opinion: Attitudes, Non Attitudes, Measurement Error, and Change* 166 (January 1, 2004).

Zervos, Cassie. "Police Vow to Target out-of-Control African Teen 'street Gangs.'" *Herald Sun*. January 2, 2018. http://www.heraldsun.com.au/news/victoria/labor-mps-warn-voters-will-punish-the-andrews-government-if-it-does-not-tackle-gang-crime/news-story/6e97fb1ef247a6697898cc59b295454f.

Zitner, Aaron, and Gabriel Gianordoli. "Divisions Among the Democrats." *Wall Street Journal*. May 1, 2018. http://www.wsj.com/graphics/divisions-among-the-democrats/.

———. "Divisions Among the Republicans." *Wall Street Journal*. May 1, 2018. http://www.wsj.com/graphics/how-trump-unites-and-divides-republicans/.

About the Author

Matthew Lesh is a Research Fellow at the Institute of Public Affairs. He regularly appears on television and radio, and has written for *The Australian*, *Sydney Morning Herald*, *Herald Sun*, *The Age*, *Canberra Times*, *ABC News*, *Australian Financial Review* and *The Huffington Post*.

Matthew graduated with First Class Honours from the *University of Melbourne* with a Bachelor of Arts (Degree with Honours), and subsequently completed a Masters in Public Policy and Administration at the *London School of Economics* where he received the Peter Self Prize for Best Overall Result.

Matthew has also worked for state and federal parliamentarians, in digital communications, and founded a mobile application development start-up.